KARMA

THE ANCIENT SCIENCE OF CAUSE AND EFFECT

MANDALA

Wisdom Library

MANDALA
PUBLISHING

Mandala Publishing
17 Paul Drive
San Rafael, Ca 94903
www.mandala.org
800.688.2218

Library of Congress Cataloging-in-Publication Data available.

ISBN 1-60109-106-0

  REPLANTED PAPER

Palace Press International, in association with Global ReLeaf ™,
will plant two trees for each tree used in the manufacturing of this
book. Global ReLeaf ™ is an international campaign by American
Forests, the nation's oldest nonprofit conservation organization
and a world leader in planting trees for environmental restora-
tion.

PALACE PRESS
INTERNATIONAL

Printed in China by Palace Press International
www.palacepress.com

10 9 8 7 6 5 4 3 2 1

Dedication

This book is dedicated to the many great teachers of the Hindu/
Vedic Sanatana Dharma knowledge. Their wisdom and personal
examples of holy living have guided my efforts in creating this
small contribution to understanding who we are and our greater
purpose for being here.

KARMA

THE ANCIENT SCIENCE OF CAUSE AND EFFECT

JEFFREY ARMSTRONG

(Kavindra Rishi)

MANDALA
PUBLISHING

TABLE OF

CONTENTS

Introduction

When you speak badly of others, you eat their karma

Of all the subjects that are crucial to us human beings, *karma*—or ultimate cause and effect—is one of the most important. Karma is about all of the things we do and the results that proceed from that doing. Karma is a Sanskrit word that comes to us from the Vedas, the library of spiritual books from India. Sanskrit is a very precise language, used throughout ancient history as a scientific language to record the results of human experience in both material and spiritual matters. Modern linguists recognize that Aramaic, Greek, Latin romance languages and English are largely rooted in Sanskrit origins. Karma is an ancient concept, with at least a ten-thousand-year cultural history in India. Before there was modern science with its notion that "every action has an equal and opposite reaction," ancient thinkers throughout the East studied karma as the science of the reactions to everything we do.

The word karma stems from the Sanskrit root *kri*, which means to do. The English word create is derived from this root. The idea is that everything that surrounds us is interconnected in causal chains that are not always obvious. And as we engage in actions, we desire the ability to predict their outcomes. It is for this reason that modern science has based its progress upon repeatable experiments. Repeatable means that there is a predictable outcome to certain specific actions. In a limited sense, this is also karma, the science of understanding how the outcome is related to our behavior: to what we do.

The scientific thinkers of ancient India also studied material nature in exactly that way, in terms of cause and effect. But they realized that in order to ultimately understand what we do and its long-term implications, we also have to understand three other things. One of those is the individual doer, the second is material nature and the third is the Supreme Controller or Divine Intelligence. In other words, cause and effect are not just about the mechanical operations of matter; they are also about who we are in essence and what our ultimate destination could be, as well as our relationship with the Supreme Being and the various laws of nature. Karma raises the questions of who we are in the final state of our being, where we come from, why we are here, who or what is in control of the universe and what possibilities are there beyond our present experiences. Karma not only asks how we can interact with and control the world around us, but also brings forward the moral questions of what right and wrong actions are and what the future consequences of our present actions will be. How long do we, and the cause and effect resulting from our actions, continue into the future?

It is for this reason that we often hear the words karma and reincarnation in the same sentence. The missing question regarding cause and effect that modern science and many religions have failed to consider is this: what if we, the doers, are neither the body nor the mind? What if we are indestructible conscious entities that move from body to body, life after life, creating and receiving the results of our various doings? It is very likely that one of the reasons science has avoided these questions is because of their problematic history with the Medieval Catholic Church. Since independent scientific thinking was persecuted and often punishable by death at the hands of religion, it is natural that the scientists of that era were apprehensive of the danger and subsequently divorced themselves from spiritual questions of life that could challenge the ruling religious elite. But in India, no such persecution of scientific thinking ever occurred. There, the widely accepted rule was tolerance of various philosophies and worldviews. Thus it was only natural for the Indian approach to karma to include materialistic, existential, scientific, philosophical and spiritual components.

The main question that lies at the root of India's spiritual schools of thought is this: who or what is the Ultimate Source of the laws of nature? These laws imply both purpose and intelligence,

including a lawmaker and finally a long-term view of the soul and its relation to cause and effect as an evolutionary process over many lifetimes. From the Indian perspective, any science is incomplete unless it addresses ultimate questions as well as temporal ones. This, at least, is the view promoted by the Vedic library of knowledge that first gave rise to the study of karma as a science. Unlike many religions or traditions that limit their source of information to one or a very few books, the culture of India has a large library of books on hundreds of material and spiritual subjects. Those texts are called the Vedas and are all written in the ancient and scientific Sanskrit language. That body of knowledge has been carefully preserved and handed down over the last ten thousand years. The information on karma in this book has been extracted and summarized from those Vedic sources. Of course, discussions on some of the principles of karmic science are present in most philosophies and traditions. You will no doubt see similarities and differences with the Vedic view as you study the subject more deeply.

Once we include the bigger questions of nature, our own eternal nature and the intention of the Supreme Being into the question of cause and effect, karma becomes a pivotal part of a much larger conversation. If, as the Vedas suggest, we really are eternal beings, then the things that we do by using our free will have the potential to unfold over very long periods of time, with very complex consequences. If we extend the boundary of our thinking beyond the limits of just one lifetime, then our continual reincarnation appears to be directed by the cause and effect that result from our personal choices and actions. In that case, cause and effect need to be studied over many lifetimes, and justice, or the balancing of the scales of action and reaction, will be played out over a much longer period of time. Such a view will also include a system of administration of cause and effect, some method by which the delivery of so many causal chains is interwoven and connected.

This is the rationale behind the ancient science of *Jyotisha*, or Vedic Astrology, which is very different from the astrology as entertainment we often see today. According to Vedic Astrology, if we are souls investing our free will through actions, then a trail of reactions is always following along behind us as the delayed result of our actions. It also follows that somewhere in us and the universe, there must be a record-keeping department concerned with the balancing of the cosmic books. Someone and something must be monitoring the delivery of the results of the actions of all these humans who are using free will to invest in certain kinds of work. The theory behind astrology then is that encoded in the positions of the planets and stars at the location and moment of birth is information about the nature and delivery schedule of the past actions carried by each soul. The delivery of that cause and effect is carried out by divine helpers working on behalf of the Supreme Being.

This means that some but not all of our life is predetermined by our previous use of free will. It means that the Divine Intelligence of the universe has a longer memory than us and that "what goes around comes around" may be on a longer trajectory than we have so far imagined. The greatness of karma as a philosophical concept and practical understanding is that it sees a soul's journey of evolution on a very grand scale. It is a view that envisions the continual evolution of countless trillions of souls over vast stretches of space and tremendous eras of cosmic time. You could say that karma is the judicial system of a great intergalactic federation of democratic action run by free will in a context of Divine law.

Seen from this perspective, each time we take on a body or are born again as a human, we are both receiving old karma and creating new karma. Finally, this also raises the questions of whether or not, and how, we might escape the limitations and suffering of this cycle of cause and effect and be restored to our original nature, which the Vedas depict as an eternal joyful soul in a transcendental world. Since cause and effect appear to us as a cycle, they may be viewed as a circle. We initiate an action and at a certain time in the future, we reap the fruit of our deeds. It resembles the agricultural cycle in the circle of the year. We sow seeds and then garner the rewards —"As you sow, so you shall reap." Karma is the science of our actions and their outcomes.

The larger process of the soul transmigrating from life to life and body to body over many lifetimes is called *samsara* in Sanskrit, the wheel of repeated birth and death from life to life. The concept of karma then includes both the short-term cause and effect cycle—the moral consequences implied in "do unto others as you would have them do unto you"—and the long-term evolution of all the souls over many lifetimes. As we will see, the implications of this view form a grand and profound cosmology that is the basis of what we have come to think of as the "Eastern" view, a view deeply influenced by Vedic thought. Now, due to the effects of technology, East and West have not only met, they are increasingly part of one world that we are changing very rapidly by all we do. Our current level of ability to alter the balance of natural law calls into question everything we do. At present we are gambling with our children's futures and perhaps the future of life on our planet. Never has there been a time when an understanding of karma was more relevant than it is today.

CHAPTER ONE

WHAT YOU DO COMES BACK TO YOU

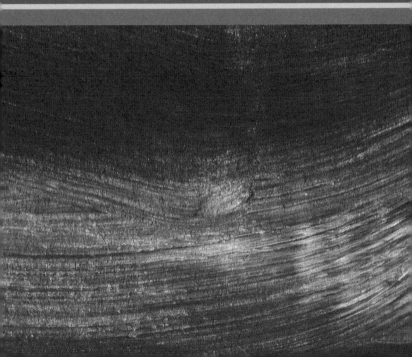

What You Do

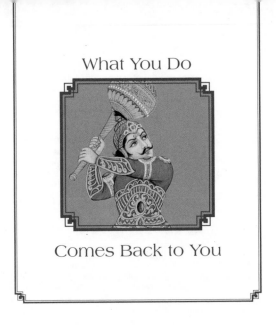

Comes Back to You

Cause is effect concealed, effect is cause revealed

The Vedic concept of karma is based upon the existence of three eternal realities. The first is a transcendental or non-material realm that is not currently visible to us. That place is described in the Vedas as existing eternally without the need for Sun, Moon or electricity. It is self-luminous, completely conscious and full of all the beauty we experience here but without the presence of birth, death, old age or disease. Naturally, from where we stand at the moment, we are inclined to doubt the existence of this other realm, since we do not have direct experience of it. But the Vedic literature is very explicit and detailed in its descriptions of that transcendental abode.

The Unconscious Realm

The second eternal reality is the material world where we currently reside. It is called *prakriti* or *maya*, the dark unconscious energy, and is real but temporary. Everything here within matter is transitory; it is created, exists for a while and is then destroyed. Unlike the transcendental abode, which is made of a conscious energy, the material world is made of an unconscious energy. In this world, everything is subject to birth, death, old age and disease or dissolution. The world we view through our senses is fraught with limitation. The beauty we experience, although real, is mixed up with the temporary qualities of matter. In simple terms, this is the cause of our frustration with life. Life is a struggle to get the things we want within matter, and then there is a struggle to keep them, often leading to conflict or war. Eventually we all lose that struggle at the final moment of the death of our bodies. Therefore, the material world is known as the place where everything dies. In spite of this transitory nature, matter itself is also described as an eternally existing reality, though it is temporary in the sense that the soul can be freed from it.

Many Eternal Souls

The third eternal reality is us, the many eternal souls, some of whom have come to visit the material world. According to the Vedas, many more like us have remained in the transcendental world. The name for these countless individual souls is *atma*. The atmas are eternal, conscious, joyful and individual in nature, but each soul eternally has the choice to reside in either the transcendental or material realms. If we choose to explore matter, as we have, then the natural result is that we go on a long journey exploring the material world. In the process, we forget our transcendental origin. The atmas who come to the material realm are then called *jiva-atmas*, since they are in touch with material life (the words "viva" and "live" come from the Sanskrit *jiva*). Since by nature we are eternal, conscious, joyful and unique, our visit to matter does not remove our original nature—it merely covers it over with layers of the dark and unconscious matter.

Unlike some traditions, the Vedas do not say that the souls coming into matter are bad or evil for doing so. Coming here is a part of our education as souls and we each personally chose to come on this material adventure. If you like, think of the material world as a grand amusement park. A long time ago, we lived in the eternal realm. Then, at a certain point we chose to enter the park, slid down a great long tunnel and began the slow and very interesting exploration of the realm of matter. Once inside, all souls need an appropriate suit to function within the park's atmosphere. This suit is the material body. Think of it as a kind of diving suit made of matter. In Sanskrit, that matter is also called *gu*, which is humorously close to the English word goo. We come to the park as eternal souls and go from one body of goo to another, temporarily forgetful of our origin and true nature. Once in the goo or *prakriti*, we are convinced that our material body is our self. This is necessary in order for us to feel we are the enjoyer, which is the reason why we entered the park in the first place. We identify self with matter from that point onward until we learn otherwise. As we will see, that step of radical evolution is only possible once we reach human life.

8,400,000 Species of Life

According to the Vedic scriptures, there are 8,400,000 different species of life throughout the material realm. 8,000,000 are sub-human, while 400,000 are varieties of human beings. The word atma is the origin of the English word atomic. Once the atomic particle of eternal consciousness enters into matter, it starts at the bottom of the evolutionary hierarchy and takes on a body. In that sense the Vedas would agree with Darwin that we do indeed evolve but our evolution is not from matter, but rather within matter, an evolution of consciousness. Our eternal soul climbs up the staircase of life, experiencing every species as a kind of learning by being and doing. From the smallest microbe up to insects, plants, birds, and mammals, we ascend the ladder of the species until we finally reach the lowest rung of human consciousness.

The Amusement Park in the Sky

Try to picture the whole process as a walk through an immense cyber-amusement park, where you put on a different body to go on each ride. For the soul it is the same. It is just like the way we change clothes yet remain the same person. The Vedas describe the universe as a grand school for gradual evolution of our consciousness, a "universe-ity" where all the *atmas* are in different grades (bodies) learning all the lessons (or going on all the rides) in the beautiful material park. Of course, in between each new birth, the last body must die. This process is called *samsara* in Sanskrit, or the wheel of birth and death. Think of it as a kind of merry-go-round or Ferris wheel, in the amusement park of material life. This wheel of repeated birth and death promises pleasures; it delivers some but with them come many pains, disappointments and sufferings of all descriptions.

The Difference between Humans and Animals

You have probably noticed that one of the differences between animals and humans is the amount of free will or choice that they can exercise. Animals and the beings below them are not able to exercise free will and self-awareness at the same level as humans. It is interesting to note that the word "mankind" comes from a Sanskrit word *manusha*. It does not mean male, as you might think. It comes from the word *manas*, meaning mind. In this context, it refers to humans as "having a mind of their own." Humans have reflexive and moral minds that can distinguish between good and bad. The difference between the reflective minds of humans and the instinctual minds of animals and the species below them is that the instinctive mind does not generate karma through its actions. It lives and dies in a life of instinctual experience with no future consequences. But at the human stage, as we begin to reawaken to

our true nature, we enter into the karma-generating stage of the evolutionary process. Once we are human, it is our actions and not our instincts that direct our evolutionary progress.

Old Souls and Young Souls

Newly arriving humans are not always certain whether they are animals or humans or some mixture of both. They have just spent many lifetimes in the various animal species, so it takes some time for the human qualities to become stronger than the animal characteristics. There are four activities that humans share with animals: eating, sleeping, mating and defending. If those four activities occupy most of our mental energy, we are more animal than human in temperament. When our human side emerges it is accompanied by questions about who we are, such as: Why was I born? Why do I get sick? Why do I age? Why must I die? If you think again of the amusement park, the question for us is: what do we want to experience in the park? Our visit to the park and the rides we choose are driven by our desires. You have no doubt heard of the term "old souls and young souls." Even though all souls are eternal, if a soul has many desires to fulfill within matter, it is likely to be relatively young or new to the park. If they are bored with the park and ready to move on, then chances are that they are older souls who have been around for many lifetimes. "Been there, done that" would be their motto and you would see them looking for the exit to the park rather than lining up to go on the next ride. In other words, humans are here in the park to collect a certain amount of experience, just as the soul had done previously by taking birth in the lower species.

The Rules of the Park

Just like in school, you can go forward and skip grades or flunk out of the human class and go backward, that is to say downward, for some time. Thus the Vedic theory of karma does not lend itself to a New Age interpretation, in which the soul only moves upward, learning lesson after lesson. Devolution instead of evolution is also possible. If a human acts like an animal, he or she can slide back into an animal body for some time before going further forward. After all, once we are humans, we start flying our own airplanes through choice and then reap the results of our choices. If we choose to act like an animal, the message we send to Nature is: "Put me in an animal body." If you were the owner of a huge amusement park, your job would be to see to it that the park ran smoothly as well as to provide a good time for the customers. In the park of Material Nature, there are rules that govern the operation of the park and those rules are mandatory for all the visitors.

CHAPTER TWO

THE LAW OF CAUSALITY

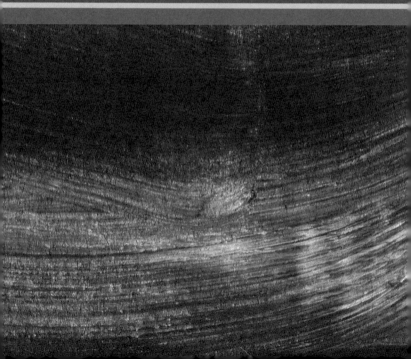

The Law

of Causality

Human actions once imparted, cannot be thwarted

No one disputes that there are laws of material nature. The first and most insistent of them, gravity, has us in its grip every moment of our lives. Every situation, every object, every transaction we experience is fraught with dos and don'ts or rules of how to do something the "right" way. In matter, if we don't do it the right way, it doesn't work. Just try filling your gas tank with water and sugar instead of gasoline. In this and a myriad of other situations, there are right and wrong ways to do everything.

The Ritam is the Laws of Nature

The English word right comes from the Sanskrit word *ritam*. Ritam simply means the invisible laws of material nature. The cosmic do's and don'ts, so to speak. The other English word derived from ritam is ritual. Doing something right is actually a series of steps or procedures. It is a ritualized way of acting that produces a predictable and desired result, conforming to the invisible laws of nature. The result of whatever you do is its karma or outcome. Remember *kri*—to do? While we are within matter, whatever we do produces reactions that were initiated by our use of free will. Extending that principle, the reactions of all our actions belong to and come back to us.

The Universal Computer

Since the discovery of computers and wireless communication, this ancient understanding that everything in nature is invisibly connected in a web of laws or rules has become much more obvious to us. For the moment, think of all of nature as a great mainframe computer with all of us as independent nodes with our own hard disk and processor. We are wirelessly connected to the mainframe in a kind of "inner-net." We are uploading and downloading information all the time. Right at this moment, some file that you created is downloading to you and "you have mail." The biological functions of our bodies are being conducted by a larger program of rules and regulations that exist as software in the mainframe. We are never independent of that larger system, even if we ignore its messages for some time. Ignoring the mainframe is never in our best interest and inevitably leads us to the nearest body shop to be looked at by the "body nerds" we call doctors.

Rule-Based Thinking and Cosmic Law

Light, air, food, electricity, various frequencies—from the obvious to the parts too small to see, packets of highly organized information are being exchanged by all the nodes on this great network of cause and effect. All of this data flow is being conducted by a rule-based system the sages of India called the *ritam*. If you ignore those rules or oppose them, your life will begin to break down. Your car will break down; your body will break down. It is for this reason that ignorance is not bliss. The simple equation for humans is "ignorance of the laws of nature = suffering." Thus, if you add the letter "m" to the Sanskrit word *ritam*, it becomes *mritam* or death. Just break all the rules all the time and see what happens— mritam.

Why Justice is Blind

The result is death or simply failure of whatever enterprise we may be attempting. If you don't believe me, just buy a new car and then violate all the rules in the driver's manual. In no time the car will be ruined. Now I'm not suggesting that you actually go do that. The point is, karma is very strict. This is the reason that justice is portrayed as a woman holding a balance while wearing a blindfold. The woman is Mother Material Nature. The scale means that nature is always seeking balance or justice. But she is blindfolded because the laws of karma are equally applicable to everyone. Once you grasp that the eternal souls have come into matter, which is conducted by strict laws, and that upon reaching human life they are held accountable for all their actions, then the importance of karma as an understanding of life's process becomes clear.

The Cosmic Investment Program ✎

Another metaphor for this system of cause and effect and how it influences our every action is to see karma as a financial arrangement. From this perspective, the whole of nature is a great bank in which all wealth is deposited. Humans have free will, which is an endowment of capital they receive by being eternal and conscious. Through the investing of their money (free will) in various actions and enterprises, they earn interest, receive payments, establish savings accounts, and open investments that eventually yield their R.O.I. (return on investment) at various future dates. This means, of course, that reincarnation is an ongoing process of paying debts and receiving the profits on our portfolios of investments. We wouldn't want it to be any other way. If you work for two weeks, you expect to receive a paycheck. The problem is, the same law that gives you your pay also holds you accountable for breaking any of the rules of the system. There is no way to have free will without having both positive and negative consequences from its use.

We Are Farmers Planting the Seeds of Karma ✎

Another way to contemplate karma is to view yourself as a farmer planting seeds. The things we do are seeds which, once planted, begin to grow. Since we are constantly acting in a variety of ways, our gardens become very complicated. In this view, our body is called the field of activities. Since the mind and body are closely connected, even our thoughts are powerful actions that set processes in motion within our body. Whatever we eat, contact, or associate with sets waves of cause and effect rippling into motion in our bodies. To continue the agricultural metaphor, our actions plant the seeds of plants whose fruit we will reap as crops of pleasure and pain sometime in the future. Of course, this also means that whatever field (body) you currently have is also the result of many actions you planted in a previous life. How many lives ago? Who knows, but since we are eternal, that would depend on what you had planted and how long it would take to be ready to harvest (experience). In this way, if you follow the logic of karma as the continual unfolding of cause and effect that was initiated by our use of free will, then we are always reaping and sowing new actions in every moment.

We Create Our Own Heaven and Hell

The final factor in this process is the vast number of beings around us, especially the humans who also have free will. At any moment, humans may use their free will to force us to open new karmic accounts with them. It is no wonder that life in the material world is complicated. There are so many visitors to the park and even though there are rules that govern the park in the long run, humans can use their free will in the short term to create considerable chaos in their own and everyone else's life. Thus it is that we can create heaven or hell on Earth by working cooperatively with the ritam or going against its inviolable rules. This applies to us as individuals, families, societies, countries and as a planet. Karmas add up and extend to every level of life on our planet.

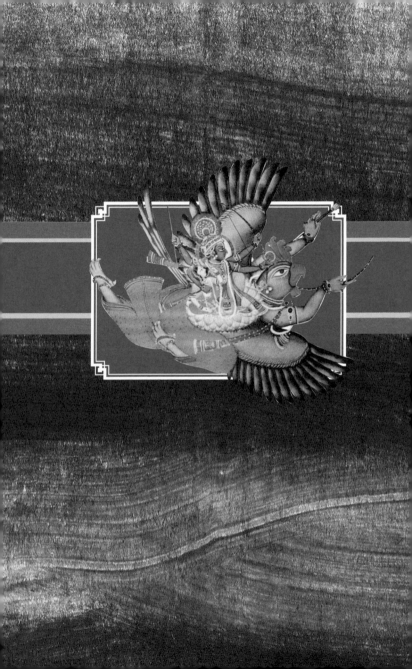

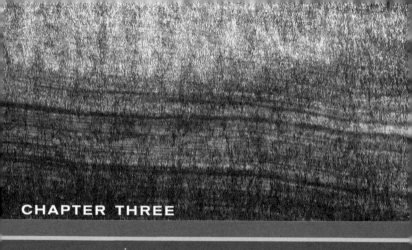

CHAPTER THREE

Universal Parcel System—UPS

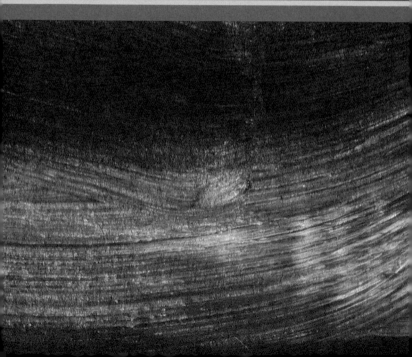

Universal Parcel

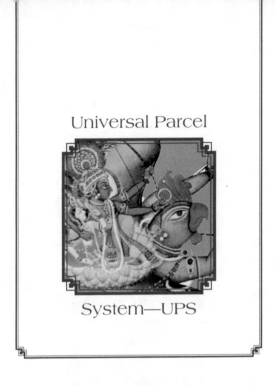

System—UPS

You are either a deva or have deviated in some way

O f all existing species, humans appear to be the only ones who ask the questions of who they are and where they come from. To answer these questions, many different religions and philosophies have arisen over time. Although there are many differences between them, they share some commonalities that show up repeatedly. One of the views found in almost every culture is that there are divine helpers, angels, or elves. They are called by these and many other names. In the Vedic literature and tradition, these divine beings are called *devas* and *devis* (since they are both male and female). The English word divine is derived from the Sanskrit *deva*, meaning "playing in the light."

Returning to the metaphor of the material world as a great amusement park, think of the devas as those beings who are acting in various roles for the purpose of maintaining the park. Sometimes these beings are also called gods because they have power over certain departments of nature, but the word "god" is misleading since it could imply that they are various competing "Gods." That is not the correct understanding of the devas. They do not compete but rather cooperate to control the flow of all natural resources. It is exactly like the city in which you live. Someone is in charge of the water department, the electricity, the gas, and collecting the garbage. They are persons just like you except they are temporarily in charge of a resource that everyone needs and uses.

Devas Have Longer Lives

So it is with the Vedic notion of the devas. They are described as souls like us or those in animals or trees, except that their current birth has given them the chance to experience being divine

helpers in the cosmic park. Instead of being tourists in the park (like we humans are) they are helping to run the park, working directly with the Park Promoter. Some devas have come to that position from the transcendental realm and others have first been human. As humans, they somehow earned the right to become a deva through their good actions. Devas are said to live longer than humans and have very sublime and pleasurable lives. The creation of the devic realm precedes the creation of humans and other creatures since their functions of maintaining the park are interwoven into the laws of nature. It is written that our year is their day: 360 of our years is their year, and multiplying by 100 equals their lifespan which then is 3,600 years. After completing their lives as devas, they also die and take their next birth as evolved humans. The angels or devas live in a place in between the earthly level and the transcendental realm. They have subtle bodies that are not directly visible to the human senses, although the devas can make themselves visible if they choose to. They are still within the material realm but are working directly in association with the Supreme Being, as the deputed managers of universal affairs.

Parks and Recreation Department

The devas work directly for the owner of the park. Whoever or whatever that Supreme Being is, the devas or angels are working directly for the Cosmic Parks and Recreation department, controlling weather and other natural processes. Of course, modern science has depersonalized all of these actions of divine intelligence into impersonal laws of nature. Remember, from the karmic point of view, both the law and the lawmaker are necessary for a complete understanding of all that exists. This means that behind every scientific process is also the personal being, or deva, managing a department of nature. Both are true at the same time. From our point of view, the devas look like processes in nature. From their point of view, we look like tourists in their park.

The devas are crucial to the understanding of karma, since they are the delivery system for our long-forgotten parcels of karma. For the moment, just imagine that whatever you do is transformed into an envelope, package or truckload of something that belongs to you. It has your name on it. Our nature as humans is to be so busy and self-preoccupied that we easily forget our past. Just as we forget our dreams from day to day, so we forget or often would like to forget our past actions.

But if there is no cosmic accountability, then there is really no cosmic justice and no continuum of free will. If that is the case, our short-term human justice would be a foolish notion. If there is no long-term cosmic justice, then why would we, who are living within the cosmos, invent a concept of justice and what would it be based upon? We all begin our lives in different positions of advantage or disadvantage. If this is our only life, then that is unjust. If we only live for one life, then the only conclusion is that life is unjust and unfair. How can we expect everyone to be accountable to a set of laws when they don't have equal opportunity to follow them? Such a system would be injustice parading as justice. So karma theory holds that since we are eternal individuals, as soon as we become humans, everything we do creates a stream of karma packets, letters, and packages with our names on them, which is constantly being "returned to sender."

Angels or Cosmic Postal Workers

The Vedas inform us that the devas are also the cosmic postal workers whose job it is to deliver humans their parcels of karma. We of course have usually forgotten the action that created a particular reaction. We don't know that winning the lottery probably gives us our old money back from a previous life. We can call the devas UPS, the Universal Parcel Service. Remember, accountability means you must also have an accounting system. Most people believe in accountability because it helps them to get what they want. But if the universal intelligence believes in accountability, then we are responsible for everything we do within the material world.

According to the Vedas, the devas are the divine accountants and the delivery system for all our trillions of karmic packages. FedEx could learn a lot from the devas.

Now this is where karma really gets interesting. In order for the delivery system to work efficiently, the many souls in the park have to be brought together again and again in various situations in order to pay back old karmic debts to each other. This is true even though they may have forgotten their connections with each other in previous births. Whoever you may be in this life bears no obvious resemblance to who you were in your previous lives. We are not the body or mind. We are the soul. The devas remember our history even when we forget. They are the continuity between our various lives. So as it turns out, not only are the devas UPS, they are also air traffic control.

Air Traffic Control

A ir traffic control means that unknown to us, the devas sometimes need to control our actions in order to position us next to someone with whom we have old karma to pay or receive. These would be parents, children, spouses, coworkers, enemies, and the like. All of the inexplicable and unavoidable coincidences, accidents, or enforced circumstances in our lives are the actions of the devic air traffic control department. At this point we can hear the human voice saying, "But, but what about my free will?" Of course, my friends, free will is how we created the results that UPS and air traffic control are kindly delivering to us. They are ensuring that over time there truly is cosmic justice. Even when we move to another body, they know our forwarding address.

Thoughts Put the Wheels in Motion

The question of free will is always at the center of any discussion of karma. In order to understand free will better, we need to take a closer look at exactly what action or doing is for us as humans. According to the Vedic theory, there are three kinds of doing that generate karmic reactions: thinking, speaking, and acting through our body. All three of these uses of our free will start the wheels of karmic reaction turning in some way.

The first and most subtle of our actions is thinking. The Vedic saying is, "everything rests upon desire." It is described that our mind is the place of contact between us and the devas. They can hear or smell our thoughts and desires and begin responding to them in real time. In other words, they are directly hearing what we think and feel. Just envision your mind as a wireless connector, a kind of cell phone, and whatever you could have, be or do in the park as something you request from the devas, just like ordering from a catalogue. In this way, thoughts and desires are received by the devas as your request to have that particular item delivered or to deliver you to where that item is. Hence, the saying "be careful what you wish for." In a similar way, every cell in your body "hears" your every thought and it reacts immediately through the mind-body link. What we think directly begins to reprogram our bio-computer. Thoughts are also picked up by other beings exactly in the way information from cell phones or wireless Internet is sent and received. Just by thinking we are doing.

Words Can Be Binding ☙

Next come words. Our speech is more powerful than we can imagine. In most cultures on our planet, until recent times a person's word was binding. All agreements were verbal. One's word was one's bond. Therefore the things we say put energies in motion that become reality. We literally speak things into manifestation. If you speak badly of others, you are cursing them. If you speak kindly of them, you are blessing them. Perhaps the image of the little devil on one shoulder and deva or angel on the other is not so far-fetched. By speaking, we create lasting impressions of who we are on all of those around us. These impressions create our futures. We have all experienced situations in life where words were spoken that put very powerful actions into motion. Sometimes words can be withdrawn and forgiven, but at other times, just by speaking, an irrevocable course of action is set in motion.

As for actions, they are the last irreversible step. With thoughts and even words, sometimes you can erase or undo a thought or word, but actions are the request for the pizza which, once ordered, cannot be sent back. The truck has left the building and the devas are about to deliver something you ordered in the now forgotten past. If you are delivered something unpleasant, you could say, "Poor me, I am a victim," or if you receive something wonderful you could say, "Lucky me, I did something right." In either case, whatever lands, in spite of your current desires or wishes, is a parcel of karma you ordered by acting in the past. If you don't accept that it was created by your own action, then it can only have been imposed by some unknown Being or force, in which case we are consigned to being perpetual victims of blind destiny.

In the karmic view we are always in a position to play the game better and by so doing change the outcome. The rules of action and reaction are obviously running the park; science has demonstrated that clearly for everyone to understand. Once you add our eternal nature into the equation, the result is long-term action and reaction with free will and personal accountability. Our dilemma is that the size of the universe seems daunting to our minds. We have trouble imagining that any system of accounting could be so complex and accurate. We are inclined to underestimate the Divine Intelligence.

All the World Is a Stage

In the final analysis, this view of karma should broaden our view of life considerably. We are souls evolving by trial and error in a vast university that is managed from top to bottom by invisible divine intelligence. Nonetheless, our free will is running the show, even though the balance is always being maintained by divine law and the constant efforts of the devas. As for us as humans, Shakespeare got it right when he said, "All the world is a stage and the men and women are merely players." Whatever we appear to be now does not at all resemble the thousand previous births that came before. Yet according to Vedic karma theory, all those births and this one as well have created and continue to create a stream of reactions that are the by-product of being in the world of matter. We are truly souls having a human experience, while the devas are souls having a heavenly material experience. But all the souls are playing at being something they are not, on the big stage of the material world. We are all in costumes made of matter. From microbes to plants to animals to humans to devas, all are eternal souls dressed in matter.

CHAPTER FOUR

KARMA, DEATH, AND DYING

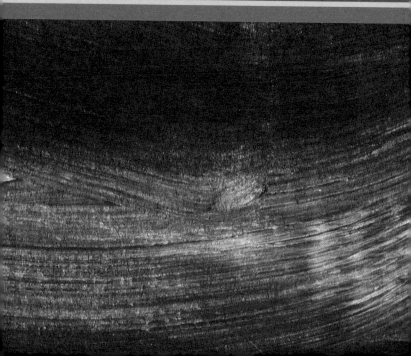

Karma,

Death, and Dying

What you resist persists, what you fear, draws near

As we have seen, by its very nature the empirical scientific methodology is not designed to answer spiritual or materially unverifiable questions. That is because its process demands a repeatable experiment for separate validation of a theory. The strength of material science is technology within matter. Its weakness is that our senses, even aided by scientific equipment, can only see so far. Beyond that point we cannot directly perceive reality. If empirical scientists insist that nothing is true beyond that point, they become priests in their own religion instead of the material technicians that they should be according to their own methodology. Empirical science does not have any special authority or qualification to speak on what is beyond the materially provable. In spite of this, in our popular culture the authority of empirical science often extends beyond the areas of its actual knowing. To the untrained mind, knowledge in one discipline creates an air of authority in other unrelated disciplines. For the same reason, we ask movie stars their opinion on many things which they have no proper qualifications to answer.

Karma Theory Originates in the Vedas

The theory of karma as taught in the Vedas of India presents itself as a body of insight into the workings of the material universe and what is beyond. Some of what it teaches is materially verifiable, like any scientific matter, and some of it is meant to be the subject of meditation by us. In the study of karma, scientific knowledge, and empirically unverifiable knowledge are both present. This chapter is devoted to the process of death. It is based on descriptions from the Vedas that attempt to convey some idea of what takes place when we make the transition from one body to the next in our continued transmigration around the Ferris wheel of samsara. Rather than thinking of these descriptions as literal, like a science textbook, think of them as a poetic or metaphorical attempt to convey some of the subtle processes that take place when we leave one body and transition to another through the divine guidance of the devas.

The first thing to remember is that the devas are mediating or assisting in all of the transitions, even when we may be unconscious or unaware. Remember that the amusement park is open 24/7, also when we are asleep or unconscious. It is just like any big city. Whether you are awake or asleep, the water, electricity, garbage, street signals, and police and fire departments are all still working. Similarly, the divine helpers are always awake whether we notice them or not. With this in mind, let's hear what the Vedas have to say about how we go from one body to another.

The Dense and Subtle Bodies

In order to understand how death works, we need to look more closely at the *gu* (remember the goo?) that surrounds our souls as our body/mind complex. According to karma theory, we actually have two bodies: one is a dense physical body made of heavy matter. That body is made up of the five great elements, earth, water, fire, air, and space, which are further broken down into the 108 or so atomic elements of modern perception. This is the dense body we are used to using as our vehicle in the material world, though some people think of it as their actual "self." Within or beyond that body is a subtle covering made up of mind, intelligence and egoic conceptions of self. That subtle body is the same one we become during dreams. While dreaming, even though our physical body is parked on the bed, we continue to be active in our subtle body. Underneath both of those coverings we find our true self as the *jiva-atma* or soul.

These two bodies, the dense and subtle, are coverings over our true selves. Thus it is often said that the physical body is our coat, the subtle body is our shirt and our naked body is like the pure soul with no material coverings. With this in mind you could say that dreaming is running around the cosmos in your nightshirt. Of course the three (body, mind, and soul) are connected once we take birth within the material world. It is said that whatever we experience from life to life is recorded on our subtle bodies. We are bar-coded with all the things we do and we carry the record of our past with us wherever we travel and from birth to birth. In addition, many things that are recorded in our subtle bodies as memories are reflected into our physical bodies as outward expressions of our inner states. That is the mind/body link. Recently the science of massage therapy and body-work such as Rolfing, Bowen, Cranial-sacral, Chiropractic and many others have acknowledged that what is stored in the subtle body is often stored in the physical body as well.

Lord Yama and the Court of Karmic Justice ⟨

For the process of leaving our bodies, the devas know that each soul has an allotment of time in a particular body. When that time is up, the devas send a few of their own workers to collect us—that is, to remove us from our physical bodies. This experience we call death. Think of those angels/devas as representatives of the cosmic judicial system. They usually have to drag us out of whatever we are doing in the physical world because of our intense attachment to the physical realm. According to some descriptions in the Vedas, the devas throw a net over our subtle bodies and pull us out of our physical bodies. We are then transported from there to a special part of the devic realm that is devoted to death and rebirth. You could think of it as the cosmic courthouse. This is where Mother Nature keeps the scales that measure and balance all we do or have done.

As you can well imagine, this process is very disorienting to most souls since they were very attached to their previous material lives. A transition period follows, during which their bodies are cremated or buried, and they are mourned and memorialized by those who

knew them. Finally they end up as faint memories. But to the devas, the deceased are eternal souls who need to continue their evolution within the realms of matter. So after some time, souls, who are still wearing the nightshirts of the subtle body, are calmed and pacified. Finally, when their turns come, they are taken into the courtroom of cosmic justice to evaluate their last lives and learn of their next ones.

In the Vedas, this entire process is described in considerable detail. The deva in charge of this process is named Yama Raja, or the Lord of Death and Judgment. He is the administrator of the ritam, or universal laws. His assistant is named Chitragupta, the court recorder. All that he records is kept in a vast library which you may have heard of; it is called the Akashic records. *Akasha* refers to the element space. The idea here is that all our thoughts, words and deeds are observed and recorded by other higher intelligences that are monitoring our long-term spiritual evolution.

The Devas Do Not Forget

At this point, the subtle body of the soul is examined and the nuances of cause and effect are explained to the soul. You could say in modern terms that the soul is shown the movie of its life and the subtle concepts of cosmic law of cause and effect are explained to him. Think of this as an educational process rather than a judgmental or punitive one. After all, some souls receive very good news at that meeting and are told of the wonderful progress they are making. Others receive not such great news as the result of things they have done to harm others or cause great pain. All of this is just the movie of what we chose to do. And the devas do not forget, or rather, they can read what we carry with us in our subtle bodies. According to the Vedic report on this, we are in their hands entirely once we are no longer in a physical body.

In the final step of this process, the soul is told of its future. To simplify this, imagine again that our use of free will is a constant process of investment. We could say that this meeting of the atma with Yama Raja and Chitragupta is a kind of meeting with your banker and accountant, who then tell you how much money you have available to spend for the next year (that is, in your next life). They tell you who your next parents will be, your siblings and relations, how much money you will have coming and your gender and type of body, as well as many other predetermined details.

After that consultation you will be readied for transition to the next womb. After nine months or so you will reemerge in another physical body (assuming you have come back as human again). You will still be the same soul with the same subtle body, filled with impressions from previous lives, but once you are born all of that will lie below the surface to unfold gradually in your new life. Picture the moment of your birth, metaphorically speaking, when the deva airplane lands (that stork we always heard about) and you are handed to your parents as their new bundle of joy. Unknown to them, your suitcases full of karmas from previous lives are stored in the basement. On them is a sign that says, "Open these when you leave home and start to use free will again."

Choices Create Our Future

Most societies don't hold children responsible for their actions with the same degree of culpability as they do adults. Of course, for us humans free will does start at a fairly young age. In no time we will be making choices that again create new reactions that will become our future. And most likely, that bully who always tormented you was a reincarnated player from your past in some forgotten previous life. The same is true for your parents, siblings, relatives and teachers. Only the Supreme Being and the devas know the secrets of our karmic past, though a good psychic or astrologer can gain some insight into the things that are in our karmic suitcases. That is because some of those karmas are already cued up for delivery. As you have probably suspected by now, there are various kinds of karmas and the whole subject is as complex as any elaborate legal system, only this legal jurisdiction is conducted on a cosmic scale for trillions of souls.

CHAPTER FIVE

FOUR DIFFERENT
TYPES OF KARMA

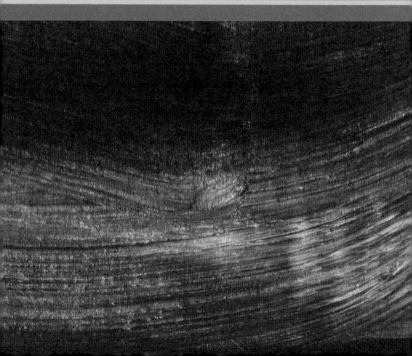

Four Different

Types of Karma

Intention is the engine of action

Almost all the ancient cultures of the world believed in concepts very similar to the atma, karma, and reincarnation. A rose by any other name would smell the same. Our modern ignorance of or resistance to karma got its start when the Western Catholic Church passed a resolution at a 5th Century Nicene council, stating that in their view the soul did not pre-exist before the body. By that vote, opposition to karma and reincarnation became Catholic dogma and have been taught as such ever since. That dogma was then also passed on to most of the Protestant branches of Christianity as well.

Before the teachings on an eternal soul and reincarnation were voted out of the Catholic doctrine, many devout Christians of the first four centuries had believed that reincarnation was the actual true understanding of Jesus' teachings. The Roman Catholic view finally prevailed and the concept of rebirth was generally referred to by them as the "Eastern Heresy." The departure from viewing the soul as eternal did later cause some considerable philosophical problems for the Catholic theologians. Since Catholics are required to be baptized at birth for the removal of their sins, the more observant among them began to ask some difficult questions. If the soul did not exist before the body, they reasoned, then how could it have sinned? If it had only existed as a baby, what sins could it possibly have committed?

Original Sin Invented

This caused the 6th Century Catholic theologian Augustine to invent an explanation for this dilemma called "Original Sin." He explained the story of Adam and Eve as a drama in which the woman tempted the man to eat the apple (have sex). They were then thrown out of the garden for that indiscretion, by an angry God. Later, their sin was somehow passed on to their children, a sort of early precursor to genetics. In this view then, although the soul did not exist before sex, it somehow came into being through sex, and the sin of being born by sex made the soul evil enough to require baptism for purification. In this way, the subject of reincarnation was temporarily avoided. There was also no attempt to define the difference between consciousness in animals or plants and in people. Why are people conscious with a soul whereas animals are also conscious yet have no soul? Where does their consciousness arise from? These and many other philosophical questions are related to reincarnation as an explanation of life.

For the last 1,500 years, the Catholic and Protestant churches have remained entrenched in this 5th Century decision. In the same way that science was persecuted, so have views like reincarnation been maligned and labeled as heresy, even though they are the most ancient spiritual teachings of our planet and also support a grand view of both individuality and divine justice. Some people think that the Nicene councils were trying to take power over common people by telling them they only have one lifetime. This tactic is well-known in the world of business as the "impending doom close." The salesman says: "Act now folks, because the sale ends tomorrow."

In other words, if I tell you that you are not divine and are a sinner and that I alone can grant you immortality, that gives me absolute power over your life and future. In the Vedic teaching, we are all souls, and consciousness is the symptom of the soul's existence in a plant, human, or animal. No one can grant you immortality, since it is already your very nature.

The Big View is Reincarnation

The Vedic view is that an eternal soul, cosmic justice, and reincarnation are the teachings that honor the individual the most and offer a big view of our potential to evolve as divine beings over long periods of time. Reincarnation also removes the rush to judge the soul and send it to hell or heaven after only one lifetime. If being judged for our actions is an ongoing process, then from life to life we are always in some condition that is a response to our previous actions. We are the drivers of our own karma.

Returning to our discussion of the types of karma performed by the souls, we are constantly engaged in various kinds of actions. This means that a steady stream of reactions will necessarily follow what we think, speak and do. Those reactions are categorized differently according to the degree of ripeness of the fruits of our deeds. For the moment, think like a farmer observing the various crops you have planted in your fields.

Ripe Fruit Karma

The first kind of karma to consider is called *prarabda* in Sanskrit, which means "ripe fruit." If you have ever picked fruit, you know that when it is ripe, the fruit falls into your hand by simply touching it. If it is unripe, it stays on the tree. The first ripe fruit karma we received this lifetime was our bodies, and with it our parents and extended family. This includes our genetic code and whatever problems and advantages come with that particular combination of factors. *Prarabda karma* is also called destiny, or manifest karma. It is the part of our reality that we cannot change by exerting any amount of free will.

Later on, if you decide to have children, whichever ones are delivered by the devas will be yours. You cannot send them back. Aside from these biological givens, most of our childhood circumstances that are beyond our control—teachers, school, classmates, our parents' relationship, their longevity, childhood diseases, and many more circumstances—are all prarabda karmas. In addition to those, there are a certain number of events or experiences that the devas are scheduled to deliver to us at a specific time in any lifetime.

We are usually unaware of the devas' delivery schedule and of the necessity of our receiving whatever they must deliver. After all, they are just giving us the things we have previously created by the use of our free will. There is the saying, "If the universe gives you lemons, make lemonade." For "universe," just think of the devas who are delivering your karma on behalf of the Supreme Being, the owner of the park. Then again, you may as easily have cherries delivered instead of lemons. It all depends on your unseen but very real karmic history.

Seedling Karma

The second variety of karma is called *sanchitta*, or the seeds of karma that are contained in our subtle bodies. Changing our bodies is very difficult to understand and at some levels impossible. Yet it is our destiny and therefore unchangeable. But changing our minds is an everyday moment-to-moment process that we understand. It is conducted by free will, or at least it could be. The Vedic definition of "mind" is "that organ of cognition that performs the activities of thinking, feeling and willing." Just as there is a tendency for us to think we are our bodies, calling the bodies our selves, so we have an even greater tendency to identify our minds as our selves. The philosopher Descartes said it very clearly: "I think, therefore I am." The Vedic view however is that we are the atma and both mind and body are the coverings of matter. If the body is made up of sticky pieces of *gu* (goo) that we have accumulated by eating, drinking, and breathing, then what is the mind made of? What are its contents and how do they affect us?

We have Hardware and Software

The simple answer is memories of past experience. These memories can be of this lifetime or of many previous lifetimes. In that sense, each person is like an archeological dig, with layer after layer of past experience encoded into his or her subtle body. A useful way to think of the dense body and subtle body is to compare them to a computer and its software. Our bodies, the computers, come with certain capabilities hardwired into their constructions, and our subtle bodies come loaded with the software downloaded through previous life experiences and acquired abilities.

Previously experienced emotions are also embedded in each person's subtle body, along with a large number of programs that have been placed there by parenting, social pressure and our own intentional learning. Along with those various programs are also old habits of thinking in certain patterns. The Vedas state it this way:

"Habit is our second nature." Our first nature is the soul, or atma, but certain patterns in our subtle bodies that are the residue of our past karma continue to control our future actions. Unless those patterns are changed, we will continue to repeat the same actions again and again. We are both preprogrammed and reprogrammable.

For this reason, our subtle bodies are the places where current desires, past impressions and habitual patterns grow like seeds. Technically speaking, those mental seeds do not have to grow into a destiny or irrevocable future if they are removed in time. This "changing our mind" is the primary aim of yoga and a variety of other Vedic arts of modifying our future by changing or reprogramming the software in the subtle body. Sanchitta karma can be altered by the use of free will. Just like changing an old habit, the mind can have old files removed from the subtle body. The result will then be a different way of doing and thus a different future destiny.

Creating our Future from Present Actions

The third variety of karma consists of the results from our current actions. If prarabda karma is the destined events we cannot prevent and sanchitta karma is the seeds of future action sitting upon the subtle body, then the third variety of karma is called *agama karma*, the karma being generated by our current actions. It has been said that there is one radio station that everyone in the world is always listening to: W.I.I.F.M. or "What's In It for Me?"

The Vedas call this *ahamkara* or material ego. The dilemma for us is that we are filled with desires for the experiences within the park, but we are not always very mindful about the effect our actions are having on the whole system and those around us. In this regard, the devas can be compared to the ecology department. They have control over the weather, the resources of nature and the ebb and flow of all other species as part of their work in maintaining the park. But we humans with our extreme free will are the wild card in the deck. We can upset the balance of nature with our tendency to want more and more. To quote Mahatma Gandhi, "The Lord has provided enough for everyone's need. He has not provided enough for everyone's greed." Our current actions can take the ecological viewpoint of the devas into consideration, or we can use our free will to override their attempts at restoring balance to the world around us.

Even though we have destined limitations and a residual set of abilities and habitual ideas, at any given moment we can make life-altering decisions with the use of free will. Some of those decisions will shape the unfolding of events in our current lives, as obvious reactions to what we choose, while the larger number of reactions to what we do will be deposited into or debited from our future karma accounts. All existing possibilities for changing our positions and locations within the park result from the conscious choices we are making in the present moment.

The Law of Association ⦀

That present moment can be run on autopilot from past habits of mind, our sanchitta karma, or we can reassert our conscious choices to dramatically redirect our destinies in the present moment. The secret of agama karma lies in two things. The first is that whatever we associate with we become like. We become like what we like. Not only is the *gu* sticky and all around us, it also has particular qualities that either improve us or degrade us. We all know that children need good role models in order not to become bad citizens. Good or bad, there are states within matter that are either destructive, and agitating, or peaceful and balanced. There is an old Chinese proverb that says, "Your parents are chosen for you, your siblings are chosen for you, your spouse is chosen for you, your children are chosen for you, so the only thing you get to choose is your friends." In a very real sense, our future karma is created by the alliances and friendships we choose with free will in the present

moment. From those associations will come actions of a particular
type which will determine our future.

Taking a Vow

The second secret of agama karma is called *vrata* in Sanskrit. Vrata
means "taking a vow." Because humans do not have a purely
instinctual nature like other creatures, we are forced to decide who
and what we are by choosing among the many choices life constantly
offers. That decision-making requires that we define our selves
and our boundaries of action. This is the tension of human life
that distinguishes us from all other births. We can choose to dive
back into the animal kingdom, or we can choose to become a deva,
or divine helper, though they must eventually return as a human.
We can remain human and by so doing involve our selves in some
enterprise of action which will definitely define our futures. Finally
we may follow some path that leads us back to the spiritual and
transcendental realm from which we originally set forth on this
journey. In every case, to maintain any path we must finally take a

vow and stick to it, in order to be self-defining in the creation of our futures. Our current vows, or the lack of them, are defining who our friends are and between them our next future is being created as our agama karma.

Action without Karma

The last major category of karma could be described as "no karma." Remember the concept of old souls vs. young souls? If we have come to this world to explore and learn, then our karmas are how we steer our ships from one place to another within the park. But what happens when a soul finishes with the park and is ready to leave? Let's just say for the purposes of this discussion that the Vedas describe this material world as having an entrance coming in from the transcendental world and also an exit back out to the transcendental world. You will know you are an old soul when playing in the park no longer excites you but the prospect of finding the exit gives you great enthusiasm. This process of finally exiting the material world is called *moksha* in Sanskrit. In English, we could call it "final liberation," or the return of the atma to its original home from which the journey into the dark realm of matter began.

Of course, the journey from young soul to old soul is usually a gradual process over many lifetimes. *Kriyamana karma* then, is something we accumulate from life to life through our various spiritual activities. This so-called karma is fundamentally different from material karma in that kriyamana karma once earned is never lost or exhausted. It accumulates from life to life until we are ready to graduate from the university. All other karmas are temporary responses to our egocentric actions. You invest money, win a million dollars, spend it, and then it is gone forever. But with kriyamana karma, certain kinds of special actions build an account of "liberation karma." That account is never diminished. In Chapter Seven, we will examine this process of final liberation in more detail.

CHAPTER SIX

ASTROLOGY, AYURVEDA, AND THE SCIENCE OF KARMA

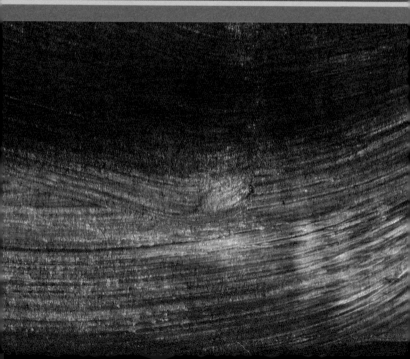

Astrology, Ayurveda, and

the Science of Karma

Mind is the soul's cocoon, body is the branch it is attached to

In modern times, the great and ancient science of astronomy/astrology has been misunderstood, maligned, and often made into trivial entertainment for consumption in the daily newspaper. In spite of the recent decline of astrology under the criticism of both modern science and various religions, it remains of interest to billions of people throughout the world. In its entertainment form it is a multi-billion-dollar industry. In the West, astrology also has a long history. When astrology was not being persecuted by church or state, as recently as 200 years ago it was taught at medical schools as a sister science of medicine. It has been studied and used regularly by some of the greatest leaders and thinkers in world history.

But long before modern times, be it the early days of Christianity, the Roman Empire or even Greek culture, astrology was practiced in India under the name of *Jyotisha*. This name means "the science of how light regulates life." In the last fifty years, along with various forms of yoga, Ayurvedic medicine and many other branches of Vedic learning, Jyotisha has spread around the world and is now sometimes called Hindu astrology, or more correctly, Vedic astrology. Jyotisha has always been associated with the Vedic knowledge and culture of India. As in the later medical schools of Europe, Vedic astrology and the medical system of India called Ayurveda were always considered sister sciences. Both medicine and astrology in India are based upon the principles of soul, karma, and reincarnation.

Ayurveda, the Medical System of Ancient India

Ayurveda is the science of preserving life whereas modern Allopathic medicine is mostly concerned with treating diseases or emergency conditions after they have arisen. Ayurveda was primarily concerned with the prevention of the imbalances in lifestyle and diet that lead to disease. Secondarily, Ayurveda had also developed very advanced surgical procedures. Only modern medicine has excelled beyond what Ayurveda had achieved. By 800 B.C.E., Ayurveda had developed procedures for brain surgery, anesthesia, cataract operations, and reconstructive plastic surgery. Ayurveda also developed an extensive herbal and pharmacological system in which thousands of plants and substances were catalogued for medical use, many of which have been patented as modern pharmacological remedies.

In those remote times, Vedic astrology was also very sophisticated in its astronomical understanding of the universe. The Vedic system of time calculation is the only culture other than our modern technological one to calculate the age of the universe in billions of years. Indian astronomers and mathematicians were the historical source of the use of zero, the so-called Arabic numerals 1-10, calculus, trigonometry, algebra, and binary mathematics, and had accurately calculated the motion of the Earth's wobble to precisely 25,920 years. They knew the Sun was the center of the solar system and had correctly calculated the distances between and relative sizes of the Earth, Moon, and Sun.

Astronomical Knowledge was used in Medicine

This considerable astronomical knowledge was applied to two principal endeavors. The first was living in harmony with the seasons and energies of the cosmos. This is crucial to Ayurvedic medicine, as it promotes harmony with nature. The second is the use of astronomical information to understand the nature, timing, and delivery of karma. In the case of Ayurveda, lunar, solar, and planetary energies surround us at all times. Those, along with seasonal influences, are the ever-changing cosmic background that we as humans need to harmonize with in order to stay balanced. Ask any traditional farmer and he or she will tell you that the success or failure of their work depends upon their knowledge of the seasons, Moon and Sun, as well as an understanding of weather, water, and the complex effect those forces have on all life.

For this chapter, Vedic astrology as the science of observing karma is our theme. As before, the place to begin our understanding of karma is first that it is rooted in the ritam, or invisible universal laws of nature. Second, that it is the devas who are the maintainers of nature and also the delivery mechanism for natural cause and effect. We call them the laws of nature. If you remember, the Sanskrit word deva means "playing in the light." Jyotisha is the science of how light is regulating all the cause and effect of life. Astrology is also called the science of time, since time is measured as the relationship between light and space measuring the unfolding of cause and effect. Light moves at 186,000 miles per second. We could say that this is the visible speed limit in matter for the unfolding of events. The ancient thinkers saw light as the action of divine intelligence, ultimately the Supreme Being acting through the devas to regulate all life in our biosphere.

The Devas are Behind the Scenes

Picture the devas as the behind-the-scenes divine agents who are constantly scheduling the delivery of all of our letters, packages and truckloads of karma. Sometimes, in order to stay on schedule, they have to get inside our minds and whisper suggestions to us, to direct us to the correct locations where the delivery or hand-off of certain karma is to be made. To us, their suggestions feel exactly like thoughts of our own creation, since they occur within our minds. Because we think we are the mind, the suggestions of the devas look like our own thoughts and ideas.

They say, "Why don't you go to the store," and we think, "Why don't I go to the store?" They say, "You are in love with this person," and we say, "I am in love with this person." This is the part of karma theory that drives ordinary humans crazy. Those who think we are alone here say: "What about my free will? If the devas are controlling my thoughts, then there is no free will." The Vedic answer to this important question is that the devas are only controlling our minds when they need to make a delivery of something we ordered in the past. At that moment they do a system override suspending our free will so we will receive the results of our past actions. The rest of the time we are running either by habit or free will. One might reply, "What right do they have to be inside my head and thoughts, telling me what to do?" The answer, of course, is simple—divine right; they work for the Supreme Being who owns the park. We have volunteered to come here and once here are forced to accept the rules of the park and the results of our own actions.

This is the conceptual framework behind Vedic astrology as the main science that gives insight into our previous karmas and their delivery schedule. For detailed information on this subject, please read my recent publication, the *Vedic Astrology Deck*, also published by Mandala. The short version of the story goes as follows. Since the souls are in the devas' hands during their transition from one life to another, the devas arrange the exact moment of birth according to the large and complex number of karmic variables and deliveries that are being given to the soul in their next life. This is the "air traffic control" part of the devas' job. The exact and complex trajectories of karmic deliveries are mapped out in advance in ways that are more complex than we can easily imagine.

The Place and Time of Birth Creates the Horoscope

Thus, the exact position in the sky of stars and planets at the precise latitude and longitude of birth creates a mathematical diagram composed of the points of light in the sky. That diagram is called a horoscope or "view of the hour" of birth. It could also be called a "karma-scope" since the devas' information regarding the individual's karma, along with the delivery schedule of when it will be delivered, is secretly encoded in the patterns in the sky at the moment of birth. However far-fetched or difficult this may be to conceive, the best minds of various great cultures have consistently found empiric and observable truth in the science of astrology throughout the ages. It is even said that the scientist and philosopher Newton, who was once criticized by one of his peers for his interest in astrology, replied curtly, "Sir, I have studied these things, whereas you have not." The critics of astrology should first learn it as a science, before they pass critical judgment on what they have not studied.

Vedic astrology, like much of the ancient wisdom of India, is still intact as an unbroken tradition for over 6,000 years. Both Vedic astrology and Ayurveda were traditionally used to monitor and correct manifest and soon-to-manifest karmic imbalances in all persons. A preventive Ayurvedic physician examines the body to determine where problematic cause and effect may be unfolding.

According to this perspective, disease of any kind is rooted in a violation of the ritam or laws of nature. That imbalance, if uncorrected, continues to develop in seven stages, culminating in what modern medicine finally calls symptoms and labels as a disease. The final stage of incurability is simply the end of a long period of imbalance that has ended in an incurable—that is to say, irreversible—physical condition. In this way, doctors, Ayurvedic or otherwise, are involved with parabda karma, the ripe fruit of long-term patterns of cause and effect.

Vedic Astrology Sees the Karmic History

Vedic astrology sees the entire karmic history unfolding over time. Some things visible in the chart will be parabda karmas that will happen because they must. Some karmas will show up as sanchitta, or tendencies, habits, abilities, and deficiencies that are the legacy from previous lives. Finally, some conditions will arise from temporary forces of nature that are transitory. In this area, before there was psychology, Vedic astrologers and Ayurvedic doctors worked as a team. They understood the mind-body connection. The mind influences the body, the body influences the mind, and nature influences both. This means that the early stages of a physical imbalance can often be altered by changing the thoughts and emotions, just as in the later stages, physical methods are also necessary. The horoscope reveals the inherent tendencies of the subtle body as well as temporary natural forces that are impinging upon us.

Finally, because we live within and are part of the complete matrix of cosmic energies, as they move we are affected by their motions. Some celestial bodies, like the Sun and Moon, push on us in very obvious and measurable ways. The planets' and stars' influence is more subtle. The changing patterns of cosmic energy are observed by the Vedic astrologer to understand how karmic patterns are unfolding. The question is often asked, "Do the planets impel or compel?" From the Vedic astrological, Ayurvedic and karmic perspectives, the answer is both. Sometimes the planets compel the delivery of an old piece of cause and effect. This will be visible to the astrologer as some movement within the sky as seen in relation to the same sky at the moment of a person's birth. Otherwise, the planets may impel by creating a climate of cosmic vibration that acts to impel us just as weather does in our daily lives. The physician will observe the same forces as changing the patterns of symptoms within the body.

To make this clearer, imagine that at the moment of conception, the exact combination of each person's genetic code is formed. From that time on, and throughout our lives, that specific gene code is programming various bodily functions as well as influencing various psychological functions and abilities. In addition, with our mental attitudes, we are reprogramming the genetic hardware by downloading new software (knowledge) into our systems. Similarly, the exact picture of the sky at your birth and all the points of light measurable in the sky, contain information about our specific karmic situation. As the planets continue their orbits around the sun, they not only move through the sky, but move through our own personal horoscope. Embedded in that horoscope are thousands of bits of information about us that can be extracted by a knowledgeable Vedic astrologer and seen by a skilled Ayurvedic medical practitioner. Similarly, a skilled geneticist could know volumes about you if he could properly interpret the relations contained in your genetic code.

Horoscope is Karma-scope

This is an important point. Just because astrology can be used to read your karmic patterns doesn't mean that everyone who claims to know astrology, in fact, does. We all understand that the same is true in medicine or genetics. That something can be done in theory is one thing; doing it in practice is another. Vedic astrology is a very complete presentation of the science of karma. Most systems

of astrology have some truth in them but how much varies widely.
The point here is "let the buyer beware." Much of modern astrology
is in a state of disrepair as a science at this moment in history
because it is underfunded in terms of scientific research and without
paid and respectable teaching positions. In spite of that, India's
Vedic astrology has kept the science alive and well with university
recognition at the highest PhD level. No conversation on karma is
complete without this proper understanding of the "karma-scope"
or horoscope. It is the view of our cause and effect from life to life as
seen by the divine intelligences of nature.

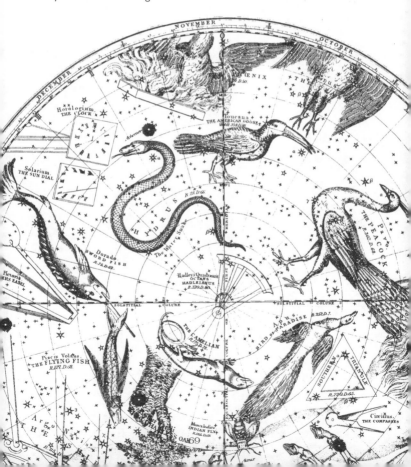

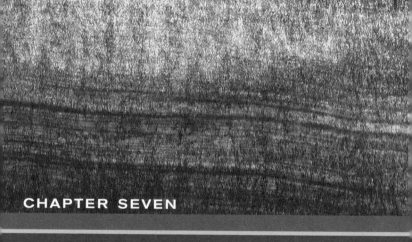

CHAPTER SEVEN

WHO IS IN CHARGE AND HOW TO GET FREE

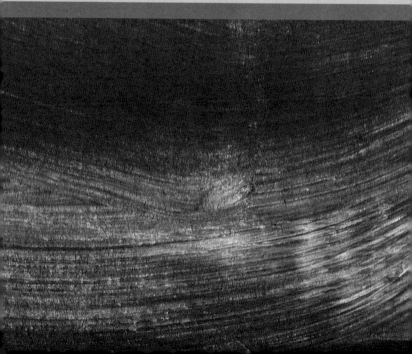

Who is in Charge

and How to Get Free

Beyond the wall of ignorance is the garden of Divinity

Since all discussions of cause and effect are examining some aspect of karma, the subject of right and wrong action is common to every spiritual tradition. As we have seen, the critical point that opens cause and effect up to its fullest extension is the view that we as individual beings are eternal and cannot die. The Vedas teach that immortality is not something we earn or that is granted to us, but that it is our true and essential nature. We are souls whose existence stretches to eternity in both directions, past and future.

The fact of our eternal nature does not remove the tension of our situation within the material world. Even though for the purpose of our discussion, I have described our visit to the realms of matter as a visit to a divinely constructed amusement park, being in the park is often less than amusing. On the darker side of things, even though we are eternal by nature, just arriving in the park guarantees that we will forget who we truly are as we pass through the countless species of life. By the time we reach human life, the poignancy of our situation is excruciatingly painful. We see the beauty of life and are madly attracted to it and then step by step lose everything we have achieved. Even if we are fortunate enough to live a relatively happy life without tragedy or disaster, we cannot help but see the misery and suffering that exist all around us. We may be sitting happily in one part of the park but in the distance, the sirens of someone's disaster can be heard.

The Four Problems of Material Life

The four concomitant processes that accompany us on our journeys through matter are birth, disease, old age, and death. No one in the material park is free from these inevitable and painful processes. From the smallest microbe to the mightiest deva, all have a beginning, then age, decay, and eventually are forced to leave their old and worn-out body to find yet another vehicle. Because we are eternal there is no end to this process as long as we are within matter. This samsara, or wheel of repeated birth and death, is nothing more than a reflection of the temporary nature of matter itself. Matter is unconscious and made of parts, whereas we are conscious and eternal by nature. This means that there is no permanent shelter or home for us within the material park. From top to bottom there is no place where we can stay, since even the park itself is periodically dissolved only to be rebuilt again and then again dissolved. This view is presented in the Vedas as the basis of karma.

It is our very nature that is frustrated by this process of birth, disease, aging, and death. What we want is a trouble-free, unlimited life of pleasure, creativity, and joy. But here there are only moments of what we want, while most of our life is interspersed with work, pain, suffering, depression, and unfulfilled desires.

In response to this dilemma, some philosophers promote the idea that there is a material or technological solution to our discomfort within matter. They say that we are material in our nature and that there is nothing beyond this current realm of our experience. From this conclusion, they continue with the view that there are no devas or distributed divine intelligences and ultimately no park Promoter or Supreme Being behind the park. Thus they define the laws of nature as arbitrary and random rules which we can bend or break as we see fit or as far as is possible. The ultimate goal of this view is either a pleasurable material life for the few while pretending to wish the same for all, or an ideal of equal distribution of material resources to all. Neither of these approaches solves the ultimate problem of our distress at the very unconscious nature of matter. No political or technological solution solves the problem of death.

The opposite view sees all living beings as of the same inherent transcendental and divine nature. It sees them all here by their own choices, evolving through the species and finally into human life, as a learning process in their souls' eternal journey to understand both each other, themselves and the Supreme Being, the Lord of Ultimate Love from whom all souls have originated. In this view, matter is the unconscious realm of the Supreme Reality and represents only one part of the total reality. The other part is our true transcendental home because it is conscious in nature, like us.

The Last Step is Final Liberation

After experimenting for an undetermined period of time and experiencing matter in both its joys and limitations, the soul becomes ready to exit the park and return to the transcendental abode. This process of return is the graduation ceremony for those souls who have finished their learning program within matter. At that stage, the souls engage in a process of gradual disassociation from matter. They begin to divest themselves of all material self-identification. Once this is accomplished, they finally achieve a state called moksha, or final liberation from identification with matter. The process of becoming ready to leave the park and resume one's true eternal nature is sometimes called *yoga*. The yoga that begins with physical postures and breathing is only one of many different yogic methodologies whose purpose is to assist the souls in achieving moksha, or final liberation from the bondage to matter. The word yoga literally means "to link or reestablish our forgotten connection to the Source of our existence in the transcendental realm."

The real aim of yoga is not health or physical fitness, or even mental balance and peace of mind. Those are by-products of achieving a state of permanent reconnection with our true eternal nature, the Supreme Reality and Being who is the source of all and the non-material home from which we originally began our journey into the realm of matter and karma. You may remember that the material energy is called the *gu* in Sanskrit. This *gu* (or goo) is the source of another well-known Sanskrit term, *guru*. *Gu* means "matter" and *ru* means "who removes it." Thus the real meaning of guru is anyone who has information on how to remove the souls' material conception of life and lead them back to their original spiritual nature.

You may remember that the subtle body is the place where the seeds of previous karmas and the desires of present actions are growing. That growth can be arrested, the desires changed and the growth of karmas prevented. Aside from the yoga of bodily postures, there are various techniques and practices that one learns from a guru that specifically remove karmas and inappropriate desires from the subtle body. By perfecting those processes it is possible for us to cultivate a divine connection that re-empowers our atma (soul) to go beyond the influence of karmas. Our oldest causes and effects, or prarabda karmas (the ripe fruit of our past actions), are not altered by these yogas. Our gene codes and bodies remain the same, but our present consciousness and future karmas can be completely transformed and removed.

By Divine Grace We Can Burn Off Our Karma

If the laws of matter that cause actions to generate reactions are called the ritam, and if the violation of those laws of nature causes death or mritam, then the remedy for the negative effects of karma is called *amritam*. Sometimes *amrita* is called "the nectar of immortality that liberates us from death." Interestingly, our English word "nectar" is made up of two words— "nec," which means death, and

"Tara," which means "she who carries us beyond." The idea here is that by some divine grace or divinely inspired process, we are able to go beyond the entire system of karma, to burn off our past karma and to live in such a way that we no longer create future karma from our present actions.

Such people are then in a state of kriyamana karma, or action that does not produce a material reaction in the future. They are becoming *jivan-mukta* and accumulate something called *sukriti*. Sukriti is spiritual merit that is collected from life to life by humans as the result of their various spiritual experiences and activities. It is not lost from birth to birth but rather grows until the atma is ready to leave matter and return to the transcendental realm. They are now "old souls."

Liberation Means Not Having to Return ⒢

Even though such atmas are still apparently in a body within the material world, they no longer generate future reactions from their actions. They appear to be acting within the material realm, but due to their connection with the transcendental realm and the Supreme Being, they are no longer generating karmas that will bind them to future reactions. They have achieved moksha, or liberation from matter and the bondage to its laws.

One could walk by such a liberated person on the street and not notice the subtle differences in his or her consciousness, although there are subtle symptoms. According to the Vedas, those who have transcended material consciousness to a sufficient degree will not experience future reactions to the laws of cause and effect. At death they will not be taken by the agents of Yamaraja but will instead be transported to the transcendental abode. They are liberated and are in the process of graduating from the "Universe-ity." They will not be returning to the material park in their next life, either as a creature, a human or a deva.

If they do return, it will be as a guru or teacher whose mission is to help other souls find liberation. Their atmas are ready to return to the transcendental abode from which we all originated. According to the Vedas and yoga philosophy, this is the end-game of karma—to have no more karma, no more material desires, to owe nothing and be owed nothing, to have no material attachments and to be completely absorbed in awareness of the transcendental world and ready to return there, to be in this world but not of it, to be a soul who had not only a human experience but all the experiences the material world has to offer. Been there, done that, got the merit badge, ready to leave, liberated from all the rules and limitations of birth, death, old age, and disease—moksha!

This raises the question what exactly life in the transcendental realm would be like. We have been within matter for a long time before we reach the point of liberation from its grasp. Therefore, not only do we need to find the way out of the material world by removing all the unconscious goo that has covered our atmas, but we also need to learn how to behave or live in the long-forgotten transcendental realm.

The library of Vedic knowledge gives extensive information about the nature of the transcendental abode. Although we don't have space to discuss the transcendental in detail in this book dedicated to karma, a few details will help illuminate the topic. The most important thing to remember is that even in how we return to the transcendental world, we remain individuals and can exercise choice. Like crossing any border, there are certain requirements for entry. When leaving the realm of prakriti, one cannot take matter or material ideas into the transcendental. No goo is allowed there. Such things are inert in nature and can only stay within the material realm.

The final knowledge of the Veda is called *Vedanta*, the knowledge of the ultimate end toward which all souls are headed when they return to the transcendental. The Vedanta literature describes that the transcendental region has a variety of places for all the souls to choose from. Just as in matter there are many galaxies and planets, so in the transcendental realm there are many abodes where life is experienced in a wide variety of ways. Some souls return to the transcendental with the desire to merge their own small being into the Supreme Being. It is as if a small light joined a big light to shine together. These souls would go to live in the "impersonal" area of the transcendental called the impersonal Brahman.

The other choice is based on the idea that the Supreme Reality is also a Supreme Person with whom all souls have the ability to enter into a loving relationship. In this second form of liberation into the transcendental, learning to love in a very pure way is the prerequisite to entering into the more personal areas of the transcendental abode. There, the many eternal beings headed by the Supreme Transcendental Being engage in a wide variety of creative and enjoyable activities uninterrupted by the problems we experienced within matter. That Supreme Person or God is called Bhagavan.

In the transcendental realm though, there is no power-based relationship between the souls and Bhagavan (God). The relationships are all sweet and loving. Such love is hard for us to comprehend while we are within the material world since here we see pain and suffering everywhere, but the Vedas say that such sweet loving worlds exist inside the Brahman where Bhagavan and his friends and lovers remain for eternity. Since we have forgotten the transcendental realm, part of returning is not only removing the goo but reactivating our loving nature to its fullest extent by a yoga that restores our lost love for Bhagavan. That learning is necessary in order to return to the personal realms of the transcendental.

It is our choice to return to the transcendental realm and to return to either the personal or impersonal areas. Yet in order to go to either, we must become qualified through the practice of a yogic process that helps restore our true eternal nature and become truly liberated souls. The Vedas are filled with stories and accounts of such liberated souls. We see this impulse for getting free from the limitations of the material world in many traditions. The Vedas would say this is because it is our true nature to desire eternal freedom, love, joy, beauty, and complete consciousness. On the one hand, the laws of karma are the necessary rules of living within the temporary material realm. Yet everyone knows within their hearts that they long for unlimited life without restriction. The Vedas say such a life is possible. It exists in the realms beyond our current perception. Whether this is true or not cannot be "proven," but the great souls of all cultures and times do say it can be experienced within the core of our true being. In the final analysis, only your own experience will give you the answer.

CHAPTER EIGHT

QUESTIONS AND ANSWERS ON KARMA

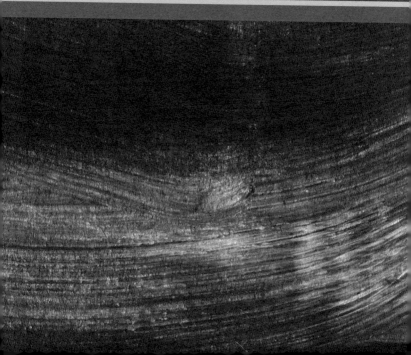

Questions and Answers

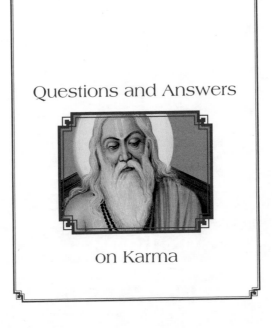

on Karma

Animals evolve,
humans involve

This chapter is designed to answer some of the most common questions asked regarding the theory of karma.

Q. If we have had many births in the past, why do we forget them?

A. The material energy, or *prakriti*, is called the unconscious energy not only because it is unconscious, but because by associating with it, we become unconscious. We are born unconscious, wrapped in the coverings of matter and in the course of our lives we forget many things. We learn things and then forget them.

We have dreams and visions and then forget them. Therefore, forgetfulness is not a proof of the nonexistence of something. This unconscious aspect of matter is so formidable that yogis say that there is really only one enemy in this world—ignorance and forgetfulness of our true nature.

Q. There are billions more people on our planet than just a few hundred years ago. If reincarnation is a true theory, where do all the new souls come from?

A. Think of all the many species of life as a grand pyramid with human beings at the apex of the triangle. There are always large numbers of souls moving upward from below us in the many species. They are constantly moving toward human life. The problem in the material world is not a shortage of souls but rather a shortage of graduates.

Q. What happens to the soul who tries to achieve liberation but somehow does not succeed?

A. According to the Vedas, if someone pursues liberation with determination but somehow does not attain that goal in one lifetime, he takes his next birth on the higher planets of the devas. To make an earthly comparison, imagine a hard working person winning a one-year vacation to Hawaii. After his or her deva vacation, the soul is placed in a good family for his or her next birth, with opportunities to continue his or her journey on the path of liberation.

Q. It looks like karma is an endless process. If that is so, what is the purpose of human life here on Earth?

A. According to the Vedas, the purpose of life on Earth is the evolution of souls in the direction of liberation. In this view, there is no particular end goal of history or final plan for being on Earth. It is just like attending a school. The purpose of the school is the education and evolution of the individual students. Other than that, the school has no separate purpose. For this reason, the karmic view is that we should maintain the Earth in perfect condition for future generations of students.

In recent times, this idea has come to be known as ecology. Previously, it was considered to be a sacred responsibility for each generation to leave the school in good shape for the next generation. Obviously, not everyone holds this view of our reason for being here. India has been trying to preserve this ideal for thousands of years, though in the last few thousand years, the forces of chaos have caused much damage to the peaceful idea of Earth as a school.

Q. Do we receive karma for killing the food we eat and is there much difference in the karma from our various choices?

A. Think again of the pyramid of spiritual evolution. We humans are the only species that does not have its food choices controlled by instinct. Thus, food choices are some of the most critical and potentially damaging we can make both for ourselves and the planet. According to the yogic theory, the higher we eat on the food chain, the more disturbance is caused in our environment. This is the main reason for adopting a vegetarian or mostly vegetarian diet. For example, to raise one bull for slaughter as food for humans requires thousands of gallons of water, creates large amounts of waste, needs acres of grazing land and produces only a relatively small amount of food protein. It is a terribly inefficient means of producing food for humans, what to speak of the violence to the animal and toxins produced by its slaughter. If the same resources were used for producing vegetarian food, thousands more people could be fed.

The modern statistics in this regard are that if we converted from beef as food to vegetarian foods, we could feed a billion more people with the same resources. Therefore, what we choose to eat as humans is much more than a personal preference or matter of taste. Our eating creates a series of causes and effects that support or displace life on Earth in complex ways for which we the consumers are held accountable. Consumers are not free from reaction simply by closing their eyes to the process. Violating these and other similar laws of nature have future consequences for the soul on many levels of responsibility.

Q. If being in this material world is so problematic, why did the souls choose to come here in the first place and why did the Supreme Being allow them to make such a dangerous choice?

A. One might also ask the question: "At what point would you like your freedom of choice taken away?" In fact there are many subtle differences in the answers to this question. Many schools of thought have accepted parts of karma theory, such as cause and effect or reincarnation, but not all are in agreement on this particular topic of individuality and free will. The widely accepted Vedic view is that we are divine in nature, which includes the right to explore all the different areas of the total existence of the Supreme Being.

Both the transcendental realm and this material realm are divine. But since we are distinctive individual sparks of divinity, we are eternally invested with free will. Using that ability to choose, we can request to explore either the conscious or unconscious realms of existence. With this in mind, in order to be here, we had to be the ones who exercised that choice in order to continue our exploration of both our own nature and limitations as well as those of the Supreme Being.

The Vedas say that although we are conscious by nature, we can get lost in the realm of the unconscious because it is so much larger than our power of consciousness can illuminate. In our own bodies we experience this. I am directly conscious of my body, the matter in it is pervaded by my consciousness, but I am unable to pervade the bodies of others or the world around me. In this sense, the definition of God or the Supreme Being would be: "that consciousness that pervades all of matter as well as the entire transcendental realm." The difference between us and the Supreme Consciousness is that we can get lost during our explorations of the unconscious realms of matter. For this reason, the Supreme Being is eternally sending search parties to the world of matter to assist us in finding the way back home.

Q. Can large groups of souls have a karmic relationship with each other?

A. Nations, cities, religions, races, tribes, villages, families, gangs, corporations, and all such groupings have a conscious idea about why they are together. That idea is often the action of their rational minds making sense out of a connection from the surface. If the same groupings are viewed from the devas' perspective, they are arranged to facilitate the acting out of various karmic agendas that may have been carried forward for many lifetimes. We see only the surface facts and try to extrapolate the plot from a few details.

The devas see the big picture, the part we have forgotten. Thus karma theory explains how we are truly players in dramas we seldom fully understand. Once understood, this view helps to remove the many artificial barriers that divide us. We have all taken birth in every gender, sect, race, party, or viewpoint imaginable. As such, this view engenders humility, understanding, compassion, and a sense that we are all part of one divine family. We are all students in the same school in spite of our differences in curriculum or view at any time. The ideal of karmic philosophy is that we will become less competitive and more cooperative as we work toward our ultimate and relative goals.

Glossary

Ahamkara: Indicates a subtle energy of matter which, when combined with the consciousness of the atma, creates the idea that we come from and are matter. Also known as the false ego.

Akasha (Akashic): The fifth of the dense material elements (earth, water, fire, air, space). Akasha is often translated as space or the accommodating principle that is filled with subtle vibrations or cosmic rays.

Amrita: A mysterious liquid substance that was the final product of the churning of the milk ocean by the demigods (devas) and demons (asuras). Amrita, or the nectar of immortality, was then fed to the devas so they could perform their various jobs of maintaining the universe. Amrita also refers to anything that counteracts the influence of death or disease due to violating the laws of material nature.

Atma: The true self that cannot die.

Ayurveda: Ayus means life; Ayurveda is the medical system based on Vedic wisdom. It creates well-being by supporting the life force in various ways.

Bhagavan: The Supreme Person who is the possessor of all opulence.

Chitragupta: The deva who acts as the court-reporter in Yamaraja's court of death and judgment.

Deva (Devi, feminine): Derived from the Sanskrit "div," meaning to play in the light. Also called the divine helpers, they are souls just like humans or animals, but they have attained posts in the administration of the laws of material nature. They work for Vishnu and Lakshmi in the function of maintaining nature.

Dharma: Based on the root "dhri," which means the essential nature of a thing, which if it is taken away, the thing is no longer itself. The dharma of fire is to burn, the dharma of water is to be liquid. The dharma of a person arises from the essential nature of his or her body. From that come certain powers and from those certain duties in the use of those powers. This is called svadharma, or a person's own dharma. Finally, the soul's eternal nature is called its Sanatana

Dharma, or its immortal nature.

Jiva: Another term indicating the atma or eternal soul. Jiva also means life or the soul in contact with the life force within matter, thus jiva-atma.

Jyotisha: The Sanskrit name for astrology. It means the science of how life is regulated by light.

Karma: Derived from the Sanskrit "kri," which means to do. The law of cause and effect.

Kriyamana: Actions on behalf of the Supreme Being that do not generate karmic reactions.

Manas (Manusha): This word is derived from the Sanskrit for mind. Applied to humans, it means possessing free will or having a mind of one's own.

Maya: Literally "not this," referring to the state of consciousness in which the atma assumes that the material reality is permanent and not causally dependent upon the Supreme Being.

Moksha: Also sometimes known as mukti. This word describes the state of a soul who has become liberated from all material entanglement and is focused upon the transcendental.

Mritam: Death, as the final outcome of violating the ritam or laws of nature.

Prakriti: That which is controlled by a greater Being; matter is called apara-prakriti, or the unconscious energy of the Supreme. The transcendental realm is called para-prakriti or the conscious realm of Divine energy.

Prarabda: This is the cause and effect that is currently manifesting as our destinies or the ripe fruit of our past actions.

Ritam: The invisible laws embedded in material nature. These rules govern all action and reaction within matter.

Samsara: Reincarnation or the repeated cycle of birth and death experienced by the eternal souls once they enter the realm of matter. Sometimes described as the wheel of birth and death.

Sanatana: Eternal or everlasting. When this word occurs along with dharma as "Sanatana Dharma," it means the true eternal nature of the atma.

Sanchitta: Used to describe the potential or future karmas that are figuratively described as seeds in the mind or subtle body. If they are not removed, they will produce fruit in the future.

Sanskrit: The name of the language in which the Vedas of India were written. The word literally means perfected, implying that Sanskrit is very scientific and consistent.

Sukriti: The merit accumulated from various forms of spiritual activity. This accumulates over lifetimes and is not used up or temporary like material karma.

Tantra: Literally means that which expands or to weave, and is the source of the English word tension. Everything in the material world is held together by a certain correct tension. Sexuality is one small subject within tantra, which is similar to the word science but is more holistic.

Tara: A devi who is known for healing and protection. Her name means to deliver or carry across. The idea is that she saves one from karmic troubles.

Vedas: A large collection of sacred writings originating in ancient India. They are considered to be one of the integral scriptural foundations of Hinduism. Many Hindus believe that the Vedas were not written by anyone, including Ishvara (the term used for God), but are eternally existing.

Vedic: Vedic may refer to ancient India, the Vedic period, the Vedas or the historical Vedic religion.

Vrata: Vow or promise. Since humans have free will, they do not act only from instinct like animals or under the ritam like devas. Instead, they act through giving their word as a promise.

Yamaraja: The superintendent of death and karmic justice.

Yoga: to link or connect. Our English word yoke is derived from yoga. This idea is that through certain specific actions, one is able to reestablish his or her lost link to the Supreme Beings in the transcendental realm.

Acknowledgments

My gratitude and appreciation goes first to my wife and partner Sandi Graham for all she has done to make this book possible. My many thanks go to Richelle Jarrell who typed, proofread, and edited the manuscript. My appreciation also goes to the creative staff at Mandala Publishing, who are dedicated to publishing beautiful books on important topics of spiritual value to the world. Finally, I would like to thank my editor Arjuna VD Kooij for his suggestions and contributions that helped greatly in perfecting this book.

JEFFREY ARMSTRONG (Kavindra Rishi)
A Western Master of Eastern Wisdom

Inspirational Speaker, Visionary Spiritual Teacher Author & Founder of VASA-The Vedic Academy of Arts and Sciences

Initiated by Masters of the mystical Eastern Traditions, Jeffrey Armstrong is a charismatic speaker and counselor who teaches the Philosophy of Yoga as a way of being, and Enlightenment as a way of life. As a student and scholar of the Vedic Philosophy for over thirty-five years, Jeffrey has mastered Raja Yoga, Tantra, and Mantra practices. Jeffrey uses humor, passion, and spiritual insights to address the needs of our current relationships. Jeffrey is also an award-winning author and mystical poet, with degrees in Psychology, Literature, and History & Comparative religion.

www.JeffreyArmstrong.com

NOTES

NOTES

NOTES

NOTES

Colophon

The main text of this book was typeset in MrsEaves. The sidebars and main header text was typeset using Berthold Akzidenz Grotesk.

All Mandala Wisdom Library books were printed on 100gsm matte art text, with endpapers printed on 120gsm woodfree paper.

Series Devolpmental Editor
Lisa Fitzpatrick

Series Editor
Arjuna van der Kooij

Series Designer
Usana Das Shadday

Mandala Publishing would like to thank Danny Grinberg and Carina Cha for their assistance.

Happy Hour Is for Amateurs

Happy Hour Is for Amateurs

A LOST DECADE IN

THE WORLD'S WORST

PROFESSION

THE PHILADELPHIA LAWYER

wm

WILLIAM MORROW

An Imprint of HarperCollins*Publishers*

HarperCollins books may be purchased for educational, business, or sales promotional use. For information please write: Special Markets Department, HarperCollins Publishers, 10 East 53rd Street, New York, NY 10022.

FIRST EDITION

Designed by Mia Risberg

Library of Congress Cataloging-in-Publication Data

The Philadelphia lawyer.
    Happy hour is for amateurs : a lost decade in the world's worst profession / the Philadelphia lawyer.
       p. cm.
    ISBN-13: 978-0-06-134949-2
    1. Philadelphia lawyer 2. Lawyers—Pennsylvania—Humor. 3. Lawyers—Pennsylvania—Anecdotes. 4. Lawyers—Pennsylvania—Biography. I. Title.
    K184.P49 2008
    340.02'07—dc22   2008023090

08 09 10 11 12 WBC/CR 10 9 8 7 6 5 4 3 2 1

To Lisa. I'm not sure if it's an indictment or a compliment, but I can't think of any woman who'd stand behind me like you have. I really, truly don't deserve you.

I mean, seriously . . . You should have run years ago.

Philadelphia Lawyer:

... [A] disparaging label for an attorney who is skillful in the manipulation of the technicalities and intricacies of the law to the advantage of his or her client, although the spirit of the law might be violated.

For example, an attorney who uses repeated motions for postponement of an action or excessive discovery requests as dilatory tactics primarily for the advantages that inure to his or her client, as opposed to legitimate grounds for such actions, might be regarded as a Philadelphia Lawyer.

—*Thomson Gale Legal Encyclopedia*

Contents

Author's Note

I have changed the names of some individuals, and modified identifying features, including physical descriptions and occupations, of other individuals in order to preserve their anonymity. In some cases, composite characters have been created or timelines have been compressed, in order to further preserve privacy and to maintain narrative flow. The dialogue has been re-created to the best of my recollection, which can vary given the circumstances of the moment. The goal in all cases was to protect people's privacy without damaging the integrity of the story. The general opinions offered about the legal profession are not intended to apply to any particular individuals or entities.

That's the legal-speak, of course. To put it in layman's terms, I've had to modify scenes and smash people together because otherwise this book would potentially expose the guilty and the innocent, contain as many "characters" as the Bible and read like shit. This is a funny riff on a funny time that happens to have some important points jammed into the mix—the written version of the discussion we might have if we sat down over a bottle of Maker's Marks and you said, "Tell me about the last ten years. And entertain me."

If anything in this disclaimer offends your standard of grit, as a wise man once said, "Lighten up, Francis."

You threw it out?" I barked into the receiver.

"I—I—I—" My roommate stammered on the other end of the line. "I—have—to—go. I have so much shit to do to-day." CLICK. The line went dead.

I put the phone on the table and stared out the window at the Dumpster in the parking lot behind my apartment. Could I dive into it? Was there a chance success was still in my grasp, thirty yards and a few feet of trash away?

RING. I answered. "Hello? Hello?"

"Look, I'm sorry. I'll make it up to you." My roommate coughed and stuttered. "I've had so much on my plate. I didn't. I mean, I didn't mean it—"

"That's nice, but what do I do now?" I pressed hard, but civil. I couldn't attack him. I had to live with the guy. But I had to vent, and the mess I was facing was his fault.

"Why didn't you ask me? Why would you just throw something like that away?" CLICK. "Hello? Hello?" He hung up on me.

I gulped the last of my coffee, slammed the cup on the table and dialed him back.

"Perimeter Funds, good morning," the operator yip-yipped in a pixie voice. I spit my roommate's name and department into the receiver. "Certainly, sir. Let me transfer you."

After a half dozen rings he picked up. "Why did you hang u—"

He cut me off. "Look, I honestly don't remember throwing it away, I just—"

"Then where is it? Give me your dishonest answer."

Silence.

"I'm fucked. You realize that." I was hyperventilating; late for work already, with a mountain of paper to clear off my desk before two. Everyone was depending on me. People were coming in from D.C., New York, and Boston. They were sitting on trains and planes and waiting in traffic. They'd cleared their schedules to make the trip and the one thing I was supposed to take care of for them—the reason they were coming—I'd fucked up, terribly and irreparably.

"Look, I have to go. I'm sorry, but I have a huge project going, and I can't deal with your shit right now. I'm sorry. What else can I say?" CLICK. He didn't give me a chance to speak another word.

I ran to the parking lot and opened the Dumpster. There was no way to rummage through it in a seersucker suit. Anything worn in the process would be destroyed. The only way to do the dive was naked, and I didn't have the luxury of risking arrest. Still, the mountains of bulging trash bags taunted me. Theoretically it was easy, a matter of finding the right one and combing through the piles of coffee grounds, rotting cold cuts, and junk mail. Then I looked a little closer. The greasy black flies buzzing around my head and the odor of diapers and spoiled fruit dragged me back to reality. It was true—I was a few feet from saving the day, but they might as well have been a thousand miles.

I trudged back into the house and called my assistant.

"I have an emergency. I'm going to be late. No. I'm fine. Just, uh . . . , I'm going to be late is all." CLICK.

Most of being a lawyer is pretending you know everything while actually knowing next to nothing, "practicing" your trade in the most literal sense of the word. Hoping some elected judge has the facility with English to understand the complicated argument you've handed him. Guessing how the court might rule on confusing language in contradictory statutes drafted by twenty-three-year-old state senators' clerks. Poring over endless pages of rules in volumes of books thicker and denser than *Atlas Shrugged* to find a simple answer as to when and how some court document has to be filed. You wake in sweats in the middle of the night. *Did I have thirty days or twenty to respond to my opponents' motion? Did I file the proper notice of appeal in the Auchincloss case? Does Rule 4:15(a)(6)(vii) supersede Rule 6:17(e)(3)(iii) when they conflict?*

These thoughts never leave, filling your head with endless tedium. Being a litigator is living in that nightmare where you're sitting in an exam and suddenly realize you haven't studied and don't know a stitch of The Information. You're as good as your last fuckup, which is just like any other job—except that unlike any other job, you have a pack of adversaries at your throat, angry little shits who live to find and exploit the tiniest error in your work and make you look stupid and illogical. You toil in constant fear of the big mistake that brings down the house of cards and sets a fellow shark or vulture upon you, suing for malpractice. This is Philadelphia—Shyster Central, Electric Lawyerland. Of course we eat our own, and statistically, sooner or later, every one of us makes a mistake.

"I'm totally fucked here." I paced back and forth through the living room, running a pointless postmortem on the situation. "I can't believe this. He threw it away!"

My girlfriend Lisa emerged from the bathroom and stared at me, combing her hair back and fiddling with a towel around her breasts.

"You still haven't found it?"

"Would I be running around like this if I had?"

"You are such a drama queen. Do you know how high your voice gets when you're mad?"

"How could he do that?"

"He was probably cleaning. You're the biggest slob I've ever met."

"Look at me. Do I look like a slob?"

"Oh no. *You* are very put together. It's everything around you that's a mess."

"I don't need a lesson now. Do you know how much this sucks? This is a serious fucking problem." I buttoned my cuffs and started tying my tie in the living room mirror.

"Great, I spilled coffee on my pants. That stains, doesn't it?"

"That's a cotton suit. It'll come out."

I blotted my pant leg with a bottle of mineral water, straightened myself, slipped on my jacket and smoothed the part in my hair. I was twenty-seven, six foot two—white teeth, clear skin, and the bright eyes of a mind with some promise. Or so they'd told me. I had "Esquire" after my name. "Attorney-at-Law." "Counselor." A man of peerage in the merchant class. I was even dressed like Atticus Finch, as if I'd stepped straight out of a Brooks Brothers catalog. Alive with pleasure . . . Living The Professional Dream.

"Are you sure you checked everywhere?" Lisa quizzed me.

"It's gone. I'm sure." I could see my roommate coming in late at night in a vodka stupor, fumbling around for a lighter or a late-night snack. He'd see it, think it was garbage, step on the trash can lever and in one flick of his wrist, in the senseless rote motion you'd use to swat an ant from the corner of a picnic table it would be Gone. Weeks of persistence, searching, phone calls—hours of work—crumpled in his fist and dropped in a plastic trash bag to be thrown in the back of a compactor, driven to a dump and lost among a universe of used tampons and crushed beer cans.

"I'm really, really late for work. We have to go." I started replacing the contents of the freezer, now scattered about the kitchen table—a bag of ice, fifth of Jim Beam, three bags of frozen fruit and a carton of freezer-burned chocolate ice cream. The cuffs of my shirt were wet with melted condensation from searching through it all morning—reopening it and scanning its white walls every few minutes, praying I'd missed some hidden compartment, secret drawer or shelf.

"Stop moping. It's a fuckup. There's nothing you can do about it." Lisa was right. Still, I couldn't bear to go to the office. Hiding seemed the better option. Take the day off, cancel the weekend plans and sit in the house. That'd be an overreaction; things would still work out. It was Friday, and no matter what happened that morning, I'd be at the beach in twelve hours, half a bottle of bourbon and a handful of bong hits into the idiot euphoria of a lost Friday night in early summer. But there was no getting around the instant issue—I was staring at a mess, and it'd be the difference between where I wanted to be and actually would be that evening. And worse than that was the shame, knowing that at least on some minor level, this was my fault—my failure to hedge a risk, however small. I never fucked up. I was trained against it, a slave to perfect execution. Always dependable. Always on time. Everyone else dropped the ball, not me. I was an "officer of the court," a professional.

"I know. It's just—it's the principle of the thing."

"The principle?" Lisa rolled her eyes.

"It's a fucking tragedy. Do you have any idea how hard it is to get that much mescaline?"

Chap Stick

WELCOME TO LAW SCHOOL

BEWARE OF POLAR BEARS

I f I had to pick the moment or place where my legal education started, I'd say the back of a truck, with an Irish girl who had an ass like a pair of watermelons.

The space was cramped and I had to strain myself just to speak. My chin was pressed into my sternum, making it difficult to breathe, and between the passing cars and the ambulance sirens from the hospital next door, I could barely hear a thing. I remember wheezing a lot, fumbling to keep my balance and thinking this must have been how trapped miners felt in the minutes before the oxygen ran out—light-headed, pinned against a wall by an avalanche of mud or water.

"Katherine, this just isn't working."

"What?"

"I said, 'This. Is. Not. Working.'"

"What do you mean?"

"I just don't think I can do this." Traction was an issue, but only the half of it. It's never easy with the large ones. They're awkward, bulky, the weight's uneven and steering them is near impossible. Positioning's half the battle, which is hard enough in a wide-open space, damn near impossible in a tight area.

"What's the problem?"

"I'm sandwiched here."

"Sandwich?"

"I can't get any, uh, leverage." Nuance seemed wrong in those conditions, but it was instinctual. "Is this really the only way?"

"I told you already—"

"I know. I know." *How in the hell am I going to do this?*

The how of it was simple physics. The bigger issue was why?

I'd been asking myself "Why?" a lot recently, from the moment I stepped inside the doors to the law school.

I remember the first day, bounding up the stairs in front of the library, dressed in flip-flops, a madras shirt and a baseball hat, sunglasses between my teeth, papers in my hand, carrying that same giddy apprehension I recalled from the first days of high school and college. New city, new school, new *women*. Possibilities.

Or not.

The front hallway of the law school was more a gauntlet than a welcome reception. None of the smiling faces I'd known from college orientation, those grins and glances of eighteen-year-olds eyeing each other like meat. The place had no carnal undercurrent at all. This was the post-college hangover, the day after the four-year party. That or the dumping ground for sorts who'd never been to the party in the first place—all the mouth-breathers stumbling around the hall with vacant gazes like Napoleon Dynamite or Dustin Hoffman in *Rain Man*. And scattered through the mix of middle-aged virgins and lost savants you could spot all the mean ones, the "cutthroats," squinting from the corners of their eyes, summing up the competition.

"Excuse me." A hulking apelike man in Bermuda shorts, white socks and sneakers slammed into me as I made my way to the registration table, knocking a folder of my papers all over the floor. No "sorry" or offer to help pick them up. Off he drove, shoving through the crowd. Standing up, I brushed the shoulder of an older man in an army jacket with the eyes of someone who might be carrying a copy of *The Catcher in the Rye* in his back pocket. He glared at me as if there'd never be enough apologies for the invasion. *Jesus Christ, where am I?* I took in the balance of the room as I arranged the papers in my hands. Ten feet in any direction, a variation on the Pat character from *Saturday Night Live* fiddled with a backpack or purse, and every fifth man was a Botero caricature, squeezed into pleated shorts and a short-sleeved oxford.

"Hello. My name is James Ellman." A Capote-like troll with heavily gelled hair pasted across a broad forehead popped out of the blue and offered me his hand. "I'm doing a little soft recruiting for the Federalist Society. Do you have a second?" He was stubby and dressed in a pink golf shirt with a sweater tied around his neck, a dwarf version of a model from a Polo ad.

"Federal what?"

"Federalist Society. It's—" Before he could finish his answer, a gray-complected man with a wispy comb-over darted between us with a pile of papers in his hand. He offered no warning or apology—just shot straight to the sign-in table, threw a pile of documents on it and started barking orders to the clerk in a grating, bitchy lisp. "I paid my first tuition installment already. I know I did. I have a receipt right here!"

"I'm sorry, sir. But I can't find it." The woman behind the desk stuttered.

"Well, it's there somewhere!"

Meanwhile, Capote was still in the middle of his pitch. "So we're, you know, just getting some people to join now. Build a membership early . . ." As he rambled on, a tanning booth casualty with bloodshot eyes and a potbelly visible through her sundress turned and shot me a "How you doin'?" glance as she angled into the line. As I backed away from her, I bumped into a holy roller laying a salvation speech on a few people. "The prayer meeting starts at noon," she chirped in a Julie Andrews accent. "Sorry about that." I apologized and turned my head as fast as possible, the only way to convey "irredeemable" in body language.

Sitting on the steps outside looking over the first-year students' welcoming literature, it was all I could do not to jump in the car, aim the vehicle down the first road out of town and mash the pedal through the floorboards. But I talked myself out of it, pouring on the rationalizations—the same ones so many of us use that first day: *You're overreacting. You're being a spoiled dick. It can't be that bad.*

It can, particularly if you live in a dorm. Yes, that's right. I lived in a dorm my first year in law school, just like a college freshman. Due to a "zest for living" that occupied most of my senior year of college, I wound up filling out my applications either at the very last minute or past the submission deadline. Not surprisingly, most of the responses I received started with "Regrettably" in the opening sentence. It wasn't until August, when I'd given up hope, that a dean from a law school I knew nothing about and only applied to on the advice of a family friend called out of the blue, offering me a spot in the incoming class.

At the time, I was living with my folks in northeastern Pennsylvania. If I wanted to get an apartment, I had to drive to the law school and hunt for one—an arduous trek west, the first few hundred miles of it through the carcasses of mining towns littering what James Carville aptly described as an "Alabama" in the middle of Pennsylvania. It was the peak of summer, and I wanted to visit friends at the beach in New Jersey. I wasn't going to burn a weekend house hunting. *A dorm will be fine. Law's a monastic calling. I'll be able to focus there, finally Get Serious.*

That didn't happen. The school gave me a room between a cruel nursing student who blasted Jimmy Buffett and a pair of graduate students who played some medieval-themed card game called "Magic" day and night, arguing about elves and wizards and dragons. The background soundtrack of the place was something out of an exorcism: *"Some people claim that there's a woman to blame/But I know it's my own damned fault."* "You cannot block my shaman by summoning a demon!" *"Cheeseburger in paradise/Heaven on earth with an onion slice."* "It's not a demon—it's a zombie lord!" And these were pre-Internet times. I had five cable channels and no pay-per-view. Not even Skinemax.

As a result, I spent a lot of time in bars, drinking around people like Katherine. I'd like to say the girl was "voluptuous," "Rubenesque" or "full-figured." "Heavy" is the only proper adjective, mostly because "obese" implies ugliness, and she did have a decent face and huge round breasts. Some might even call her a "convertible girl," the sort who looks hot until she gets out of the ragtop and you see her monstrous backyard and piano legs. Your grandmother would have called her "big-boned." And been upset if you brought her home.

Katherine was what I'd recognize years later in the office setting as a "polar bear." Huge, alabaster, and hunting men like meat. Polar bears rarely see prey on the tundra, so when they spot anything alive they kill it. Katherine's kind apply the same selection process to men. We've all seen the polar bear in action, falling down drunk at company functions while nervous managers debate who'll take her home and a busybody demands her car keys. She doesn't care what anyone thinks. The only thing that's going to stanch her heroic intake of White Russians and chardonnay is sex, no matter how humiliating and career-threatening getting there might be. Usually she winds up with the same kill—an IT drone with volcanic acne or the mailroom guy who wears Doc Martens to work and talks about Fugazi all the time. Or a hopeless drunk like me.

Sitting in the back of her truck, it was easy to blame the situation on Katherine, that she'd overpowered me, that I didn't have a choice. Bullshit. I was complicit. I told her she could sit down, and sometimes that's all it takes.

"Can I take this seat?" she asked, saddling up next to me in a dive bar just off campus. "I'm waiting for friends, but I think I missed them."

"Sure."

"I'm Katherine."

"I'm P.J."

Katherine wasn't unlike anything else a person might pick up in a dingy college bar. The place was filthy, stinking of mold, stale beer and that acrid chemical smoke from the Marlboro Lights sorority girls chained. But it had women and drinks, and both were cheap, and when you're penniless and living in a dorm, that's an oasis.

One of the meaner realities you run into during the first month of law school is the dating pool. Like college, the place *should* provide all the opportunities you need. I say *should,* of course, because in reality, law school is the photographic negative of college, an anti-beauty pageant in every regard. And I'm not being sexist here. In fact, the law school singles scene is probably a lot crueler to females than males. A lazy woman looking for anything from a fuck buddy to Mr. Right is faced with endless varieties of Dustin Diamond, Beavis, Bobcat Goldthwait and the guy who played the subway ghoul in *Ghost.* Whatever your sex, living in this world your standards drop like an anchor.

Katherine and I knocked back beer after beer, trading the usual dreck—dreams, desires, career goals. She wanted to be a nurse, or maybe it was a pharmacist.

"When did you know you wanted to be a lawyer?"

"I don't know. It just kind of happened." I was twenty-two and had spent more of the past four years drunk than sober. In that mind-set I believed any work would be tolerable for the right-sized paycheck. I also figured I was a natural for the job. I liked the sound of my own voice, I could talk, and I had great hair. And more than that, I had a truckload of experience. I'd been talking my way out of trouble with parents, teachers, girl-friends, doctors, coaches, policemen, professors, deans, bosses, and supervisors of every stripe for as long as I could remember. It wasn't that I was a bad person, just the sort who never paid attention to orders, directives, plans, procedures, or fine print of any kind. I'd try, but it was all so tedious and dull. Arguing my way out of the penalties after the fact was more fun—a challenge, and the more absurd the defense, the more amusing it was. "Advocate" seemed like a synonym for "overpaid performance artist"—Andy Kaufman in a pinstripe suit. I couldn't think of a more inviting job description.

So, yes, like 50 percent of any incoming class, lack of direction and greed brought me to law school, but I wasn't altogether shocked to find myself in the business. In the catalog of aspirations for a kid like me, "lawyer" fit perfectly. It even looked respectable. A middle-class fantasy—doctor, attorney, CPA. The road most traveled . . .

Straight to a barstool in this filthy tavern.

"I've been out west but never east." Katherine brushed her hair back. "What's it like?"

"Gorgeous country this time of year. Beautiful foliage . . . and you should really see Philadelphia. They have a massive statue of Sylvester Stallone."

"That's like—like New Jersey, isn't it?" Her thighs flopped off the sides of the chair like sandbags.

"Not exactly." I signaled the bartender for a reload. Beer's a terrible, slow drunk, but eventually it works. Somewhere around five or eight of them, I made out with Katherine in the ladies' room.

"Let's go back to my place."

"But my car's back near the library."

"So leave it there."

"My folks expect me home."

"You're drunk."

"I just have to make sure I'm home before seven, when my father gets up."

"So come back to my room."

"Just walk me to the car."

As we passed the parking lot, Katherine pressed me up against a wall and shoved her tongue down my throat. When she started grinding into me, I could feel the grain of the concrete wall through my shirt. The girl had no idea of her strength; I felt like Lenny's ill-fated pet in *Of Mice and Men*. I figured this was what it felt like to be a cheerleader getting manhandled by a pasted lummox after the prom and was starting to understand why some women never have orgasms.

"There. You found it." When we finally made it to the street, I saw what I figured was her truck ahead of us.

"Come on. Get in." She opened the driver's-side back door.

"This is dumb. My room's right over there."

"Just get in." She yanked my hand.

Fighting was useless. I was prey, about to get date-raped by a girl with a neck like Nate Newton, and judging from her booze-fueled lack of coordination, destined to stumble away from it with hips like Bo Jackson. Thankfully, I was numb—lucid but detached, in that perfect calm zone you hit between More Than I Needed and Way Too Many.

Katherine wasted no time. The moment we got in the truck she was on me, over me, holding me down. Her massive breasts were pressed into my face, a set of jelly-filled freezer bags with baseball-diameter nipples eclipsing everything in my view. The girl had been in a dry spell, that much was obvious. She was jerky and aggressive, with lumberjack hands and the touch of a black-smith—squeezing my testicles like stress balls and charley-horsing my left quadricep with her knee. I practically had to put her in a choke hold to gain leverage so I could lean forward and pull a condom from my pocket.

"Let me up for a second. I need to get something."

"What?"

"You know . . ."

"Um, we're not having sex."

"What are we doing then?"

"I don't . . . I don't have sex."

"Are you religious or something?"

"Well, I am Catholic."

"Cool. So am I." I reached into my pocket.

"So? What does that mean?" She had me on that point. There's no fornication exception for screwing other Catholics, but I didn't know what else to say. I was too confused by the whole thing. I'd never met anyone who held on to the "marriage first" rule. It was a throwback, like the prohibition of meat on Fridays or the rule against using artificial contraception.

But then, I grew up out east.

This was a different planet. People here still believed in things, or at least in notions of how things ought to be—that the old rules are good, right, and every synonym of "American." These parts know they're Rust Belt–Fucked and yet they cling to the idea that if they hold steady, the world will eventually come back to them. And why not? This was Big Ten Country, the part of the world where the Big Red Machine owned the National League in the seventies, the Browns and Steelers waged the Turnpike Rivalry for decades, and the Buckeyes roll to the Conference Championship every few years. It's a proud part of the nation, and not without reason. Tradition's bedrock out there because, in one sense, it's always the right choice, or at least the safe one. In another, less appealing sense, a person could say tradition's all they have left.

And Katherine was holding fast to hers.

"Seriously?" I was still hoping she was joking.

"Seriously. But that's not the only way to have sex."

"What do you mean?" Anything oral was out of the question; the quid pro quo from my end carried a risk of suffocation. And there was no way I was taking a hand job from anything with Katherine's biceps.

"You've tried the other side? You know, the other way?" She smiled.

"Really? That?" There was no mistaking the offer. And no point in lecturing her about Leviticus or the cosmic illogic of her strategy. I'd dealt with pious girls before; it's part of growing up in an Irish county. Most are blow-job queens or hand-job artists. Katherine's angle was a little unique.

"No. I've done that . . . It's just, well . . ." *Completely fucking ridiculous? The worst misapprehension of a loophole in history?* Suddenly I was back in the law school classroom listening to one of my professors explain a legal technicality—how to game your way through a pile of administrative rules and all of the ways to exploit them.

As I sat there pondering the offer, knowing I'd accept it, a horrible irony took hold. Here I was in law school, spending thousands of dollars and hours listening to old men in cheap suits flog the simple notion that in any pile of rules, there's always a string of verbs and nouns that will allow you to rationalize doing what you want. A horny Catholic girl could teach you that in fifteen minutes.

Katherine would cram an assembly line of cock in her cornhole before she'd find a man willing to marry a woman of her girth, but she would keep her maidenhead, at least as they defined it in some Gospel. She'd wear white on her wedding day and the ugly truth of her carnal degradation would only be known to her and the Holy Ghost. And her proctologist.

"I'm going to need something . . . Do you have any lotion in your purse?"

"Try the glove compartment."

I found pens, maps, nail polish remover, manuals, lip balm, ticket stubs, napkins . . . No lotion.

"What about lip balm?" I knew the answer to the question before I asked.

Jergens, Vaseline, Oil of Olay . . . Hawaiian Tropic, Johnson's baby oil, Ivory soap . . . Irish Spring, shampoo, sunscreen, tanning oil, conditioner . . . The variety of lubricants men have slathered on their penises would fill a supermarket aisle. Some are no-brainers, obvious aids for the process (Lubriderm). Some are tragedies-in-waiting (Ben-Gay). Most are found out of sudden necessity.

Add Chap Stick to the list. Twist out the stick, mash it in your palm, and spackle on multiple coats. I'll never know the genesis of that discovery; we could just as easily have missed it. Was it subconscious? Experience? Maybe Jesus, blessing Katherine for navigating Rome's rule book so well?

"You've got to lean forward more." I was still hitting my head on the ceiling.

"I'm trying."

"My head's smacking the roof."

"Is this better?" She leaned down onto her elbows. "Does it work now?"

Unfortunately, it did.

I woke with the first rays of the morning sun, my face drool-pasted to the back of a folded leather passenger seat. "Shit. Shit. Shit." Katherine was scurrying around the truck, searching for keys and furiously arranging herself in the rearview mirror. "Get out. Please. I have to go."

"Thanks. That was, uh, fun." What could I say? I wasn't kissing her goodbye or getting her number and she knew it. The fewer syllables the better. She put on her sunglasses, turned the key and peeled away.

Back at the dorm, I remember standing in the shower, straining to scrub the fruity wax off myself with a washcloth and listening to the grad students arguing over the stalls nearby:

"A dragon beats a hill goblin every time."

"Not if the goblin has flying powers."

"A hill goblin can't get flying powers!"

I wonder if I can still get my tuition refunded?

Breaking and Entering

MISDEMEANORS AND HYPOTHERMIA . . .

A SORT OF HOMECOMING

'd always considered Thanksgiving a B-grade holiday, nothing more than a teaser for Christmas and New Year's Eve. In college it was just a lost weekend at home, with high school friends in local bars, doing exactly what you'd be doing back at school. I liked it fine, but the idea that it was a "break" of any sort, or that a person even needed a break from that four-year vacation, seemed ludicrous. Half the time I didn't even realize it was approaching. My mother would call one Sunday and say, "When will you be home next week?" I'd look at the calendar and think, *Shit, November already? Again? I'm going to wind up graduating one of these years.*

That first semester of law school was completely different. By Thanksgiving I needed to get as far as possible from the place. The problem, of course, was I had no money. Luckily, my alma mater was halfway between my hometown and law school. The plan was a no-brainer. I'd take a long weekend, drop in and stay with some friends who were still undergraduates. Recharge the mind. Relive a better time. Don't think about law, or the school, or the people. In fact, don't think at all.

The biggest annoyance in law school isn't the demanding

professors or the difficult nature of the work. It's actually the students. Most people hear "law student" and immediately think "nerd"—a terrible and unfounded insult to geeks everywhere. The average law student isn't a nerd at all. Many are "angry insignificants," people who can look, sound, and appear utterly normal, but just below the surface have this terminal insecurity, manifesting itself in a pathological need to fight and impress everyone, always get in the last word and be the smartest person in the room. It's like they're still stuck in high school, coming to terms with wanting to be the varsity quarterback or prom king, but realizing their physical gifts were more aligned with the audiovisual club. They're all irritating in their own unique ways, but in that first year, it's a subspecies known as "gunners" and the obnoxious, inane debates they start in every class that make you want to step out and hang yourself in the men's room.

> **Professor:** So you all see, whether an act is a true proximate cause of an injury, and compensable under tort law, depends on whether a chain of events that caused the injury can be reasonably connected to the negligence of the defendant. And in this case, in regard to Mr. Jones, that linkage does not exist.

> **Gunner:** I disagree. Mr. Jones set off the Roman candle, and that set in motion the chain of events leading to the fire truck hitting the pole and causing the blackout which caused Mrs. Smith to trip on her way down the basement stairs and herniate her knee.

> **Professor:** Yes, but the neighbor's unleashed dog running in front of the fire truck, causing it to swerve and hit the pole, would be a superseding cause that negates all of the negligence of Mr. Jones.

> **Gunner:** Again, I disagree. Mr. Jones is still liable. A fire truck swerving to avoid a stray dog and hitting a telephone pole while responding to a gazebo fire caused by Mr. Jones's reckless use of illegal Roman candles,

and that crash causing a blackout, is a foreseeable occurrence.

A couple months of that is more than any normal person can stand. I'd try to listen to a few main points the professor made, only to have the lecture hijacked by some thirtyish virgin in acid-washed jorts or a creepy Young Republican attempting to start an argument about the Second Amendment or *Roe v. Wade*. Sometimes it would go on for the entire class—one gunner starting a debate that led to a "pile-on," where a team of gunners would start raising their hands in every corner of the classroom, firing off endless hypothetical scenarios. "What if . . ." "Suppose that . . ." "Let's assume that . . ." A bukkake session for the mental masturbation crowd, with all "money shots" on the professor. And none of them seemed to care or have any clue how cruel it was to the rest of the people in the room to start asking a question with two minutes left in the class. *Some of us have lives. We want to leave class early.* The only way I stifled the urge to scream was by reminding myself, over and over, *The job will be different . . . Practice will be different . . . It will be better . . . Normal.*

I pulled into my old college on the Sunday after Thanksgiving, and my first stop was an off-campus apartment called "the Shithole," where my buddy Mason lived. Mason was a six-foot-four ex-basketball player, large enough to be menacing, strong as an ox, but in every regard harmless, polite, downright Midwestern in his demeanor. Until he drank. On a few glasses of whiskey Mason devolved into a baboon, the sort of hopeless, infantile drunk who'd sit on the toilet to urinate because he was too trashed to aim for the bowl. His eyes would gloss over like a mako shark diving at kill, and you never had a clue what he was thinking—who he'd tackle, what piece of furniture he'd throw across the room or appliance he'd smash to bits. Of all the reckless drunks I've known, there was never a wilder Jekyll and Hyde act than Mason. On the right night, in the right circumstances, bourbon might as well have been PCP to him.

Walking into the Shithole, I heard the unmistakable dialogue of *Dazed and Confused* pouring out of the house. "Motherfucker!" Mason screamed as I opened the door, grabbing a can of Rainier from a case on the floor and throwing it at my head. "Just in time!"

"Didn't think I'd come empty-handed, did you?" I took a seat on the couch and broke out a box of nitrous oxide cartridges. For the next hour or so, shots of Jim Beam and the hiss of gas canisters emptying into balloons filled the room as the movie rolled along, one memorized line to the next.

When *Dazed and Confused* ended, Mason immediately put on *Easy Rider*. I didn't say a word, but I remember thinking it was a terrible choice. Not in the sense that it didn't fit in the moment, but that it fit all too well. The one-two effect was overwhelming. Watching the clueless seventies stoners stumble through *Dazed*, you're left thinking, *Why didn't I write this?* Watching *Easy Rider*, you're asking yourself, *Why didn't I join the circus?* As cartoonish as they appear on the surface, the characters in the films are strangely familiar, and they speak to those priceless privileges of youth that are only truly understood in hindsight, after college is over. Sitting there staring at the screen, I knew that perfect mix of freedom and irresponsibility was gone forever, but on a deep psychic level, free of the cheap pragmatism that told me its loss was necessary, acting like I still had those liberties—at least for a night or two—seemed the only dignified course. Not the mind-set you want on a headful of bourbon and laughing gas.

"We need to go somewhere. Now!" I leapt from the couch as the credits to *Easy Rider* rolled over the shot of Captain America's bike blazing a cloud of black smoke from the side of the highway. "I need to do something. Anything."

"Right." Mason threw on his jacket and pulled from the whiskey bottle. "Let's get the fuck out of here." I followed as he stomped out the door. No use in asking where we were headed. Mason had those mako eyes going.

We trudged uphill, through three inches of snow, to a keg party at a fraternity house, which I knew was a mistake the minute I opened the door. Walking into one of those scenes as a recent alumnus is like stepping into the living embodiment of the bleakest Leonard Cohen dirge. You've only been gone seven months, but the stink of reality hovers around you like spoiled meat. Dead, graduated, a reminder of a day the sorority pixies and tattered hatters swilling Milwaukee's Best are all busy pretending will never happen. I suddenly felt very alone, in a place that had been home just seven months ago.

"Come on," Mason growled and grabbed my arm. "Let's check out the house." We left the party and headed down Fraternity Row, to our old fraternity house.

If you closed your eyes and imagined what an ideal "college" looks like, you'd probably imagine something like mine. *U.S. News* called the place "a resort" a few years before I got there, and you could see how an uncreative reporter could default to that nickname. Part of it is the students. The place is a finishing school for future businessmen in the Not Quite Ivy bracket. Nobody's there to change the world. The school uniform is J. Crew, even the Deadheads are moderate Republicans and graduation weekend looks like a Brooks Brothers and Ann Taylor fashion show. The other part's the campus. A short walk through Fraternity Row alone supports the name, passing all the hedge-lined, Greek-columned fraternity mansions framing the red brick, white-trimmed academic halls and manicured quads ringed in rows of cherry trees.

And past it all, near the end of the road, hidden behind overgrown trees and shrubs, guarded by a red door and skull-and-crossbones lawn sign, was our house, or what was left of it. The school had sent the State Police and campus security to shut it down my senior year, to padlock it, throw out all the brothers, and board up the windows. Something about "inadequate risk management," they claimed. Looking back, I guess they had a point. The house was less a fraternity than something along the lines of a tailgate at an Allman Brothers concert. It was usually pleasant—people roaming around twisted out of their heads, throwing Frisbees and dancing to Dead bootlegs blasting from the basement. But it could also be scary—a pack of wired lunatics tearing the piano to toothpicks with axes and a chainsaw or a crowd of bourbonized maniacs punching out windows and firing dinner plates into the parking lot like clay pigeons.

And now it was over.

Mason and I stood outside in the snow staring at the brick edifice of the house, dead as rot, boarded up and collecting snowflakes. We hadn't spoken about why we were going there, but the reason was obvious.

"I'll bet the kitchen is still easy to get into," I said, wrapping my ski jacket around my hand. I punched out a pane of glass and turned the lock inside the door.

Mason pushed ahead of me, through the kitchen and into the dining area. It wasn't the old basement anymore. The murals of smiling sunflowers, Jerry Garcia, and American flags were painted over in gray-white lacquer. The school had taken over the basement of the house and turned it into an office suite of some sort, filled with rows of grey cubicles, lit from the little green and red diode bulbs of fax machines, copiers and computer drives blinking on and off.

Mason strode a walkway to the end of the basement, turned, grabbed an answering machine by the power cord, and swung it onto the floor. For a moment I was concerned. Were we out of our depth? Committing an actual crime? But then I figured, *When in Rome* . . . I mean, this was *college*. Or at least it used to be.

I grabbed a computer keyboard, yanked the power cord from the hard drive, wrapped the end of it around my hand and started spinning it over my head like a helicopter blade, whipping it into the sides of the cubicles. If I hadn't seen the lights coming through the windows I'd probably have kept going until the dizziness dropped me.

Shit. As soon as I saw the glare came through the windows I knew it was the cops. We'd clearly tripped some sort of alarm.

"Mason!" I staggered toward him, trying to gain my balance. "Mason!" He looked at me but didn't process the problem. "It's the cops! Get the fuck out of here!" He stood motionless, staring at me, grinning and flipping the remnants of whatever doomed piece of machinery he'd been murdering in the air like a cowboy playing with a lasso.

"Come on. Let's fucking go!" I waited at the door for a moment, screaming at him. Out of the corner of my eye I could see men in uniforms running toward me, lights behind them obscuring the distance between us. I had to run up a short set of stairs and spin around a brick wall to get loose and the window of escape was closing quickly. "Mason!" I looked back at him one last time, jumped up the stairs and cut around the wall. "Hey! Hey! Stop!" the officers screamed and a flashlight hit me in the eyes. There were two of them, ten feet away. *Would they split up, one cornering Mason while the other chased me? Did it matter?*

If you've ever run from cops, you know there's an instant at the outset, just before the jets fire, when your feet suddenly weigh a thousand pounds. The body seizes for a moment, every synapse in the flight system pouring adrenaline into the bloodstream at once. The engine redlines and your pulse stretches the arteries, first in your stomach, then your neck. Your hands go numb and your jaw clamps like a vise while your mind games the next ten moves, all in an instant. *Do I bolt for another fraternity house, run inside and hide in a random room? Make a dead run straight into the woods across the street? Is the guy with the flashlight fast enough to chase me? Could I burn him? Why the fuck am I wearing boat shoes this time of year?*

Thankfully, the drunken mind doesn't vacillate. I just ran— up the driveway, across the street and into a neighboring field, sprinting through the snow, pulling my jacket on as I went—never looking back. If I turned I'd slide. If I slid I'd buy it. If I bought it I was caught, and I wasn't getting caught. Not for this silly shit.

The distant streetlights faded as the woods closed in. I smashed into the brush at full speed, darting between the crush of thin trees sprouting out of the snow in every direction like a massive bamboo patch. Plowing ahead, I found myself falling sideways, forward and backward, slipping on icy leaves under the snow, tripping over dead branches, and stumbling on the uneven terrain meeting my feet at odd angles. The hood of the ski parka was tight over my face, barely allowing any peripheral vision. Head down I went, like a running back guarding the ball from being stripped, using the jacket as a shield against the jagged branches whipping and tearing me along the way. Two, three, five, maybe a dozen times I found myself hoisted on a branch jousting into me. I knew it hurt, but the pain didn't register. *Forward* was the only thought in my head.

About a hundred yards in, the barbed wire caught me. I'd been running so fast and shielding my eyes I never even saw the fence until I was caught in its thorns. "Motherfucker." I tore the North Face jacket off, bunched it atop the wires and leaned over it until my weight pulled the top wire down and I tipped over to the other side. Once on the ground I laid back in the snow, panting, writhing from booze shivers or hypothermia. *Fuck. I'm caught.* I was certain they'd be on me in an instant. But when I finally sat up and looked back, there was nothing but trees and snow. No flashlights or figures crunching toward me. I'd escaped.

The only question now was, Where the hell was I? I knew which way the open field was, but I couldn't go there. The cops could have been waiting for me to come back out. I had to keep plowing ahead.

Ten years old and lost in the woods is scary. You're going to hear the Riot Act for being home three hours late. Still it's an adventure, and there's a thrill and independence in being lost. Twenty-three, plastered, and stumbling around the woods in the freezing cold is a different experience. The first ten minutes I plunged through the dark aimlessly, waiting to run into a street or a yard. Neither came, and flashes of *Deliverance* and the end of *The Shining* passed through my head. *People die in the woods. They find lost escapees from psych wards and Alzheimer's patients frozen to Popsicles in these straits.* And I was weak, delirious, and desperately in need of a bed. *How did I get lost so close to campus?* I looked back in the snow to gauge direction. My footprints wound through the brush like spaghetti. I felt like I was in one of those computer-simulated reenactments of the final moments of a small plane crash, illustrating how a pilot could get disoriented and confuse the horizon with empty sky. I knew up from down, but east, west, north, and south were all the same. The only thing to do was keep walking and hope. *This isn't Siberia. There's a house ahead somewhere.*

I eventually popped out of the woods, onto a road about a mile from campus. It was a long walk back to the Shithole, where I crashed in a fetal position on a couch, using my ski parka as a blanket. By this time, my adrenaline stores were dead and every joint in my body was starting to ache. The lacerations on my hands and face were pulsing, my feet were numb and my jeans were soaked in ice water to the knees. I lay there shivering for hours, too wired to sleep, too drunk to drive to a hotel.

Sunrise came and I looked for Mason, but he wasn't there. Probably at his girlfriend's across town. Or in a cell. I didn't stick around to find out. If someone was looking for me, campus security, the cops, whoever, the best place to be was as far from town as possible. I chugged two coffees, started the car and drove back to law school. When I got there I walked straight into my dorm and went to bed. The phone woke me the next day at 9 A.M.

"This is Chuck DeNardo, head of security back at your alma mater." *Son of a bitch! Mason dimed me out.* For a moment I was mad, but then I realized it wasn't intentional. He was so drunk they probably gave him the "good cop, bad cop" treatment, and the minute he started talking he accidentally used my name. "We have reason to believe you were involved in a breaking and entering on campus two nights ago."

I didn't know how to respond. Embarrassment? Mea culpa? Feigned ignorance? Chuck had me by the balls. Of course I'd broken into the place.

"Look, Chuck. I don't know what happened. It was just one of those things. We didn't intend to do it. Things just kind of erupted—"

"Yeah." He cut me off. "I understand. But you're a graduate now. It's a crime and it's out of my hands. They report it to the local police."

"I just graduated last year. There's got to be something you can do. You don't want to prosecute alumni. I mean . . . I think it'd screw up my career."

"You're not a student anymore."

"Yes, but I—"

"I'll tell you what. I'll see what I can do."

Was it just that quick? One day you've got the privileges of youth, the next you're a criminal?

Sitting through days of classes wondering what Chuck would do—whether I'd get a call from the police asking me to turn myself in for booking—was maddening. I read criminal law books and gamed my strategy. They had a confession from an accomplice, fingerprints, and dozens of people who could verify I was there. Still, if they sent my case to the real cops and handled Mason in-house, I could pin it all on him. I had rights. There had to be a law against selective prosecution. I could beat this thing.

Whatever.

The solution wasn't in a legal book. Anyone with any sense knew that. In real life, for nine out of ten disputes, the abstract hyperanalysis they drag you through in law school is as useful as a condom machine at an Indigo Girls concert. The actual application of law isn't string theory. There's a human element. The professors tell you to strategize, organize, assume the worst motive of the opponent and vet every silly angle. Grow a "lawyer's mind," and faced with any dispute, dig in, fight, and engage the endless, tedious legal processes. Even if you don't win, it's cynically brilliant advice, at least from a lawyer's perspective. The longer and more complex the solution, the more the attorneys get paid.

That's probably giving them too much credit. Most just realy, really need hobbies.

Chuck eventually called back. "Well, I went to bat for you."

"And?"

"Well, they're not real keen about this."

"Look, I'll be thrown out of law school if I'm convicted."

"I'm not saying we can't work this out. I'm saying we need something from you."

"What?"

"A formal letter of apology, admitting everything."

"Consider it done. I really appreciate this and it won't happen again. I mean that."

"I know. Look, we all like to have a good time. You just can't do this kind of stuff anymore."

No shit.

THREE WOMEN AND A WOODEN SPOON

Are you nuts?" I turned my head and leapt backward off the bed. "I'm not kissing you. Not *now*."

Actually, I shouldn't have been kissing Rachel at all. The girl wasn't attractive, in any regard. Not even a three-beers-and-you-realize-she-has-nice-eyes kind of fuck. More in the realm of six whiskeys and a half hour of heavy glue-sniffing—the sort who only become tolerable when your image of them is warped like a funhouse mirror. She had a fat ass, pancake breasts, bloodshot eyes, and this bowl haircut that made it appear I was sodomizing a fat young boy when I took her from behind. And those were just the secondary annoyances. The worst part of Rachel was her voice—this grating Joan Rivers baritone she never stopped exercising:

"I fucking hated Puck, didn't you? He was the worst character on *The Real World*." "My father's been in San Diego for, like, fifteen years. They let you jog on the beach with dogs. It's really cool. I like the sun." "Wow, this couch is comfortable. It's like these seats in my boss's car. He's got one of those ones that looks like it's driving backwards. Not a Volvo. The other one . . . What's it called? You know—it's made in Scandinavia. Or maybe Finland."

Listening to her talk was like turning the dial on a radio playing at full blast, and I'd have forgotten about the girl long ago—blotted her from my memory like some awful childhood trauma—except for this one memorable thing. Rachel ate assholes.

You don't really know awkward until you're on your back, legs in the air, with a woman licking your anus. It's a total reversal of the sex roles. Suddenly you're "catching"—exposed, open and invaded, far past the usual "kink" of role playing, bondage, or any of the other common closet fetishes.

We all know the anus more than we ought to. Every man attempts anal sex on his girlfriend sooner or later, and every woman expects it at some point. The location of the thing screams for exploration—that cold mocking eye, taunting you when you take her from behind. *You're a big man in the front door. But you haven't brought that game into my house.* And most men have known women who liked to give "prostate massages" or had a girlfriend shove her finger inside them during sex after she read how it gave us "mind-blowing orgasms" in *Cosmopolitan.* But licking, sucking, *tasting* the anus? That's just disturbing, wrong on every level. A crime against hygiene.

As I laid there in shock, her tongue flicking back and forth like a cat at the milk bowl, that horrible Massengill douche commercial dialogue kept rolling through my head. Was I "springtime-fresh"? Could I ever be? I've owned a male anus for decades. Kept by a toothless hillbilly or a metrosexual with a waxed taint, it's a toxic cavern of festering bacteria knotted into the filthiest dreadlocks imaginable. And worse than all of that, how was it supposed to end? Was I expected to give some unholy form of a "money shot"? The concept alone tripped my gag reflex.

I assumed I was getting a blow job when Rachel pushed me onto my back and slid her head down my torso. When she passed my penis, I figured she was going to "teabag" my testicles. It wasn't until she bypassed those and started licking the inside of my thigh that I started to get concerned. *Wait a minute . . . Where's this going?* But before I could do anything she grabbed my legs, spread them, thrust them in the air and plunged her tongue straight into my ass.

I'd like to say I handled it like an old pro, that I discovered some new, intense form of orgasm. That wasn't the case. I fumbled, shook, and when she hit those odd nerves you never knew you had I scratched the air like a badger on its back. As I imagined her raking out shreds of toilet paper and the vilest residue imaginable with her teeth, all I could think about was how I had to get her out of the house as soon as she was done. That face wasn't touching my pillows. But how could I upset her enough to leave? There's no demeaning a person who'll suck an asshole like an oyster. Staring at the ceiling listening to the sickening licking sounds, I repeated the same thought in my head, over and over. *It's all for a bigger cause.*

A week before, I'd bet my buddy Alex that I could fuck three women in three days. Nothing shocking, but recall, I was in law school, so the handicaps weren't insignificant. How the bet came about I don't fully recall. It just seemed natural, the right thing to do, one of those random "just to see if you can" ideas, like having sex on the fifty-yard line of your college's football field or trying to do a hundred bong hits in one day. It was the end of my second year in law school, one of my last chances to get away with this sort of nonsense. In a situation like that, the only question that seems to make sense is, Why not?

Below that surface explanation, of course, part of the deeper reason was necessity. Every man knows sex comes in waves—a game of momentum where the more you get, the more you get. Women sense which men are having sex and which aren't, and they only fuck those who are already getting fucked. And just like any other wave, a run of luck with women inevitably peaks and crashes. The highest point is always bittersweet because you know, it's all downhill from there—only a matter of time until you're in the trough again, screwing your hand and cursing your luck. So when you catch that wave, the only course is to ride the fucker into the rocks, even if it means taking "volume" scores like Rachel just to keep it going.

The other part of it was what junkies call "chasing the dragon," racing after a high that grows more elusive the more you chase it. Have you ever gone out and bought a large-screen television just to have something to do? Do you flip your car leases early and shop new models compulsively even though you only drive to the train station every morning? Ever go out to pick up lunch and come back with five hundred dollars' worth of crap from the closest clothing store just because using or buying something temporarily blots out the bigger consideration of how you'll be spending the rest of your afternoon? Then you understand.

In school things are different. There's no cash for exotic distractions. The only things you can afford to consume are screwed or ingested. Which is how you find yourself in boxers in the living room, gulping a glass of Knob Creek and praying the woman in your bedroom who'd just used her tongue as a bidet would either pass out and leave you to sleep on the couch or take the hint that you're not coming back to "cuddle" and have the pride to slink out the front door.

It took two glasses of whiskey to put me down, but eventually, somewhere in the middle of a late-night showing of *True Romance,* I passed out. I don't know what Rachel did and I don't care. All I know is when I got up in the morning she was gone. "Thank God." *One down.*

Day Two was Melissa, a grad student at another university I'd met through my friend Lewis. She lived in the suburbs, on some tree-lined street, fifteen minutes out of town. It took me forever to get there in heavy traffic, which would have been annoying but for a mild beer-and-dope buzz lingering around from the afternoon. I didn't even realize I was half an hour late until I glanced at my watch outside her door. In any other circumstance, I'd invent an excuse, but with Melissa it didn't matter. I'd say nothing, and that'd be fine. Another generic evening. Eat. Drink. Fuck. Leave. The lateness only forced me to work faster. I aimed to be back in the neighborhood before midnight, to catch a few drinks with friends. The pre-sex dialogue with Melissa was always short, but now it had to be compressed to haiku length.

You look very nice
Fascinating . . . Some more wine?
Where is the K-Y?

I should have liked Melissa. She was a perky brunette with great tits, a pretty face, and she was tighter than any woman I'd ever known, enough that I could feel every undulation inside the girl. But her performance didn't approach the quality of her equipment, at least with me. She was a Porsche with a cracked gasket; should have been a fun ride—only she never got out of the garage. As a simple matter of biology it's next to impossible for a male to have bad sex. Somehow, with Melissa, it happened. She'd just laid there, like she was going through the motions—that it was all just a means to an end. Usually that's a sign of a husband hunter, a woman looking for the "Mrs." degree. But the problem with Melissa was far more complicated than that simple, cynical explanation—a slippery issue I could never put my finger on.

I remember trying to figure it out one night at my friend Lewis's place.

"There's two kinds of fucking." Lewis slugged back on his Sierra Nevada. "You have fucking just to fuck, and then there's fucking where it's not only about the fucking—where the fucking's, like, part of some bigger concept."

"How baked are you?"

"Let me use a metaphor. Your school had sororities, right?"

"You are baked. Did you order Thai food yet?"

"No."

"No which? You didn't order Thai yet?"

"Listen. Remember the hot good girls' sorority and the hot party girls' sorority?" Of course I did. He knew that. It's a cliché, but every school has exactly those competing factions. "Both kinds of chicks fucked, but the good girls got pinned by their boyfriends and all that shit, remember?"

"I guess." I never even owned a fraternity pin.

"You think those chicks were thinking the same thing when they were fucking their steady boyfriends as the crazy chicks were when they were hooking up?"

"I don't know." Actually, I did. Every guy understands the difference between women who fuck to fuck and women who fuck with a purpose, however subconscious it might be.

"Ever try to fuck thinking about something other than fucking? If you're fucking for any reason other than just fucking, it's not going to be a good fuck. It's Fucking, but not really 'fucking,' you know?"

"You sure that wasn't a simile?"

"Huh?"

"Never mind."

I didn't admit it, but Lewis's point made perfect sense. Some people are in it for the fucking. The basal animal attraction is the start, and if that takes them further, so be it. Others are in it for the relationship, working in reverse. Fucking's a secondary process, or an instrument, one of the things they do to manage the bigger project. I can't say one approach is right or wrong or better than the other, but I will say this about the latter: There aren't many sensations creepier than being inside someone and at the same time feeling like the two of you are on separate planes, flying toward opposite coasts.

The night at Melissa's played out the usual way. We drank a bottle of red wine as the food cooked, then shoveled down dinner. When that was done we watched part of a movie and had a few beers. Halfway through it, I put my arm around her, like a high school student trying to get to second base. Melissa took the cue, we started fooling around, then we fucked on the couch, from just the right angle so that I came almost instantly. The whole time I remember smelling the garlic from the sautéed spinach on my breath, certain I was exhaling it in her face. The smell had to be awful, but she didn't seem to care. She just smiled, or winced every now and again, never even asking me to slow down or try a different position. The process felt like one of those National Geographic specials where they showed lions ramming away on each other in the brush, both of the beasts staring across the Serengeti, bored shitless, just rolling through the motions of the mating season. The whole thing took three, maybe four minutes from start to finish. I'm pretty sure I didn't even take off my shoes.

"That was great." She smiled when it was over.

The mind's usually blank when you come. No deep thoughts.

Just the sound of your breath, echoing through an empty head, at least until the high wears off. But when I heard her say that, I immediately wanted to snap. *Are you fucking serious? Do you really expect me to believe that?* The lie didn't offend me. We were both doing that. It was her half-assed effort—assuming I'd be complimented with that flattery.

But then, I had to admit, her "phoning it in" was only fair. Melissa and I gave nothing and we each got exactly what we deserved. It wasn't much, but in my case, it was good enough—all that I needed.

"Yeah, that was great." As soon as I finished dressing I started looking for my car keys. "And thanks for the food." *Two down.*

Day Three was Loren, the one I was really into. Loren was an "Automatic," one of those women you meet and immediately know you're going to fuck. You don't know when or where, but it's going to happen. And both of you realize it. Neither of you is the love of each other's lives. There won't be any brunch, meeting the parents or walking her chocolate lab through the park. You won't settle down and raise children with an Automatic. The relationship, if you can call it that, is far too intense to go long term—more in the way of a release, like runner's high or the blessed cold fingers of that first drink on a Friday at five-thirty. You're into the woman on an animal level. Maybe it's the curve of her cheekbones, or the slope of her breasts. Maybe the tendon running up the side of her neck when she turns her head. Whatever the reason, not fucking her seems a crime against karma.

Loren was a predator, the polar opposite of Melissa. She didn't care about finding a man or having a relationship. She just liked to fuck—sideways, upside down, tied up, blindfolded, over the sink/table/car hood/gas grille. She was pushing thirty, moody, impulsive, and utterly rudderless. She'd been in marketing, advertising, and real estate and didn't like any of them. When I first met her, she'd just quit an MBA program, the latest in a long line of futile efforts to find a direction.

And I think it was that shared aimless ambition that attracted us to each other. I saw something in Loren I saw in most people

I'd found interesting. She wanted to get ahead, but she also wanted an endless run of new *experiences*—to sample as many careers as she could until she found something she liked. Most would say that's mad, impatient and immature, a childish refusal to settle for the realities of the working world. But I understood. I sympathized. Fuck, it turned me on. She mirrored every reason I was sticking it out in law school. As bad as the career was looking, I knew law infected every corner of commerce. I thought as a lawyer I could work on a smorgasbord of different cases involving different industries until I ran into a real career I liked. Then I could quit law and use the dilettante's primer I'd picked up litigating in the industry I was interested in as the experience I needed to get a job in it. Or at least that's what I thought I could do.

"Hey babe." Loren answered the doorbell. I didn't say anything, just pushed her into the hall and closed the door behind me. At that point, the only thing on my mind were her nipples, poking through a frayed T-shirt. A handful of bong hits and Amstels later we were on the floor and I had one of them between my teeth. "Wait, I need to put something on." She jumped up and ran to the bedroom.

I sat on the floor sipping a beer, watching her walk away. Loren wasn't model-hot, but she was very well crafted. Five foot eight, blond, with long hair, long legs, and a body tight in all the right places. She'd have been a solid 8.0 if not for her pussy. That pushed her to a 9.0.

From an aesthetic perspective, the pussy's personality is all in the bush. It tells you everything you need to know about the owner. The "Disco Mitt," a patch of hair crawling near the thighs like ivy, says Granola Chick. The "Vertical Hitler," a tiny rectangle of hair just above the opening, indicates a *Girls Gone Wild* alumna with a similarly sized IQ. The "Landing Strip," basically an elongated Vertical Hitler, is the same girl at twenty-nine, working at a job with "manager" in the title. As to the Brazilian, well, that has no profile. She could be a stripper or a CEO or a schoolteacher. The only thing you know for sure is she expects you to spend a lot of time with your face in it.

My favorite's the old "Standard Cut." The two-and-a-half-inch wide, close-cropped style is the Two-Button Brooks Brothers Classic of pubic fashion—dependable, tasteful, and always in style. It's never overpowering, a bush content not being the center of attention, exuding a quiet, understated dignity. The Barbara Bush of bushes, one could say. Only you'll want to fuck it.

Loren's pussy pushed her to a 9.0 because of its originality. Where most women crop the Standard Cut only on the sides, allowing the body to grow high and curly, Loren trimmed hers like a green at the U.S. Open, a rare, high-maintenance cut. Too close and you've got a patch of porcupine stubble; too high and the hair stands up straight like a Johnny Unitas buzz cut. When it works, however, and hers did, you get a refreshing modern spin on the Standard Cut—an exotic but practical pussy.

I was sucking back an Amstel, flipping through a magazine on the floor, when Loren came back from the bedroom. She was wearing a black latex dress and steel high heels, eyes ringed in heavy black liner, and holding a huge wooden cooking spoon. "I like to get spanked in this." She handed me the thing, walked back into the bathroom, leaned over the sink and pulled the dress up over her ass.

I stood behind her for a moment, feeling the rubbery fabric of the dress as I held it halfway up her back. Latex fetishes are something I'll never understand. So plasticky and clinical, raising so many questions—questions I'd never ask. There's a confessional element to fetishes and the rule is always, like the title of that old Kinks record, *Give the People What They Want*. Never judge; never ask why. I pulled my arm back, took two slow practice swings, then—CRACK. The wood connecting with her flesh sounded like a line drive slapped off a fastball, but Loren didn't flinch. "Come on." She smiled in the mirror. "Now *really* hit me."

If you're looking to beat someone, try a wooden cooking spoon. It's light and clips through the air with minimal drag, slapping flush against the skin with a sickening crispness. By the tenth or so swing, I'd found a perfect DiMaggio slice, and the spoon's sweet spot. "I think I'm doing damage here."

"Use the belt." A tear streamed down her face.

"That thing on the door?" A heavy-gauge leather strap with a broad iron buckle was hanging from a towel hook. "That's a fucking elephant crop."

"Focus on the right side." In my half-baked laziness, I'd swatted her almost exclusively on the left, which was swelling into an argyle pattern of welts.

"This room's too small." I tried to use the belt but wound up hitting the wall behind me with my backswing. "I can't get a proper arc."

"Let's move to the bedroom." She pulled the dress over her head and walked out.

I'd like to say the bedroom was too small as well, but it was huge, with twelve-foot ceilings, and when we were done in there I felt like the slave master in *Roots*. "You should really put some ice on that."

I was grabbing a quick beer in the kitchen, blurring what had just happened from my mind, when Loren brought out the video camera. We'd talked about taping sex in the past, but neither of us was ambitious or organized enough to set the thing up.

"Now?"

"It's as good a time as any."

Here's a tip: Never videotape yourself naked. First, it's not a myth—everyone's fat on camera. At the time, I wasn't buff or anything, but I thought I looked pretty good. Until I saw the tape. "Jesus Christ. That's awful. I have tits."

"That's just shadowing." Loren laughed.

"And I look translucent." Second, the devil's in the lighting. On video, the rosiest tint may as well be a halogen lamp. I was Day-glo porcelain white, with scattered patches of hair and a whiffle-bat-sized member jutting out of my form. Yes, there is one benefit to video—the "John Holmes Effect." It adds twenty pounds *everywhere*. The widening effect that bloats your face into that of a *Family Circus* cartoon strip character does the same to your conveniently horizontal member.

"Damn . . . I'm hung."

"I love this part." She started snickering to herself.

"You kept that? Erase it. It's horrible." Here's another tip: Never feign masturbation for a camera.

"Why did you bite your lip like that?" She laughed. "Does it hurt?"

"Erase that."

"Why? It's not like you're running for office."

"That's not the issue. It's a piss-poor performance." The images gave me a new appreciation for the skills of porn actors. Pretending to be approaching orgasm on film is no task for the layman, which is probably a symptom of the act. Women look sexy working themselves over—licking their fingers, sliding them between their thighs, breathing heavy, sighing and shaking. A man looks like that Internet movie of a chimp diddling himself in a tree at the zoo. Frantic and uncoordinated—0 to 100 and across the finish line like a funny car, graceful as the motion you'd apply sanding an old banister. Faking it's even harder. I thought I gave a solid performance, but it was terrible, robotic porn karaoke.

"Here, tie me up." Loren placed the camera on the elevated slate base in front of the fireplace and handed me two scarves from the closet. "This one's a blindfold." I put her on the floor in front of the camera and tied her hands behind her back, arching her upward, forcing her breasts apart.

"Is the video on?"

"Yes, but I can't get into position." I tried to angle Loren sideways, to make sure my ass wouldn't be between her and the camera lens. "The space is too tight. I'm just going to do it myself." I strained to move a coffee table next to her so I could lean on something, grabbed the camera with my left hand and began running my right hand across her breasts, working my way down her stomach, glancing back and forth over the spaces just inside her hip bones. Trying to adjust the focus was making me dizzy, and the commands she was firing at me made it all the more difficult.

"Pull inside, like a trigger. Not that hard. Stay right there."

Loren rattled her hips and screamed, but it sounded too loud, too forced, like she was just acting for the camera. That's the biggest problem with "filming it." Lewis was right. Fucking with any agenda other than just fucking isn't fucking at all. Loren wasn't on the same page as Melissa in that regard, but the minute I turned on the camera, it wasn't about getting off anymore. We were putting on a show for a fantasy audience, and the oddity was, at that point, out of the three of them, Rachel seemed the most honest. Say what you will about the foulness of the thing, nobody eats assholes with an ulterior motive.

"I want you in me."

"Lemme take this crap off you first." As I leaned over and looked down, I realized I'd been so focused on managing the camera I'd completely lost my erection. "Actually, uh . . . hold on just one second." I ran to the bathroom.

The fallacy that men can be kept titanium-stiff indefinitely by anything with breasts and a pliable orifice is exactly that. There are myriad little things that crush our libidos. If she disturbs you in one small way, that's one small issue you'll be thinking about, and it can snowball, eclipsing everything else. Hearing a woman moan like a man, talk about her love of hermit crabs or show you a ceramic unicorn collection can turn a man limp in seconds. Discovering she has a "treasure trail" or breath like a golden retriever can kill an erection faster than a dry hand job. And fiddling drunk and stoned with a video camera, like some alcoholic porn cameraman, will bore you flaccid. After a while, anything's just images through a viewfinder.

"Shit." I ran into Loren's medicine cabinet and pulled out a tube of Estée Lauder moisturizer, slathered it on and went to work. After about thirty seconds, I realized I had bigger problems than I'd thought. *Oh, come on.* There's no feeling in the world as desperate and low as pulling a flaccid penis. Nothing—not Buckner letting that ground ball trickle through his feet, Webber calling that fourth time out for Michigan, or Duran *no más*-ing Leonard—crystallizes the agony of defeat like a limp dick in your palm.

But I wasn't giving up just yet. This was my fourth and goal, inches, literally, from the end zone and I still had a couple seconds on the clock. I ran it up the middle, Big Ten-style. No fancy strokes. No "Western" or "Interlock" grips. No two-hand action. I just closed my eyes and yanked the fucker until it responded, then checked my profile in the mirror. It wasn't a raging hard-on, but it was holding steady, just north of 90 degrees. And every man knows, no matter how weak it might be, as soon as you get it inside her it turns to steel.

"What were you doing?" She heard me running back from the bathroom.

"Nothing." I tore off the scarves and got inside her as fast as I could, before the damned organ could betray me again. And after a few thrusts, the tepid erection shifted to a wrought-iron rod. Finally, success. *Three down.*

The odyssey was over. I came, I saw, I came a couple more times.

I didn't see Alex in school until Wednesday of the following week. "Where have you been?"

"I was supposed to head out for a few drinks on Sunday night with this chick. We wound up doing shots at my place until three."

"You were hungover through Tuesday?"

"No. I had to put a CD changer and a new subwoofer in the car yesterday."

"You didn't do that Monday?"

"I was hungover."

"Remember that bet? Well, I got all three, in three days."

"Really? Good for you."

"What do I win? I forget."

He held out his hand. "Congratulations."

"What's that mean?"

"That means we didn't bet anything, dumbass."

Ten Percenter

BATTING .100—

A PROPER END TO LAW SCHOOL

Maybe you wake up like I do every day—amazed the boss or professor or whoever's in charge hasn't caught on to the fraud, wondering when the other shoe's going to drop. When they'll find out you have a split personality, that you're only playing a game and if they had the slightest clue what you were really like—what you were thinking or how you got your kicks when you weren't around them—they'd fire you, expel you, have security drag you from the property in cuffs. All for good reason.

You don't deserve the paychecks, bonus, grades, or whatever else they might be giving you. You're not a team player. You're not even playing the same sport. Every day that goes by is one more successful charade—another scene in the longest-running comedy you'll ever see; feigning interest in all sorts of conversations about the acceptable topics—the weather, lawn care, the satisfaction of having a new roof with a five-year warranty. But you never discuss anything that lets the actual "you" out of the box. This stifling of the self can be maddening, and you might feel the need to be honest with those in your work or school world—dueling to fuse the spheres of your existence. Suppress that urge. Bury it. The merger doesn't work, and attempting it only leads to disaster.

Back in my first semester of law school, a third-year student named Wallace schooled me on a fundamental truth—there were two kinds of people in the place, and the chasm between them was wider than the Grand Canyon.

"Why are the people here so fucking stressed and angry?" I asked.

"They're cutthroats. This is their whole world," Wallace replied, as if that alone would explain the problem.

"It's grad school, not a gladiator match."

"Dude, this is everything in life for a lot of people. If they're not at the top of the class, they don't make law review, and if they don't make law review, they won't get a job at the most prestigious firm. And if they don't get that job, there's no reason to live."

"That's deranged."

"Never underestimate how desperate these people can be. Look around. What else are they going to do to make money?"

"Come on. It's not that bad."

"I'm serious. Maybe, *maybe* ten percent of the people here are worth knowing. Be happy you're one of them and stay away from this place. I'd never mix my actual life with this world."

"How do you locate that ten percent?"

"They just kind of find each other. How'd you know to ask me this question?"

I didn't think much about that conversation my first year. Most of my second semester was spent away from the school, on four-day weekends with college friends, or hanging out at Alex's place, freeloading off his kegerator.

It wasn't until my last year of law school, facing down graduation, that I truly learned the wisdom of Wallace's advice.

The mess started with the best of intentions—free alcohol. I'd been drinking one night with a friend who worked for a company that sold bar exam study materials on campus. To promote the product, she rented bars and invited law students from the schools in the city. Somehow, in a Guinness haze, we hit on the idea of throwing a promotional party at my place.

"That's a great idea." She laughed. "I'll buy you a few kegs," and just like that it began.

My roommates and I quickly invited all of our friends, and most agreed to come. The only regret I heard was from Alex, who was the last person anyone would expect to turn down free booze. "Dude, your timing sucks. I'll be returning from a hockey tournament late that night. And I just got a quarter sheet."

"Where'd you get that?"

"Remember that stripper I bought the Olds '98 from? She couldn't get the title together. It's payment for doing the paperwork for her."

"Took her long enough."

"You tried to buy acid lately?"

When I learned that he'd be dosing, I was glad Alex couldn't make it. Alex was one of those rare personalities that defy simple definition—a huge, hulking freak, equal parts menacing and absurd, and one of those strange minds who could be the smartest and dumbest person in the room at once. On a headful of whiskey, he was a violent force of nature—reckless, monstrous, unbridled by boundaries of money, time, distance, or common sense, the sort of lunatic who'd start the weekend at the corner pub and end it two states away, penniless, wandering around a hotel with nothing but *How?* in his head. Whacked on psychedelics, Alex was simply uncontrollable, the frantic mind of a hapless hippie losing his shit in the body of a NFL lineman, banging around the house like a wild boar, pouring liquor down his throat and screaming the lyrics to "Monkey Man" over and over.

"Anyway," he went on, "the team is renting a U-Haul. We're going to drive back from the tournament with a keg in the back. If your place is still going then, I'll stop by."

I'd already lost my share of the security deposit due to the holes Alex put in the walls during a drunken argument about whether to watch *Shakes the Clown* or *Cocksucker Blues* that had degraded to a wrestling match. The last thing I needed was to wind up in hock to my housemates for a set of blown speakers because he decided again, in the midst of psychedelic mania, that he needed to hear Black Sabbath's "Supernaut" at "eleven." Bringing a hockey team of people like him to the house, all dosed out of their trees, might as well have been burning the place down.

"Sure, great. The more the better." *They'll never make it. They might not even make it back over the state line.* I got a mental snapshot of highway patrolmen forcing an acid-crazed hockey team into a paddy wagon. Guns and flashlights look like toys with acid eyes, the sort of thing you can't help grabbing. *God be with them.*

Alex lived in two very different worlds, and if there was any truth to Wallace's claim that the decent people in law school—"Ten Percenters"—find one another, it was running into him. The first time I met the guy I was just sitting in the library, reading a magazine, nothing to distinguish me from any of the other people in the place. All of a sudden this guy sits down across from me, opens a newspaper, scans the thing for a second, then slams it down on the coffee table. "Is there a worse hangover than Mad Dog? I can't even fucking read."

Some people would have figured that a strange introduction, possibly off-putting. I wasn't one of them. "I haven't touched that shit since college." I laughed and introduced myself. Anyone dropping that line as an opener was good people.

After about five minutes of conversation, I knew Alex was part of the decent ten percent. I knew that because I'd known his kind my whole life. I'd gravitated toward them, and they to me. At every juncture—high school, college, and now grad school, I found myself surrounded by people who thought in a fashion just outside what the types who enforced the "norm" defined that to be. I'm not talking about bizarre counterculture sorts. Not stoners, geeks, goths, computer freaks, rebels or loners. These Ten Percenters aren't rebelling against anything. They look and act entirely average in every regard, something akin to highly functioning alcoholics. One may have performed surgery on you, piloted the plane you were on last week, or done your estate planning. The difference is so subtle you could easily miss it.

There's no secret bond between these people, and it's not an elite fraternity. In fact, in the greater world beyond law school it's probably more like twenty percent of everybody. And they're not easy to find. Sure, if a coworker signs the weekend security log in your building "John Cocktoasten," hums "Dear Mr. Fantasy" around the office, or has dog-eared Bukowski novels on his windowsill, chances are he's one. But those are just cheap, superficial traits. If there's any deep common link to these types it's not realizing they're part of any "type" at all. They just roll through their days, always operating in two worlds—appearing engaged on the surface while utterly disconnected from the reindeer games the other ninety percent get caught up in, knowing it's all just a comedy in the end.

To the average law student biting his nails, scribbling notes furiously, chain smoking outside the library and mainlining espresso to stay up studying into the early morning, this thinking is insane. The job is the brass ring, and if you're not pathologically devoted to "the law," you're at odds with almost everyone and everything around you. The statements professors routinely made about commitment to the field—"I never had time to read a newspaper in law school," or "Law becomes your life"—struck me as signs of mental illness, low intellect, or a person trying to escape himself. To the heads around me in the classroom nodding in agreement, this sounded normal.

I didn't think much about the party until the day it was supposed to happen, when, as they always do, the unexpected contingencies started appearing.

"It's snowing!" My friend Lewis called that afternoon. "Kas got some Mexican shit. It's crazy strong."

"Excellent." *Coke monkeys—just what this party needs.*

Kas was a sixth-year college student majoring in black-market pharmacy studies. A loud girl who never stopped talking or smoking, she was a drug-buddy confidante—the sort who never had a man but was always around them. Half starfucker, half granola chick, pinballing between endless inane topics—from seeing Marky Mark at some resort, to the last Aquarium Rescue Unit show she'd attended—all of it rolled together into a streaming beatnik riff. Conversing with Kas was nodding or saying "cool" or "yeah" a lot, but no one ever complained. She could say whatever she liked. She had drugs.

Lewis stomped in around seven. "Where are the kegs? Sierra Nevada, right?" He spit into a "dip cup" in his hand.

"Yeah, if you're buying them." Which Lewis could do. He had a job paying him far more than he was worth. I'd met the guy my first year in town, through Alex. He was twenty-six and already a player at some financial services outfit downtown, high enough on the ladder to afford a huge luxury apartment up the street from my place. How he did it was a mystery. Lewis never worked more than eight hours a day, which I knew because he was always hanging out at my house or the bar up the road where I ate all my meals.

Kas arrived a short time after Lewis, toting a kid with dreadlocks who introduced himself as Reggie and a couple of "dead bodies," those perma-baked couch stains who drink your beer, flip through your Dead and Dylan discs and never offer anything to the conversation. The only time either of that pair spoke was to ask me for some obscure microbrew I clearly wouldn't have.

"It's the best ale. I had it at a show at Red Rocks."

"I saw the Allman Brothers at Red Rocks. Do you see them here?"

And so on.

After a few drinks Kas tapped the side of her nostril. "Anybody want a little 'ahem, ahem'?"

"I don't need that right now."

"I have some mushrooms." She laughed.

"Well . . ." There's never a reason to turn down fungus. Ever. "Maybe just a few."

I was fixing a drink in the kitchen a little while later when Alex called. "Hey motherfucker! The last team didn't have enough guys. Forfeit! I should be there around ten."

"Great."

"Do you have any Jack? Beer isn't going to work." I could hear drunken hockey players and team groupies screaming in the background. "These are strong doses. I'm already tattooed to the ceiling."

"I don't know."

"You don't mind if the team comes, right? We'll bring another keg."

"No problem, but I don't see any Jack in the liquor cabinet. You'll have to stop and buy some."

"I can't handle buying anything right now." Acid's an odd drug, capricious and subjective. The difference between brilliance and idiocy on the stuff can be as thin as the doors to a package store. You can be debating Stanley Cavell outside but then suddenly, faced with a cash register and the simplest transaction, your mind turns to mush, the words "Jack Daniel's" seem impossible to form and when the clerk asks for identification you can't tell your license from your MasterCard.

"Send somebody else into the store."

"I won't know where to stop. We're riding in the back of a U-Haul truck. No windows."

"You could literally be killed by beer tonight." The image of a group of tripping hockey players crammed into the back of a moving van, doing 75 on the interstate with sixteen-gallon metal kegs which would instantly turn into body-crushing projectiles with any sudden application of the brakes was coursing through my head, among a lot of other things. At that point, the mushrooms were kicking in and the appliances in the kitchen taking on that 3-D-without-the-glasses appearance, where the colors of an object bleed slightly outside its perimeter. The music started echoing, the room got brighter, and the colors began erupting. Everything was eye candy, from the Kandinsky print above the fireplace to the red diode lights on the stereo. I looked into my beer and its appearance was reversed, a cup of white foam topped with sprinkles of yellow liquid. Watching water soak into a blue dish towel was mesmerizing.

No reason to panic, but with mushrooms there's always a fleeting moment of concern. Strong ones grab you quickly, a sharp rocket ride into the sky. Forty-five minutes in, you're doing 600 miles per hour and every so often, somewhere in a primitive circuit of the brain that doesn't grasp the simple reality you're on a drug you know like the curve at the base of your girlfriend's spine, a twinge of fear and the notion "this wasn't a good idea" jumps into your head. But there's no turning it off—no talking or thinking your way out of the mess. You're powerless save the dulling effect of whiskey, which only provides an illusion of calm and control. I sipped a Maker's Mark and checked my pupils in the mirror—wide as saucers.

People started piling in half an hour later.

"Hey, is this your place? Nice. You have wine, right?"

"You don't let people smoke inside, do you? I'm allergic."

"Hey, nice to see you survived Secured Transactions. You looked pretty shocked when the professor called on you. How did you not know the priority liens?"

Fifteen minutes was enough. I ducked upstairs, to the front bedroom, the "Studio 54" area. Reggie the Rastafarian was fiddling with a mirror laid flat on a dresser. "Just one." I smiled, cutting a small line. Why not? A little, for lucidity.

When my drink ran out I headed back downstairs, to get a reload in the kitchen. The house was two stories, thin and long, like a row home, and the only way to the kitchen was back the way I'd come. It was a long walk, and by the time I reached it my temporary clarity was gone. I scanned the room for a conversation in which to inject myself, but it was all just mouths, snapping back and forth like Trekkies debating whether season one was better than season five.

"If the motorcycle were to go off the cliff because it skidded on the dead squirrel, then the driver who killed the squirrel, were he to have been driving recklessly, could be responsible. I mean, I guess it all turns on where the squirrel was located. If it's outside the yellow lines, that would indicate the driver who hit it was driving recklessly."

"What if the squirrel walked to where it was after it was struck? Who's responsible then?"

It may as well have been a pack of twenty-five-year-old virgins discussing computer games. "If I get the invisibility cloak, and I'm on my last life, and I'm slain, will I become visible again before I die? I mean, if I die invisible, is it possible no one would know I'm dead?"

I darted to the front of the house, to get back upstairs. How had it come to this? Where did I make the wrong turn? Two and a half years ago I was standing in a bar full of cute girls and witty people making jokes and planning to get apartments together after graduation. And then this? Was it a sentence? Punishment for playing mailbox baseball in junior high? Taking Jenny McConnell's virginity sophomore year?

The voices came from every direction as I climbed the stairs, some of them live, some a cruel, repeating echo. "Parol evidence should only apply where there's an ambiguity about the terms of the agreement and . . ." "Actually, the proper citation since the 1977 Commentary has been a semicolon, and no italics . . ." "A deliberate act qualifies as a superceding cause only when . . ."

The reality was clear. I was a misfit among misfits, which I guess should have been comforting, but it didn't feel that way in the moment, and my head wasn't processing the "double negative" compliment in the epiphany. Watching the crowd as I walked up the stairs, I felt like I was in that famous long fade-away from *Gone With the Wind,* where the camera slowly cranes back over thousands of dead and injured bodies on the battlefield, surveying the wreckage.

There's a myth that all lawyers are merely greedy bastards—that we do what we do out of cash lust and nothing more. That's true for some, but for a much larger sector, the career is a calling, or a lifeline, a magnet for thousands of lost minds all buying into the "law as life" lie—that collecting the cheapest, easiest professional degree somehow elevates an utterly unremarkable existence.

But where did that leave me, the man on the stairs? Was I trapped in this warped reality, doomed to play their game? What became of lawyers like me, just looking to beat a nice paycheck out of the degree? Did I have to split myself in two, and if I did, how long could that last? There'd be a witching hour when side took over the other. Which would it be? Would I give up. Spend my life arguing minutiae? *Jesus, these mushrooms really have me by the eyelids. I need a huge glass of something.* I darted upstairs, where I knew there'd be a bottle of Beam.

As I reached the second floor, Mason came barreling over the top of the stairs in a Gene Simmons wig. He was visiting from Chicago, where he was now in graduate school, and still very much what health professionals would call a "binge drinker." As I watched him flip over the banister into the front hallway, I knew something would get broken. Mason was prone to great physical feats in a strong drunk and he had no concept of his own strength. The first time he'd visited, he drank a bottle of Glenlivet and kicked the bathroom door off the hinges believing he'd somehow been locked inside and had no other way out.

"What are you doing?" Kas barked in my ear.

"Just stealing a quick one." I closed the door to the front room and chopped a short bump on the mirror.

"Fag. That's a girl's line. You can't get high on a line that size."

"I'm not trying to get high. Just get a little grip." I put the mirror back in the dresser and went back down the stairs.

A thin man in a sweater vest grabbed my arm near the front door. "Your friend just knocked a beer all over me, and I think I speak for everyone when I say nobody wants to hear Ozzy Osbourne."

"Does he look like Ozzy?" I nodded in Mason's direction. "That's a Kiss wig he's wearing."

Mason was in the other room, his arms flapping and head jerking up and down to Foghat's "Slow Ride." As I tried to reach him, one of the "dead bodies" moved in his direction, holding out a compact disc, which I knew meant certain disaster. Mason was a music Nazi—the mere suggestion that he endure something he didn't like could provoke an outlandish response.

"Godstreet Wine? Fuck that!" Mason slapped the disc from the kid's hand and threw him onto the couch, into a pile of doughy men drinking beers.

"What the fuck? That guy assaulted me." A man on the couch stood up.

"Careful with the legalese." I smiled.

"Don't fucking tell me—"

"Excuse me." I laid a hand on his shoulder. "Someone needs me upstairs." The last thing I needed was an argument, and there was no point staying in that scene. It would only degrade, quickly. Somebody would ask to hear Dave Matthews and Mason would put him through the coffee table.

As I turned to run up the steps, a round little woman who was coming down berated me. "You know people upstairs are using drugs right out in the open. We could all get in trouble and—" *Oh Jesus.* She looked like a little pug dog—crinkled face, spitting slobber and barking. She even had a thin layer of whiskers on her upper lip. "I'm no prude, but . . . yarf yarf yarf yarf . . ." *You should be on all fours, collared, shitting in the yard.* The more the images came, the harder it was to keep my mouth straight.

"What? What's so fucking funny?"

"Nothing . . . I—I—" Explaining was impossible and she'd never understand anyway. I leaned on the banister, coughing to stifle giggles.

"You fucking asshole," she snapped.

The front door swung open a moment later, slamming into the wall as Alex and a couple of hockey players dragged in a keg. "Hey fuckhead, where's that Jack?"

The round little girl immediately bolted down the stairs and scampered out the front door, saddlebags flapping back and forth in her khaki stretch pants.

"What the hell was that?" Alex asked.

"We're in love. You just fucked it up."

The hockey players and their girlfriends poured into the house, and the rising noise level piqued the interest of the upstairs crowd, which slowly began working its way downstairs. The mingling began, changing the scene from folk to electric. Within minutes, all the liquor in the house was being passed around the kitchen. Alcohol-immune from the acid, the hockey crowd was swigging Glenfiddich, Knob Creek, and Stoli from the bottle. It was a terrible waste of good booze, but there was nothing anyone could do to stop it. Alex was grabbing people and demanding they do shots.

"But I don't want a sh—"

"Then you can't get into the kitchen."

"But I want a beer."

Reggie ran past with a green-complected girl throwing up into her hands. The force of the vomit was causing it to shoot out of the spaces between her cupped fingers like little fountains, leaving reddish yellow clumps of half-digested salsa, chips and red wine slurry on the tile. "When she gets cleaned up, can I use your room?" I didn't bother to answer his question. He'd use it either way. Kas was pinballing around the place, searching for any pliable male. "So do you want to be a judge someday? That seems pretty cool." Out of the corner of my eye I could see "Fetus," one of Alex's roommates, half naked, wearing Mason's Kiss wig. He'd tucked his penis between his testicles and pulled it back between his legs and was screaming at two of the hockey players' girlfriends, "Look at my pussy! Look at my pussy!"

"Dude, tell him to stop that. It's upsetting the chicks." A man in a Notre Dame hat was barking directives at Alex.

"You stop him."

"It's fucking gross."

"They've never seen a vagina?"

It was sometime after midnight when the cops arrived. I was upstairs, smoking a cigarette with Lewis and licking the last of the coke residue from the cover of *Rust Never Sleeps* when the red and blue lights poured through the windows, coloring the room like a disco.

"Shit. That's not good."

I darted down the steps, before some acidhead could open the door and invite the cops in for drinks. A skinny kid was running his mouth off to a girl near the door. "They can't come in. The Fourth Amendment requires—"

"No talk like that. Not a word," I snapped, and opened the door.

"Hello, officer."

"We have numerous complaints of noise and people urinating in the street. We found a person vomiting in your yard." I stared and nodded, as polite as possible. Cops aren't abstract legal concepts or hypotheticals in law exams regarding recent *Miranda* rulings. Most are a decent sort; they'd prefer to sit in their patrol cars, bullshitting and drinking coffee. The best course is to act friendly. Never argue and never stand on principle. The only "winning" with a cop is him turning and leaving.

"What's going on in there?" The other officer stepped up the porch stairs.

"Nothing too crazy, just some beer and pool." I pulled the door almost completely closed. We didn't have much to fear, I figured. Anything illegal was hidden. Still, even then, there's nothing gained by giving a cop a peek inside. Once in the door, they can take a look around, and considering the mess of empty bottles and cups and smoke everywhere, they could easily get curious. Cops are human, and some folks have an odd moral order—what's "wrong" is worse than illegal. I was pretty sure Fetus, nude and grinning, with glazed eyes and his cock in his hand, qualified as universally Wrong. "You know, a bunch of law students letting off some steam." *Imagine the paperwork.*

His partner pursed his lips and stepped forward. "Okay. Just make sure people aren't running around outside. It's late. You might want to shut this down."

"Gladly."

How to Not Get a Job Offer

LOOK BOTH WAYS BEFORE YOU CROSS

Getting hit by a car the morning of my first law firm interview was probably a sign from above. An omen—God or nature or whatever cosmic puppet master runs the program giving me a hint, and me too stupid to take it.

It was the summer of 1997. I'd graduated from law school and was living with my parents, studying for bar exams. The sun woke me up on the morning of the interview. *Shit.* I'd wanted to be up at six-thirty, but my watch said seven. I had barely three hours to get to Philadelphia, ninety-eight miles down the highway and Turnpike, park, then run inside a law firm in Center City. I showered, shaved, ran out the door and jumped in the truck. *Son of a bitch.* I slammed my hand on the dashboard. The gas tank was empty. I'd reminded myself half a dozen times the night before—*Make sure the truck has gas. Fill the gas tank. You didn't fill the gas tank yet!*

The self-nagging was wasted. As soon as I started watching television the night before, I forgot about the interview. It's always been like that. Try as I might to plan in advance or stay on focus, the minute anything sidetracked me—a newspaper open on the kitchen counter or a phone call from a friend—I forgot everything I was doing. It was annoying to have to run like a madman to make the interview on time, but it wasn't surprising. I seemed to do everything at the last second, and though I never admitted it out loud, that was how I liked things—running, confused, planning as I went. Menacing deadlines kill the pain of having to organize your thoughts. Instinct takes over and you surf the situation, however it unfolds.

I raced downtown, to stop at a gas station near the entrance for the highway. On my way there I reached into the center console, to grab my antacid pills. When I shook the box it was empty. *Motherfucker.* There was no way I was going to talk to a bunch of lawyers without antacid. As the gas tank was filling I darted across the street to a drugstore. On the way back, I crossed the street in front of a parked bus, scanning a newspaper as I walked, totally oblivious to everything around me.

Then I heard the horn.

The sedan was coming from the left, a midsize Honda with more than enough mass to maim, cripple and disfigure. Through the windshield I could see the driver cringing, slamming the brakes in what was clearly too little space. *Shit. I'm going to have to jump on the fucker. That or it's going to break one of my legs.*

I threw the newspaper into the air and leapt with everything I had, which wasn't enough. The top of the grille slammed into my left ankle and I'd probably have bought it right there—face-planted straight into the hood—if I hadn't been wearing wingtips, which happen to be excellent shoes for car jumping (at least with moving vehicles). The sharp rubber heel of the shoe on my right foot dug into the vehicle's hood, and between that traction and the forward motion of the car moving under me, I was almost able to run right over the vehicle. And I might have done exactly that if the damn car hadn't finally screeched to a halt as I was still leaping across it, stealing my momentum and causing me to bounce off the hood and roll into the street.

This is going to hurt later, when the adrenaline fades. I jumped up from the pavement, brushed myself off, and gave the driver a thumbs-up. "Are you all right? I am so sorry. I didn't see you and—" She was thirtyish, attractive, and white with fear, hands flailing around the inside of the car, searching for a phone and apologizing over and over.

"Don't worry about it. Don't call the cops." I knew the minute she calmed down she'd realize I dented her hood. Legally, I had a case against her—reckless driving, failure to stop. Ethically, I was a jackass who'd walked into traffic reading the newspaper. I owed her a new hood, which I couldn't afford.

"Are you sure you're okay? I can take you somewhere." The woman was still rattled.

"I'm fine, really. Thank you." *Just don't look at that hood until I can get in the truck and head for the Turnpike.* I probably could have postponed the interview at that point. Getting hit by a car was a pretty solid excuse. But I went ahead with it anyway, figuring I'd already put on the suit, committed a day to the project. So it was a rough start. I was a little shaken. I'd taken my share of exams hungover. How much worse could an interview be?

I stood on the gas pedal the whole way to Philadelphia, thinking about what I'd say when they started asking me questions. Most law students interview with firms during the second year of law school to get a clerkship over the following summer. I remembered walking through one of those "cattle call" interview scenes in the law school lobby, glimpsing the rows of bodies in two-button blue and gray corporate uniforms, black lace-ups and white shirts and rep ties, standing around the lobby fidgeting with their résumé folders. The girls with their makeup toned down and their hair pulled back, the men in their fresh John F. Kennedy haircuts. Everybody's nervously looking at each other and smiling, waiting for the firm representatives sitting behind lunch tables to call their names out and process them into classrooms for interviews. "Gilbert Felcher? Step right this way . . ."

Watching them disappear into those rooms reminded me of that awful horror tale, "The Lottery," where the residents of the town had to draw lots to decide who'll be stoned at the conclusion of the raffle. The tension in the lobby made me nervous, and I was just passing through, in jeans and a hat, sipping coffee. I could see the gears turning in the candidates' heads and imagine the internal prep-talk dialogue:

Smile. Stand up straight. Hands at your side and don't bite your nails. You know the lines, right? "I was excited reading about Underphephler & Munklow's approach to litigation because . . ."

Some of them looked like they were about to snap, grinding their teeth, eyes darting around the room, barely holding it together. *Oh God, I need this job. If I don't get it, what will I do? I'll be a failure . . . A loser . . . I'll die in shame! They'll mark it on my tombstone! "Here lies Gilbert Felcher. Rejected by Lipshitz & Limptwiddle, 1997."*

I didn't apply for any of these on-campus interviews with law firms. Hell, I didn't even know the process was going on until I saw it happening in the library. At the time, I was happy to be avoiding it, but in the drunken recesses of my brain I knew—the future would inevitably catch up with me. When graduation finally rolled around, I called some friends and family for favors. They rounded up a handful of interviews for me, all in Philadelphia.

With each passing minute I drove, I was that much closer to the city, to that moment of truth or, more accurately, the test of my ability to lie with a straight face. I called Candace when I passed through the tollbooth onto the Schuylkill Expressway.

"Hey, I'm almost in town. I should be done with this thing before noon. I'm meeting Martin for lunch near your office. Stop by."

Candace was an ex-fuck buddy. I'd met her in the spring of 1997, on a trip to visit friends in Philadelphia. She was a friend of my buddy Martin and I wound up sitting next to her over drinks at a bar on South Street called Bridget Foy's. She didn't seem to like me at first and was a couple years older. Normally that wouldn't be a big deal, but a twenty-six-year-old man just getting out of seven years of school and a twenty-eight-year-old woman in her sixth year in the workforce have very little in common. She told me point-blank I was immature, but as we talked and the margaritas kept coming, it became obvious we'd be going back to her place. It was also clear she intended to use me as a toy. Which was fine with me.

Candace and I had a few amazing weekends after that. Sex with her was exhausting. My shoulders would ache the next morning as though I'd done a hundred bench presses the night before, which, in a sense, I had. The only problem was that every one of these marathon sessions ended with regret. On Candace's part, not mine. "Conflicted" barely described the woman. I'd never met anybody so confused. That first night she told me over and over how we weren't going to have casual sex, then we got to her place and did exactly that. She was clearly a libertine by nature, but for some pathological reasons I had no interest in uncovering, she was intent on reinventing herself as this überconservative businesswoman looking for a mature, professional man. It was obvious she felt guilty about screwing me, like she was wasting time better spent on "serious" prospects. I didn't care as long as I was getting laid, but the little criticisms—juxtaposing my attitude against the suits she worked around—could get annoying.

"There's something hot about a man working, concentrating and really driven to succeed." "Getting drunk is for kids." It was always the same nagging. She talked to me like Mr. Hand lecturing Jeff Spicoli in *Fast Times at Ridgemont High,* and all of it was cheap Dale Carnegie horseshit. "You need to get a portfolio for interviews. *Professionals* carry a portfolio—a *leather* portfolio." I'd stand there and listen, wondering when she was going to hand me a dog-eared copy of *The Seven Habits of Highly Effective People.*

Candace told me a month before my interviews in Philadelphia that she'd started seriously dating someone—that we couldn't screw around anymore. "I want to stay friends, because I really like you."

"Of course. But I don't understand why we can't have sex."

"Because I'm in a relationship now."

"Let me know if you get bored. He's not as good as I am."

"*Ah.* I'm going to miss that. You were always so romantic."

I called Candace in advance of the interview because I wanted some inside information on the process. She worked in a law firm, so there was value in picking her brain. I also wanted to see if she'd be up for a random fuck. I hadn't gotten any action in weeks. For all I knew, she'd broken up with her boyfriend, and it's always easier to grab a quick screw off someone you've slept with before.

"Are you prepared for the interview?" she asked.

"I read Harrison & Wentworth's website. I think I have the firm history down."

"That's it?"

"I printed out some pages of it so I could read the information right before I walk into the room, to keep it fresh."

"Keep those printouts in your folder. You have a résumé folder, right?"

"Yes. I have a, uh, folder." I didn't mention its manila cardboard construction, but she knew.

"Do you know how hard people fight to get interviews at big firms? And you're just walking in there clueless. You're going to be grilled."

"I called my cousin for advice. He works for a big firm in Boston. He said I should just be myself."

—Cue long silence and tumbleweeds rolling by—

"Hello? Candace?"

"Be yourself? Really? Tell me how that goes afterward."

"What does that mean?"

"I can't do this. I have to take another call." She hung up.

Flying down the Schuylkill seeing the tips of the Philadelphia skyline emerging on the horizon, I suddenly started getting nervous. Try as I might, I couldn't jar Candace's warning from my head. *You will be grilled.* She sounded so severe, so dire. Was I walking into a firing squad? *She's nuts*, I told myself. *Paranoid and crazy.* But that didn't mean she was wrong.

Harrison & Wentworth's offices were nice but unimpressive. The building was a drab concrete box and the waiting room would barely hold a standard pool table. I'd expected an imperial space, something imposing. I knew dermatologists with swankier lobbies.

"Hello. Can I help you?" A pert blonde girl trying to mask a Philly accent leaned over the desk.

"Yes. My name is P.J. I have to meet with a group of law-yers."

"Oh yes. A committee. On this floor. Have a seat. Would you like a coffee?"

"No thanks." I sat on the couch and tore into the firm's mar-keting brochures, looking for miscellanea to sprinkle through the interview. The more arcane the fact you can cite, the more home-work it appears you've done. If you didn't understand a concept, memorize some footnote dicta and sprinkle them through your essay. Or at least that's how it worked in college and law school. No reason to think this should be any different.

It wasn't until I crossed my legs that I spotted the red streak running up the left side of my suit, from the outside of my ankle to my thigh, then picking up again on my left arm. *Shit.* I'd hit the car hard enough that its paint had rubbed off onto my suit. "Excuse me. Can you point me to the men's room?" I asked the receptionist, licking my finger and furiously trying to rub the streak off the fabric.

"Got a coffee stain there?" An old man stepped out of a stall and fixed his hair in the mirror as I leaned against the sink in the men's room, scrubbing off the paint with wet hand towels.

Yes. Bright, shiny, candy-apple red coffee.

When I got back to the waiting area, the receptionist smiled and pointed me to the conference room just off the lobby. "They're wait-ing in there." The space was a claustrophobic's worst nightmare, stuffy and cramped with four lawyers sitting around a conference table far too large for the room, leaving barely two feet between the walls and any of its sides. After we did the introductions, I sat at the head of it, smiling and waiting for the inquisition. To my immediate left was a tall Italian-looking man with a permanent grin and tie undone, leaning back in his swivel chair. Behind him was a younger, pasty man in glasses, leaning on his elbows and run-ning his hands through the back of his hair. Both of them were reading my résumé when I walked in the door and seemed half in-terested at best—probably pulled into the interview at the last sec-ond by some senior partner. They were the easy side of the room.

The right side of the table was going to be the problem. Immediately next to me was an older, round-faced man, the quiet, smart sort who listens and takes in every detail. Not what I needed in a presentation where I'd be inventing a professional persona on the fly, but at least he wouldn't take me on right there, face-to-face. That was the job for the man behind him, the "Little Guy" with his hands folded over my résumé.

Law is the world's biggest repository of fragile male egos, and some of the worst belong to "Little Guys." It's a bit unfair to use that adjective, of course, since they come in all shapes and sizes, but there's no better description for these congenital Napoleons. I'm a little over six feet tall, 200 pounds, and moderately decent-looking, or so I've been told. Nothing fancy. Not a male model or the picture of athletic fitness, but I keep up appearances. And though I'm not the funniest person in the room, I can tell a story or a joke. It's hard not to form some "salesman's charisma" growing up Irish. We're bred to work the room, and for a lot of us, decent looks and a fast mouth are our only means of survival. Held against society at large, I'd place myself on the high end of the "utterly average male": smart enough to know my limitations, with no urge to prove myself to every other man I encounter. The last thing I'd ever be interested in is a dick-size comparison with someone who still had an ax to grind for having to stay home on prom night. I'm the sort of person who just wants to make money so I can live the life I want to, away from the people who live for all the bullshit of the office.

That attitude put me at odds with a lot of lawyers, starting most immediately with this Napoleon. He was the size of Dennis Kucinich, with an Eric Estrada haircut and one of those strange upturned noses, with wide, flared nostrils. Think Henry Waxman, the obnoxious congressman from California, with a toupee. And from the way he dropped his voice and spoke like a drill sergeant to his deliberately strong handshake, it was obvious he took everything about his job—even this silly interview—very fucking seriously. But then, how couldn't he? We all know his type—you could recite his yearbook profile from memory.

This was the guy who ran for student council president and lost.
Twice.

EUGENE NIDERMAN

Student Council Treasurer; Glee Club; Students for Reagan

Favorite Movie: *Top Gun*
Favorite Song: "Born in the USA"
Quote: "There is no substitute for victory."—Douglas MacArthur

The first five minutes of an interview are supposed to be easy
questions, icebreakers to get you into the flow of a polite but inva-
sive Q&A. Why'd you come to this city? Why'd you choose this
firm? How was your law school experience? You're supposed to
have positive answers for each, things like "I came to Philadelphia
because I've always enjoyed the city and wanted to live here," "I
chose Harrison & Wentworth because I think it's got a great platform for the type of work I can see myself doing down the road,"
and "Law school was tough, but I found it really rewarding."

I was prepared to jump right in, start saying whatever I
thought they wanted to hear. But when I opened my lips, I realized there were no good answers, even for the easy questions.
*Why'd I come to Philadelphia? Because a couple of connections got
me job interviews here. I'd rather be in D.C., but my contacts down
there haven't come through. Which explains how I wound up in this
firm. And law school? I didn't even buy books the last two years. I
could probably translate Cantonese as well as tell you anything the
Supreme Court's done in the past decade.*

Obviously you can't say any of that in an interview, so I
wound up spitting idiot gibberish. "I've always liked Philadelphia. It's a good midpoint between New York and D.C." "I liked
your firm because it has a strong Pennsylvania background, with
your main office being located here. I grew up in Pennsylvania,
it's a nice state." "Oh, law school was a tremendous learning experience. You can't help but come out different than you went in.
You learn so many things there."

Yes, it was that bad. I'd never flailed like that before. As I sat there listening to myself, I wondered, *Was the part of my brain responsible for bullshitting damaged in the accident? Do I have a mild concussion?* No, that wasn't the case. The problem was my expertise, or lack thereof. I was skilled in alibis and excuses, not straight-up lies. When someone's accusing you of something, they hit you with facts and you try to weasel out of them. The responses are always limited. Baroque lies—the sort of background story I was crafting there, with an imaginary persona justifying why I was in Philadelphia, why I'd gone to law school and why I wanted to work for a firm full of people I'd never have spoken to otherwise—are impossible to construct and even harder to control. My hands started sweating and I could feel the pulse pounding in my neck as I answered the seemingly endless questions. I'd say it was nerves but this was fear, horror at the process and the people and the *institutional* character of it all. I wanted to run so badly and the whole time I had to sit there, telling these people how much I wanted to work in the place. I'd sworn I could stomach anything for the $70,000 good firms were paying then, but sitting in the jaws of the beast, I realized that's a lot easier said than done.

Fifteen minutes into the thing, it was obvious I'd blown the interview, that we'd reached the stage where everybody would run out the clock, talking sports or current events, with an occasional job-related question just to be polite. But of course the Little Guy didn't play that game. He saw blood in the water and moved in for a pound of flesh:

"So you weren't on law review. What about the moot court team?"

"Those classes were at odd hours. I was working." *If I was on the moot court team, it would have been on my fucking résumé, you tool.*

"You had a job through law school?"

"A few. I needed spending money." *Shit. He's probably hearing "drinking money" there.* "For rent. To pay for rent."

"I assume you studied very late at night."

"I was up late an awful lot."

"What kind of cases did you work on?"

"All sorts. A lot of issues similar to the memo I gave you as a writing sample."

"Yes. I read that. What was the issue in that case again?"

"Well, it's really complicated." *Ahhh, so you think I didn't write the thing?*

"Refresh me."

"You know, it's been a while. Let me take a look so I can be sure." I figured he'd say no and move along, rather than put me through the embarrassment of having to scan the thing in silence while everyone watched. I was wrong.

"Certainly. Go ahead."

Prick. I scanned the memo but the ink blurred together. All I could feel was the deafening silence of time passing and eyes on my lapels. *Fuck it. You've already blown this. Stop embarrassing yourself.* "I can't recall exactly."

"You don't recall the issue the case turned on?"

For a second I considered using the incident with the car as an excuse—pretending to go into convulsions from a latent head injury. If they took me out of the place in an ambulance, maybe the firm would feel guilty, fear a lawsuit or think I was *really* committed to the career and give me a job. At a minimum, it might explain my obvious retardation.

"I don't know if the issue's in there. One of the back-office guys worked on that case. I codified a lot of his research."

"What's a 'back-office guy'?" He leaned in and squinted at me.

"You know. Those lawyers who are best allocated to the research angle of cases." *Someone with a personality for undertaking. Someone like you.*

"You don't research?"

"Oh no, no, I can research. But my skills are more in writing and talking." *When I have a clue what I'm talking about, of course. Unlike, say, right now.*

"Do you understand what an associate does?"

Honestly? No. I didn't know a goddamn thing about what it

meant to be an associate. I didn't even know what it meant to be a law student. I'd gone through most of the last three years asleep, reading magazines or talking to Alex through class, turning my brain on once a semester, just enough to memorize a pile of course outlines a few nights before exams and spit the information back in the test booklet. You could get away with that in an academic setting, where it's all about surface knowledge. But here, now, these people were testing whether I was invested in the career, whether I saw it as the end and not just the means to one. Candace had been right about the grilling, but she was wrong about my lack of preparation or a proper résumé folder. You can't cram for a test like that. It was obvious I was just another slacker trawling for a bloated paycheck, which translated to an F.

The sloppy lawyer to my immediate right interjected, to kill the tension. "Okay, okay. Do you have any questions for us?"

I opened my thin manila folder and pretended to scan some papers. "No. I think my questions were answered in our back-and-forth."

"Okay, then." He smiled, we shook hands, and I headed for the lobby. It wasn't even eleven-thirty yet. I called Martin to confirm our lunch plans, then rang Candace.

"Hey. You still game for lunch with Martin and me?"

"You're done?"

"Yeah, I'm done."

"That's quick."

"We, uh . . . started early."

"Did you know Harrison & Wentworth pays seventy grand? I asked an associate here. That's exciting. I didn't know they paid that well." She didn't sound as judgmental as she'd been on the earlier call.

"Yep. I know all about that."

"How do you think it went?"

"Did I mention earlier that I got hit by a car?"

Twenty-six

LIFESTYLES OF THE DESPERATE

AND SEXLESS

Jeezzzuzz . . . fuhhh . . . blurry . . . so blurry . . . You take the . . . wheel." Harris's head was nodding forward, toward his chest.

"Keep your foot on the gas." I spoke low, careful not to excite him. Any sudden spasm—slamming down on the brake pedal, jerking his arm and throwing the shifter into reverse or spinning the wheel—we were Done. The nose would lurch and tip sideways, the back wheels lift into the air and the force of three thousand pounds of metal moving 80 miles per hour flip the car end over end, spraying us across the highway, a comet of steel, glass, and tan leather upholstery.

The New Jersey Turnpike outside New York City in December is no place to lose control in fourth gear. The road's as wide as a football field and straight as a runway, but around you, barreling through the four or five lanes of traffic at any given moment on a Saturday afternoon, are hundreds of four-wheeled projectiles. An eighteen-wheeler roared past us on the left, a pimp in a gold-package Lexus was riding our tail and a bread truck eclipsed the view of Manhattan coming up on the right. We were in a tunnel of industrial machinery, walls of gears and wheels blurring by on either side, all screaming down the artery, racing to be first to wait in line outside the tunnels.

I kept one eye on the road and one on Harris, to gauge where he'd be over the next ten seconds. I'd seen people in his state go limp, seize, and shake like epileptics. Sometimes they'd drop cigarettes in their laps and spill drinks over themselves, mouths open, eyes rolling back in their heads in something near a death rattle. Harris wasn't there. He was conscious, smiling and mumbling, still tethered to the moment, but for how long? Would he lose it entirely, start drooling and moaning and fall into the wheel? My elbow was cocked, ready to strike him if he lurched suddenly. A drastic measure, of course, but one could never be too safe under these circumstances. I knew this, sensed it, even if it wasn't registering on the surface. But as I looked at the white-knuckle grip of my hands on the steering wheel, all I felt was calm, a sense of déjà vu, that this was business as usual. And it was. One last idiot moment—the climax of a run of senseless, desperate drunks I'd known as the fall of 1997.

Twenty-six is a rotten age. You're not an adult by any stretch, but you're way past college jackass, going through the tail end of those lost years we all have just after graduation. You're facing thirty, but half of you is still eighteen. What you really want to say, think, or do is unacceptable. Suddenly everything's serious, staid and stoic, every day another exercise in acting "businesslike" and "professional," suffocating your personality, stifling all the rancid jokes in your head to play a bland office caricature. But that live wire of adrenaline you've been living on for the last decade— the fuel of that mad stretch from sixteen to twenty-five—doesn't just fade away. It builds—relentless, demanding release with no-where to go, like the pressure in a clogged steam pipe on the edge of exploding.

The only cure for the pain of twenty-six is pussy. Without it, you're all but legally insane. Everything a man does comes down to two simple ends—fucking and avoiding boredom. When you're young, stuck in an office in a new city, and not getting any action, you're an unpinned grenade. There seems no reason to live, and you don't give a shit about anything. Lock a guy who isn't getting laid in a box with nothing but stacks of paperwork and you'll create a dangerous, desperate mutant, a fearless freak with nothing in his head but escape, fuck the risks.

The fall of 1997 was a shit sandwich from the start. After a couple of interviews with large firms in the spring and early summer, followed by lightning-fast rejection letters, I landed a job with a solo practitioner named Sean O'Malley. Sean had a white-collar criminal defense practice and was considered one of the better trial attorneys in the city. I hadn't expected much going into the interview, but I wound up liking the guy from the moment we met. He was a decent mick—quick-witted, open, and real, an actual human being. After the corporatespeak and stuffed shirts I'd endured in formal law firm interviews, talking to him felt like therapy. His practice area was also a huge draw. Sean needed help defending a rogues' gallery of alleged corporate criminals he represented. During my interview he told me about a brand-new case involving a pair of Colombian businessmen indicted for money laundering. "I have to do a conference call with one of their business lawyers in Bogotá this afternoon."

Some people might have been creeped out at the mention of "business lawyers in Bogotá." I was intrigued. Sure, the money Sean was offering could have been better. I could have done more interviews and gotten a better salary in straight civil litigation, but I wasn't going to work on multinational money laundering conspiracies and nine-figure corporate frauds doing that. And let's face it, his practice work was right up my alley. Ten minutes into the conversation, I knew I'd be taking the job. He made me an offer over lunch and I accepted.

The first few weeks of the job didn't let me down. The white-collar criminal defense bar in which Sean operated is a small, elite fraternity—heavy hitters who command staggering retainers from well-heeled business criminals. I went from clueless law student to case strategy discussions with some of the biggest defense lawyers in the country in four months. It was gratifying to wander through the orbit of those players, to have a case you were working on written about in the *New York Times*.

But even with those amusements, I was still stuck in an office, studying the paint on the walls. The fact remains, whatever the position, no matter how much the pay or how interesting the work might seem, that first desk job is a horrible shock. You realize you're on the bottom of a learning curve, slogging through grunt work and putting in the sunken costs they tell you will reap dividends down the road. It's not supposed to be easy, that's understood. What hits you like a train wreck is the realization it's Permanent. There's no summer break. No return to school in September and no monthlong Christmas holiday. This is what you'll wake up and get dressed to do every day for the rest of your working life.

School is the worst preparation in the world for a career. Getting a degree is a project, as opposed to a job, and the difference between those two concepts is the difference between Saturday and Monday mornings. A project has a start and finish date. You know when it's done and then you're on to the next thing, which is usually just about the time you're sick of it. Up to the point of that first legal job, all I'd ever known was one semester-long project after another, each stimulating because it involved a different subject.

Even my previous work experience was limited to projects. The last summer job I'd known was driving from Pennsylvania to New York City at three in the morning to deliver computer files around lower Manhattan. I'd find myself on Canal Street with a forty-pound box in my hand, wheezing as I sprinted through clouds of exhaust fumes, running myself ragged just to save a minute or two. But I never stopped to question why I was pushing myself, or why I'd taken a job that only allowed me to sleep four hours a night. The sooner I did the deliveries, the sooner I got home. If I pushed myself fast enough, I could be done in six hours, back on my parents' deck reading the paper before noon. Work was something to be done to get as much money as possible as quickly as possible, entered grudgingly and finished furiously so I could get back to living my life. My employer probably thought I had a tremendous work ethic. And I did. But who wouldn't? There's no incentive on earth stronger than a promise that the faster and harder you work, the sooner you can stop.

Not a good mind-set for law, where you bill your time in six-minute increments.

But the pain of the office was only half the problem. That can be rationalized—a necessary evil to pay the bills, a sad reality accruing from the lack of robber barons or software kingpins in your family tree. The bigger problem was not getting laid.

That fall, I'd been degraded to chasing Candace, hoping she'd break up with her boyfriend. She lived a couple of miles away from me and we'd have drinks every now and again after work. It was friendly, but awkward. She'd stare at me, running her teeth over her lower lip. I knew she liked fucking me more than that insurance coverage lawyer she was dating. She'd all but said as much. She also said I had no goals. He was a go-getter, with crisp white shirts and George Will's hair.

The fact that I lived near a pair of college friends trapped in miserable jobs who also weren't getting laid only made things worse. Harris worked at a small bank in town and had recently been dumped by his girlfriend. He'd call me buzzed on a Wednesday afternoon, somewhere in his third hour of lunch, asking if I wanted to go to Atlantic City on the weekend. Martin toiled for a local credit card operation outside of town and had recently ended a long-distance relationship. He spent his days staring at the clock, waiting for five, when he could race to the parking lot, go home, bake himself, and watch a Sixers game with the sound muted, listening to *The Pros and Cons of Hitchhiking*.

You couldn't find three more desperate people in the average Third World refugee camp. Putting us together in the presence of alcohol was lighting sparklers in a gas refinery. Pushed against the wall some people make changes—finding Jesus, joining "awareness" campaigns or taking up mountain biking. The rest of us follow the old wisdom. We go on benders.

I don't know when the bender of 1997 started exactly. But if I had to pick the first peak, or low point, of the thing, I'd start on a September afternoon in Baltimore, in Fells Point, a sliver of bars and souvenir shops in the city's DMZ.

We were in town because Martin's uncle lived in a suburb of the city. He was out west for a few weeks on vacation and had asked Martin to look in on the place. Martin invited Harris and me down, figuring it would be a good change of scenery, and provide a top-shelf liquor cabinet to pillage.

I sensed ugliness when Martin started ordering bourbon shots for us at three o'clock. Three's an odd hour for whiskey, long past the breakfast Bloody Mary hours and luncheon wine window. Three's a beer hour. And the whiskey concerned me because our plan, at least in theory, was to drink slowly and meet up with girls later. Harris had asked an ex-girlfriend, Liz, to meet us that night. She lived in Philadelphia but happened to be staying with friends just outside Baltimore that weekend. They were supposed to meet us around seven, but as the day wore on and the shots kept coming, I was sure we'd never make it.

"To evil!" Every time a round came, Harris raised the same toast. By six there was no way to count how much whiskey and beer we'd had, and there seemed no way to stop more from appearing. Every time I turned around the waitress was bringing more. The conversation had degraded to shouting, random profanity, and hand gestures. "U.S.A! U.S.A!" Harris would scream and pound the table every few minutes for no reason. At one point Martin took a flailing roundhouse swing at me.

"Why the fuck did you do that?" I ducked the haymaker at the last second as Martin fell into a stool under the force of his own momentum.

"I don't know. I just wanted to hit you."

By the time Liz finally met up with us, the table was littered with empty glasses, cigarette butts, remnants of fried oyster sandwiches, and piles of shrimp peelings. Martin was already passed out and I was chain-smoking to stay awake. Normally you'd hide this display from women, but Liz hadn't brought any friends, and she knew us well. Harris sat at the end of the table, pondering his watch and muttering. "I've had a dozen shots, I think."

"Well, you're not stopping now." Liz laughed. Liz was a spit-fire brunette who cursed like a convict and only knew how to binge-drink. She and Harris had a long, sordid history of one-night stands, which wasn't uncommon for Harris. Up to the last girl he'd dated, Harris often kept as many as three girlfriends at once. And he never juggled them the traditional way—sleeping at one girl's house one night, another's the next. He'd see one at lunch, one for dinner, and stay at a third's house, mixing the order from day to day. This would drive the average person mad. Not Harris. The guy never slept and the defining characteristic of his personality was a terminal inability to sit still. We'd go out drinking until four in the morning and he'd call at nine, already showered and driving somewhere to get food. He was always talking fast and in a hurry to get somewhere, fueled by some incurable need to keep moving and doing something, anything. I understood him on that level. And so did Liz. She knew she was a target—that Harris was trying to get a quick screw. She had bad news for him—she had a boyfriend. After Harris heard that, the whiskey orders came faster.

Somewhere around nine Martin woke up, which spurred one last order of doubles, a pointless stress test for the organs since we clinically couldn't get any drunker. Martin was somewhere between sleep and a blackout, Harris and I could barely speak and the last thing Liz needed was more liquor. She'd been steadily downing vodka and cranberry juices for the past two hours—flailing, spilling drinks and burning anyone standing near her with her cigarettes. Thankfully, our waitress finished her shift after the last order of shots, forcing us to pay the tab so she could close out the table.

"Where are we going now?" Liz bleated through a spout of cigarette smoke.

"Back to your friends' place."

A Jeep Cherokee with high miles on it is a bag of bolts, built of recycled beer cans, North Korean pleather and balsa wood. At anything over 70 miles per hour, the wheel might as well be a paint shaker. I could feel the truck bouncing over grooves in the pavement, swaying with the wind and the drafts from passing tractor-trailers barreling down the beltway. "This *really* fucking sucks," Harris sneered through his teeth as he held a bull rider's grip on the wheel.

"Do you have a lighter? I need a lighter." Liz slapped my shoulder and screamed in Harris's ear, "I don't want to go home. Let's hit another bar."

"No more bars." Martin was imprisoned with her in the backseat.

"I need another drink! Vodka and cranberry!" She pulled at Martin's shirt, yanking him sideways into the center of the bench seats. Harris turned up the music and stepped on the gas. The engine wheezed and we bucked forward.

"We need to get some food." Martin leaned in, between the front seats.

"Let's get her home first." Harris put a dip of tobacco in his lip.

"Do you have any water? I need water." Liz was hollering from the back.

"Are you still going to try to fuck her?" Martin whispered.

"I can't think about that right now." Harris blinked and stared ahead, squinting to make out an exit sign hundreds of yards up the road.

"Motherfuuuhhhh!" A split second later I heard Martin scream and turned my head to face the backseat.

There are those moments in life when you realize, *Where I am, what I will be doing, my happiness—my future—depends on how an event taking place in front of me, that I have no control over, plays out.* I'm not talking about the SAT or a job interview or any of the other "make-or-break" moments with endless second chances we're too naïve and brainwashed to see at the time. What I'm talking about is unexpected and random in every regard, an incident that catapults you from the routine to a life-and-death flashpoint in seconds.

As I looked into the backseat I realized we were in one of those moments.

Martin was leaping to grab Liz's ass as she pushed the door open with one hand and tried to jump from the truck. She was fully committed to the project, leaning out, aiming toward the pavement. Gravel at 75. She'd be skinned and what was left torn to bits under the wheels of the cars speeding along behind us. The physics of it were ugly from every angle. If he lost her, she was done, pulled meat strewn across the lanes.

I didn't say a word as I watched the scene play out. I looked at Harris for a millisecond. He knew the door was open, but processing the situation was beyond him. He was just the driver. His eyes never left the road, as if looking forward put him in another universe, far away from the backseat, from Martin lunging for Liz and yanking her back from the front page of tomorrow's *Baltimore Sun.*

The rush of fear must have flushed the booze out of Martin's head. His grab was gymnastic. Lightning-fast and sticky-fingered, he lurched sideways, snagged Liz's thighs and dragged her back into the truck. She barked about getting another drink, then set about fixing her hair, oblivious to the fact that she'd almost been road kill. Harris clicked the automatic lock button and no one said a word for the rest of the ride—just stared ahead at the road, imagining what could have been. All the investigations, lawsuits, fines and sentences . . . We'd have to bolt, run for protectorates past the grasp of any civil judgment for gross, wanton negligence.

We all thanked Martin, but looking back, he got lucky. We all got lucky. Liz was a curvy girl, with huge tits and a round ass Martin was able to palm like a pair of rugby balls. A waif model would have been through his fingers and out the door. I'd probably be writing this from Nauru.

I asked Liz the next morning why she'd tried to jump out of a speeding truck. She didn't recall. Anything.

A month or so later I was in a neighborhood bar outside Philadelphia with Martin and Liz. It started at five as a quick run

for a burger and beers, but rapidly evolved into a cocktail marathon. The last thing I recall inside the bar was Liz giving us tips
on women.

"You're spoiled from college. You guys never had to lay rap
and now you do."

"It's so much fucking work." Martin stared at his drink. "I
don't want to play the 'game' or put on an act. I used to just have
a good time with girls."

Liz was right, of course. Martin and I were spoiled. Suburban
kids who'd spent the last decade hunting captured game in high
school and college, moving from one drunken hookup to the next.
Martin was five foot ten, an ex-athlete who dressed like a J.Crew
ad and desperately needed some sun—standard post-college white
fraternity guy. That was just appearance, of course. If I had to sum
Martin up, the only image that comes to mind is Jack Lemmon.
Lemmon always played straight men—self-deprecating and decent to a fault, which pretty much describes Martin. There was no
bullshit to the guy, none of the craven self-promotion or alpha-
male act you needed in the post-college pickup scene. I think it
frustrated him that he was being pushed to act like something he
found offensive, and every now and again, with the right amount
of liquor in his blood, the pent-up annoyance would boil over and
explode.

"I *just* want a nice chick, in torn jean shorts, wearing one of
those shirts that looks like a tapestry. A laid-back, normal girl.
Where'd they all go?"

"That's sweet, Martin, but things don't work that way anymore. Women are on a different wavelength." Liz drew on a cigarette and another round of drinks arrived.

"Yeah, they want some douche who'll run around acting like
he's a player." I snickered.

"You know what your problem is? You expect them to come
to you." She shoved a finger in my face.

"I don't need the speech."

"Hey, it's your celibacy."

"You're cruel, Liz—a cruel, rotten woman." I passed around

the drinks. "Chug these and let's get the fuck out of here." It was another sexless Saturday. I just wanted to go home, get high, and pass out.

We were half a block from the bar when we realized Martin wasn't behind us. At the same time I heard the sound of glass smashing and turned in the direction of the noise. Martin was outside the bar, stomping pieces of a brass lamp he'd torn from the side of the building.

"Get the fuck out of there!" I screamed. We were in a yuppie town, but it was a blue-collar bar, filled with the sort of natives who hated our kind. If any of them caught Martin, they'd beat him to hamburger. Luckily, due to the noise and loud music inside, no one seemed to hear.

I thought about running back and pulling him away, but it was pointless. There's no way to stop a man on a destruction high. It's incredibly immature, and in the pantheon of things that really turn women off, it's near the top, but destroying things in a drunken rage is a near-orgasmic release. The joy of shattering inanimate objects hasn't seduced John Daly, Keith Moon, and Johnny Depp for no good reason. I never understood exactly why watching something explode, burn, or crack into a million bits felt as satisfying as it did. My guess was it had something to do with rejection—total disregard for the value of property and the notion that it stands for an accomplishment of some sort. But I'd never know for sure, it's such a subjective high. All I knew was, whatever Martin was experiencing was intense, personal, and very fucking illegal, and I wasn't going anywhere near him.

"That's going to be expensive." I listened to the glass in the fixture shattering. "Come on, Martin! Get the fuck out of there!" I shouted again, loud enough to get through to him. He picked his head up and stared at us and the wave of anger seemed to break. Lucidity grabbed him first, then panic. He looked at the shredded fixture and it dawned on him: *This is a crime. What the hell am I doing?*

He ran, and he was halfway to us when I spotted the round little cop bolting from across the street. The guy was solid, perfectly round in the center—an egg with feet. His gut bounced up and down as he ran and his footwork was clumsy and robotic, but he was fast. I'd have yelled, told Martin to spin, weave, or juke left. All he needed to do was miss the initial hit and the fat little man would have fallen under the force of his own momentum trying to turn. He'd land on the sidewalk like a beetle on its back, scurrying to right himself. We'd be a block away by the time he got up. Sadly, I was slow from the booze. By the time I got "Look left!" out of my mouth, the cop was clotheslining Martin. A moment later they were rolling on the ground, the officer struggling to straddle Martin between his knees and cuff him.

"Are we in Russia?" Martin was snapping as the cop frisked him. "Is this a Communist state?"

The cop turned and glared at me.

"Martin, let him do his job."

"I am. I'm not in fucking Russia. I'm a U.S. citizen."

"Russia's not Communist." I figured I had to say something.

"This is Russia! Russia!" The adrenaline had clearly melted Martin's synapses. "I pay my taxes!" I prayed he wasn't going to use the "I pay your salary" argument with the cop. Of the many different ways to offend a civil servant, that's guaranteed doom.

"That doesn't allow you to destroy property, sir." Cop 2; Martin 0. The officer sifted through Martin's identification cards. "Are any of you sober?"

"I'm a lawyer and—"

"That's nice. I asked who's sober."

Silence.

"What's your name?" He turned and addressed Liz. She stiffened and took on a formal tone. "I've had a few, but I'm okay. I can take care of him."

"I'll go with her, comrade," Martin snapped off.

"You want me to take you to jail instead? You can spend the weekend in a cell."

I walked over to the car where Martin was standing. "Russia. Is. A. Democracy."

"This is Gestapo shit."

"The Gestapo were Nazis."

Martin hung his head and stared at the sidewalk. I walked back to the cop, who was lecturing Liz. "I'm remanding him to your custody. If I see him out tonight, he's going to jail. Understood?"

"What's with the 'Russia' thing?" I asked as we trudged away.

"Fuck it. I don't know. It's all wrong. Everything's wrong."

He was right. Facing what you think is the only future—an autopilot skid, phoning in forty years at a desk, with an immediate lack of pussy on top of it—everything is wrong, and none of the epic drunks of that fall seemed in any way illogical. If anything, they were the only rational course. How many good years were left? If not now, never. If it killed us, so be it.

And that's how I found myself barreling down the Jersey Turnpike on the way into Manhattan that December afternoon, steering from the passenger seat as Harris came out of a nitrous oxide stupor. The idea was stupid and senseless on the surface, but at that point it just seemed right, almost normal. This was the tail end of a long and brutal binge, a carnival of abuse finally collapsing under the weight of its own degradation. The holidays were here, a new year was coming, and though we never discussed it, this bender was clearly coming to an end. The only question now was how far to push the thing before it finally flamed out. Let it fizzle, or send it off with a twenty-one-gun salute?

We were on our way to New York, to go to a party thrown by some college friends. I was fishing for compact discs on the floor when I remembered we had a box of nitrous cartridges with us, as an appetizer for the evening, to get us in the right frame of mind before we headed out. "*Oooooh.* I forgot about these." I laughed to Harris, filling a balloon and sucking down a hit. "*Yesssssss.*" Everything on the road immediately slowed down, and the Ramones song thrashing out of the stereo suddenly turned into a plodding Black Sabbath dirge.

"Give me one of those." Harris laughed.

"Are you serious?" I was still a little confused from the gas when he asked.

"It's a straight road." He had a point. It was a dead-ahead run on a long, wide highway. *Sssssssssssss.* I watched him inhale the balloon in one shot and fall back in his seat. "*Jeezzzuzz...fuhhh...*blurry...so blurry...You take the...wheel..." His head nodded forward.

I was already holding it, watching the road and imagining what anyone pulling even with us—perhaps some van full of seniors on the way to the Radio City Christmas show—would think if they looked in the window. "Jesus, Mary and Joseph! Ethel, Ethel! Will you look at this! The man in the car next to us is having a heart attack!"

The crazy thing was, everything was under control. After the past five months of wretched lost weekends, this was just standard operating procedure. Warped on laughing gas, we were probably safer than most of the people on that road. In our element, more in control than we'd have been stone sober.

"I got it. I got it." Harris came back to life, shaking off the last trails of the gas. "*Whew.* I don't know if that was a great idea."

"It's a straight road."

"Well, I wouldn't do it alone." He took the wheel back and I pulled a nitrous cartridge from the bag on the floor. *Sssssssssssssssss,* the cracker released the gas into the balloon. I sucked it down and slid back into the seat, mouth breathing, a grinning short bus mongoloid. "*Ahhhhhhhh...*" Perfect oblivion. Nothing in the mind but the skyline of the city coming fast on the right and the joy of knowing this was just a teaser. I was half an hour from my first glass of whiskey. By midnight I'd be a million miles out of my mind. Who knew? Maybe I'd even get some.

Squirrelfucker

The whole mess started with an email. I was sitting in the office one afternoon, just minding my own business, when I received this from myself:

> From: PJ <XXXXXX@hotmail.com>
> To: PJ <XXXX@XXXXXXXXXlawoffices.com>
> Re: Greetings from Yourself
>
> Hey,
> Fuck you.
> Best,
> You

Today, everyone has a private Gmail, Hotmail or Yahoo! mail account they use at the office. It's the only way to get around the IT goons reading personal information or those furiously typed "[Insert partner here] is the biggest cocksucking douchebag" emails. With so many of these addresses out there today, you can't open an account on any of the free email servers without having some random number, the year of your birth or the abbreviation for the state you live in attached to the end of your name.

But back in the late nineties, those free email services weren't well known, and you could still set up email accounts with names exactly the way they appeared on a person's credit card. And if you set up a believable-looking email address, people would accept that you were whoever your address purported to be. They called it "spoofing," and it's exactly what you'd think. Once you created an email account in the name of a friend, to everyone online, you were him, and the only question was how unmercifully you intended to screw with the poor bastard.

The second I saw that email, I knew who'd sent it. It had to be Bennett. Most of my friends had an odd sense of humor, but only Bennett was the sort who'd take the time to open a phony online account in my name and zip off a profane message to my work address. Harris probably had the idea first, but he was too passive to prank a person like that. Bennett didn't give a shit about me or anyone else getting upset at one of his jokes.

Hell, half of Bennett's humor was offending people by saying whatever came into his head or chucking an ugly truth at someone in the form of a joke. I'm not talking about some Howard Stern shtick here. Bennett's sense of humor was subtle, but knife-like. He could dismantle the biggest ego in less than thirty syllables, and what made it truly amusing was that his target would never expect it. Part of it was appearance. If you ran into Bennett on the street, you'd think he was a vice president of some plastics conglomerate or a merchant bank—company man all the way, from his boy scout haircut to his button-down collars and red striped ties. Part of it was his demeanor. Bennett was a listener, soft-spoken and impeccably polite, and he knew that the sort of people who were worth laughing at would always give you an opening—exhaust themselves talking, then look around the room and gauge people's reactions. That's when he'd open his mouth.

Other times, usually involving bourbon, Bennett was flat-out insane, the guest people didn't invite back. One of the more notorious stories about him involved an incident where he put a knife to a guest's throat at a friend's party because the guy refused to take a shot of whiskey Bennett had been demanding he drink, totally unaware that his victim had just been released from rehab.

The minute I received the email from "myself" I called Bennett, to make an alliance before he started using my name on white supremacist or NAMBLA chat boards.

"Excellent work."

"What?" Bennett coyly replied in his thin Southern accent.

"The email address. That's pretty funny."

"I don't know what you're talking about."

"Stop fucking with me." I wasn't about to indulge any of his pathetic alibis. "We have work to do."

As my one-year anniversary as an associate ticked closer, it was getting harder and harder to remain interested in the job. The criminal cases I worked on were exciting in description, as anyone would expect. The problem was, the more I read about clients living life on the edge, the more I realized I wasn't. I was just a mouthpiece, living vicariously through them, immersed in the facts of their lives more than my own, which, when you're spending most of your waking hours reading legal dicta and writing procedural arguments, isn't very exciting. I liked Sean O'Malley's practice, but the more I worked in it, the more I wanted to be the client rather than the lawyer, actually make decisions instead of arguing about the legality of someone else's.

Luckily, I had the Internet to amuse myself, spending my every spare moment surfing "nude celebrity" websites, shopping for music and posting bogus profiles on dating websites to solicit amusing responses. There were many low and desperate moments in those days, instants where I'd find myself ordering Deep Purple's *Made in Japan* from Amazon.com in one window while posting the description of "Arnold Gobel, Ph.D." on a dating website in another—"I'm six foot four, dark and buff, looking for a woman who loves Journey and doesn't shave *any* body hair." Every now and again I'd stop and wonder what the hell I was doing. *Look at yourself, what you've come to, man. For Christ's sake, does anyone ever need a twenty-minute live version of "Smoke on the Water"?* The worst moment of those months, however, involved Bennett and the "squirrelfucker" situation.

Immediately after he sent me that first phony email under my own name, Bennett and I set about opening Hotmail, Yahoo!, and Excite accounts in the names of people we knew and started sending out all sorts of embarrassing announcements. The trick was to bury the "kicker"—the tidbit that turned an otherwise innocuous email into grist for the rumor mill—in the text.

From: Baker, Gary <XXXXXX@hotmail.com>
To: [insert a dozen or so of Gary Baker's college friends' addresses]
Re: New Contact Info

Hello all:

Just a note to update my contact information. You can reach me at the above email for the next few months.
    I know it's been a long time since many of you heard from me. As some of you might know I've met a wonderful person and am taking a few months off to hike and decompress from the rat race. There have been a lot of changes in my life recently, all positive. Right now I'm between places and spending the next few weeks in the Sierra Nevada mountains. I'll forward some permanent information when my partner, Lance, and I get into our new home, hopefully with some amazing nature shots.
All the best,
Gary

Or send out something surprising but believable:

From: Berman, Katie <XXXXXXXXXXX@hotmail.com>
To: [list of sorority contacts]
Re: Baby Shower

Hello all,
If you haven't heard, Marybeth Nicholson and her husband Jerry are preggers! The girls and I are planning a baby shower

for March 23. Please save the date. RSVP to come shortly!
We're going to be doing it coed at Marybeth's parents'
country club so the boys can play golf if they want to.
Can't wait to see you there,
Katie

And then, as they always do, things degraded quickly:

From: Flynn, Thomas <XXXXXXXXX@excite.com>
To: [list]
Re: Making a Change

Hey all,
I just wanted to pop off a note to you all that I'll be out of
pocket for 30 days starting Monday. So if I don't answer your
emails, don't hold it against me. It's nothing terribly serious,
just an issue I've wanted to take care of before it becomes a
serious problem. I'm looking at this program as a fresh start,
a new chapter in my life. I'll give you all a ring on the other
side of it.
Thanks,
Tom

Sometimes we'd get responses from recipients on the mailing
list:

From: Regina Peterson <XXXXXXXXXXX@erols.com>
To: Baker, Gary <XXXXXX@hotmail.com>
Re: New Contact Info

Hey Gary,
I don't know what to say. Congrats! I'm so happy for you, and
I hope your family was supportive. I know that's important.
Can't wait to meet Lance. Please give me a shout when
you're settled.
Gina

From: Kelleher, Jen <XXXXXX@aol.com>
To: Berman, Katie <XXXXXXXXXXX@hotmail.com>
Re: Baby Shower

K—
Is she registered anywhere yet? Please let me know when
you know. That is *soooo* exciting!!!
Can't wait!
Jen

From: Anne Falloway <XXXXXXX@XXXsystems.com>
To: Flynn, Thomas <XXXXXXXXX@excite.com>
Re: Making a Change

Tom,
I just wanted to offer my support for you. If you need anything,
and I mean anything at all, I'm here to help. I know how that
can be. My uncle was in AA. Please let me know if you need
anyone to watch your place or feed pets or whatever.
     Best wishes and I can't wait to see you when you come
back.
Love,
Anne

Sometimes the subject of the emails would find out about it
and send a scathing missive to the fake address:

From: Gary Baker <XXXXXX@XXXXXXXXpartners.com>
To: Baker, Gary <XXXXXX@hotmail.com>
Re: Phony Announcement

Whoever you are, stop sending emails under my name. This
shit is not funny. Stop being an asshole.
I'm serious.

The response back to that was easy:

From: Baker, Gary XXXXXX@hotmail.com>
To: Gary Baker <XXXXXX@XXXXXXXXpartners.com>
Re: Phony Announcement

Unless you have some proof you're me, you'd better stop
sending emails under my name.

   Trust me. I'll find out who you are, and if you're not me,
you're in a shitload of trouble. Trust me, or you, on that.

Pulling these gags off involved the two of us working multiple
email accounts simultaneously. Sometimes I had three or four
different web browsers going at the same time—each with a different email account. And you'd think between that and my job,
I had enough to keep me amused at work. You'd be wrong.

Over the past few years, numerous studies have shown that
employees are spending more and more time at work and getting
less done. Talking heads on the news channels and business con-
sultants blame it on our warp-speed lifestyles, the pitfalls of multi-
tasking, and our lack of sleep. Some warn we're having a national
nervous breakdown—a country of terminally wired imbeciles
doing a million things at once, all badly.

Bullshit.

The reason workers are spending more time at work but not
producing more is because of the Internet. The average toil of an
office monkey is hopelessly dull, and even the best corporate environment is stultifying. I mean, let's face it—80 to 90 percent of
what we do is dressed up administrative task work. In the past
that was fine. You sat there in your gray flannel suit and sucked up
the drudgery, maybe had drinks at lunch to speed the day away.
But now, thanks to technology, the ultimate cure for that terminal
office boredom is right in front of you, inside the very machine
they pay you to sit and stare at all day long. Giving workers the
Internet might as well be putting Stolichnaya in the watercooler or
joints in the candy machine. Giving the thing to a person whose
idea of Nirvana was reading the *New York Times* and *Wall Street
Journal* within arm's reach of a laptop and a television switching

between Comedy Central, CNN, and the History Channel was like saddling me with a crystal meth addiction.

In many ways, having the Internet in the office killed any chance of me having a normal legal career before I really even started. If it weren't insidious enough as a source of pranks, it also provided endless information about all the thousands of more interesting lives I could lead or places I could be. On a speedboat rolling through a jungle river, taking notes for a *National Geographic* article on Nigerian warlords. Working at an Internet company where they served microbrews at lunch and kept a Ping-Pong table in the boardroom. Maybe just tending bar in some island resort, writing screenplays in my spare time. The choices seemed endless. With every click on a site showing all the better things I could be doing, the damn thing taunted me, planting seeds of discontent no office drone would have felt sitting behind a desk in 1964.

And, of course, there was the porn. I didn't surf for that too much at the office, but that had little impact on the volume of it I ended up viewing there. The same way people used fax machines to send filthy comics to one another in the seventies, in the earlier Wild West days of office Internet abuse, everybody sent porn to one another.* A few months earlier, Harris, Martin, our friend Les, and I had started exchanging foul material with one another and with every more bizarre or obscene link or picture someone sent, the bar was raised—"Who can top *this*?" At first it was tame, outtakes from porn shoots or slide shows of *Playboy* centerfolds. As people gained more facility with search engines, however, the raunch level picked up, quickly and exponentially.

This wasn't surprising, of course. Les never did anything halfway. Not a bet, a challenge, or any sort of contest. To this day, even among all the vicious lawyers I've known, he remains one of the meanest competitors I've ever met. Darts, chess, basketball, Xbox, Fantasy Football, you name it. The guy just had to

---

*One friend of mine actually crashed his company's server sending a particularly large movie to fifty or so close friends.

win at whatever he was playing. It wasn't long before he took the game of who-could-find-the-most-disgusting-thing-on-the-Internet to a new level. The titles of images and links in the emails shifted from "centerfolds" and "lesbians" to "midgets," "she-male," and "'facial' collage #12."

Around the same time Bennett and I were in the middle of our phony email prank, I received a cryptic email from Les addressed to Martin, Harris, and me:

From: Faulheit, Les <XXXXXXXX@yahoo.com>
Re: Scat

Careful opening this at work. You'll never be able to explain yourself.
—L

That was a woefully inadequate warning, which I realized the moment I clicked on the attached images. These days, most of us have seen it all by twenty-five: dwarf porn, anorexic beauty pageants, eighty-year-old women wearing ball gags and nipple clamps, Japanese schoolgirls making love to Wiffle bats, women expelling Ping-Pong balls, softballs, grapefruits, mangos and those tiny plastic footballs you get on fan appreciation day, "Sparky the Wonderdog" mounting a toothless sixtyish crack whore, golden showers, fist fucks, triple entry, she-male double penetration, conga lines held together with double-sided dildos, hidden-camera gynecological exam videos, and, of course, endless variations on the "he sticks his whole head inside" video.

The list of things that will always be shocking, to which no one could ever become desensitized, gets shorter and shorter every day. But even in that rarified air, "scat" holds a special place near the top. Scat's what separates the iron stomachs from the rest of the amateur sex voyeurs, a very deep line in the sand, enough to swallow a car. Don't believe me? Go to your computer and look up the word in a Google "Image Search," with the "SafeSearch" setting turned off. You'll quickly find yourself in a very ugly universe.

"Jesus, man." I called Les after I'd opened his email. "This is making me gag. I think you can get *E. coli* from doing that."

"Let me send you ones of the Asian girl with the blindfold on." He laughed. "It's astounding. You won't believe the human body is capable of what she's doing."

"Who is the guy in these photos? He looks famous, like I ought to know him, but the pictures are fuzzy. It's hard to make out his face."

"Yeah, they're from a slideshow with better resolution. Let me find that."

"I want to say Cheech, but that's not it."

"He kind of looks like Oates."

"Oates?"

"From Hall & Oates. The short one."

"Nah, that's not it. It's on the tip of my tongue. I can see the guy, but I can't think of his name, or what movie or show he was in."

"Did you get the email I just sent you?"

The new mail icon blinked on my screen. "What is this?"

"The Asian thing."

"This has fifty photos in it. Where are you getting this shit, a white slavery ring?"

"I could be killed if I told you. Let me see if I can find that slideshow."

The problem with this endless barrage of information was that it started to become overwhelming. Between Martin, Les, Bennett, and dozens of college and high school friends, I was opening and closing more files and sending and receiving more emails than any one mind could manage. It was confusing as hell and unnerving at times. I'd frequently catch myself accidentally typing the wrong response into the wrong email window, which could have been a real problem. There's no way to explain to opposing counsel why you sent them a folder of amputee porn or a link to www.rotten.com. Yet I knew it was only a matter of time until something like that happened.

When the "mistake" inevitably occurred, it was exactly as I'd expected, an errant message shot off in a flurry of emails pinballing back and forth between a dozen different people. Bennett and I were trying a prank on a group of college friends living together in a house in Hoboken. The idea was to use several fake email accounts at once to start arguments among the roommates, which would lead to confrontations when they all got home after work. This was a trickier gag than usual because, rather than a simple one-shot announcement, there was a back-and-forth involving several email threads, with Bennett and me pretending to be different people at the same time:

From me:

From: Carter, James <XXXXXXX@hotmail.com>
To: Ellis, Jon <XXXX@XXXllc.com>
Re: Sink

Dude, the disposal is broken and we can't use the kitchen sink because of all that crap you threw into it last night. I expect you to get a plumber and pay to have it fixed. Now.

Response:

From: Ellis, Jon <XXXX@XXXllc.com>
To: Carter, James <XXXXXXX@hotmail.com>
Re: Sink

Chris? Is this you? What is this address? I didn't put anything in the sink. I didn't even eat in the house last night.

My reply back:

From: Carter, James <XXXXXXX@hotmail.com>
To: Ellis, Jon <XXXX@XXXllc.com>
Cc: Fuller, Mark <XXXXXXX@excite.com>
Re: Sink

This is my private email address. They don't want us using the work email for anything personal anymore.

I call bullshit on your excuse. Mark told me you were eating Mexican in the kitchen last night. You threw something into the disposal. Nobody else ate in there last night.

Is that accurate, Mark?

Bennett, playing Mark, responding to my reply:

From: Fuller, Mark <XXXXXXX@excite.com>
To: Carter James <XXXXXXX@hotmail.com>; Ellis, Jon <XXXX@XXXllc.com>
Re: Sink

I don't want to get in the middle of this. I just want the sink fixed.

As that thread was going on, in another window, I was also corresponding with Candace. Somehow, despite our history, we remained friends, and in an amazing lapse of judgment, she'd even put me on an email distribution list, one of those collections of people where recipients hit "Reply to All" on every email, using the group as an informal chat board. Hers involved an assortment of work friends, largely young female lawyers.

At the time, it was still common practice for people to circulate those idiot chain emails where some authentic-looking article described how Microsoft was monitoring all of our computers for the United Nations, or NutraSweet caused multiple sclerosis. Every firm had at least one superstitious receptionist or assistant who believed whatever she read in electronic type, particularly a conspiracy theory. They'd get these "articles" or "public service warnings" from their manicurist or niece in junior college and compulsively forward them through the firm to anyone too polite to tell them to stop. Lawyers being native skeptics, and 99 percent of these missives being filled with fantastic nonsense, they usually didn't circulate too far.

Every now and again, however, one of the things used just the right pitch, discussing just the right subject matter that even a cynical lawyer would pass it along. That day, Candace's distribution list had circulated a story about frozen yogurt having dangerously high fat content. Apparently Big Yogurt was secretly using lard to thicken their product—a war crime against the borderline bulimic set.

Normally, an email about the calories in yogurt was a strange thing for a twenty-seven-year-old male to receive, but I was used to getting all sorts of material from Candace's group. I had no problem reading about the slimming properties of black stretch pants or sales at Neiman Marcus. It was like reading *Cosmopolitan* at your girlfriend's house; keeps you in touch with your feminine side. The only problem this time was that somehow, in the mix of emails, photos, web browsers, and work documents open on my computer screen, I forwarded the yogurt email to Bennett, in a format where he could reply to everyone on Candace's distribution list by simply opening the thing and hitting "Reply to All."

I was too caught up in the scheme with the Hoboken roommates to realize what I'd done. And after sending out and handling the responses from the initial emails to the roommates, I got caught up in legal work, drafting a motion for court. I shut down every open window except my private email and started writing the motion longhand on a legal memo pad, only looking up at the computer screen every now and again. Les, Martin, and Harris continued swapping jokes and porn, and from the subject lines and commentary of the first few emails between them, the content of what they were exchanging held immense promise:

From: Faulheit, Les <XXXXXXXX@yahoo.com>
Re: Superscat

M/R—
Scroll down. The "Dinner is Served!" one is disgusting.

From: Lennard, Martin <XXXX@hotmail.com>
Re: Superscat

M/R—
Oh my god . . . That camera is far too close. I swear I can see
corn kernels. I feel like I'm going to vomit.

I was barely pages into the motion when the phone rang.
"What the fuck is the matter with your friend Bennett?" It was
Candace, and she was seriously pissed off.

"What are you talking about?" I'd lied with that phrase so
many times it felt strange using it earnestly.

"You know what I'm talking about."

"No I don't. I was just sitting here, writing a brief."

"That email? 'Squirrel-fucking'?"

"I honestly don't know what you're talking about." I pulled up
my email and scanned the in-box to locate the offending corre-
spondence. Smack in the middle of a pile of emails between Harris, Martin and Les, I found it:

From: Bennett Lawrence <XXXXXXXXX@XXXXXXXXllc.
com>
To: [Candace's distribution list]
Re: The Inside Skinny on Yogurt

Lard in yogurt? I blame the Bilderbergers and Trilateral
Commission!

But seriously, food safety's no laughing matter. I know a
girl who died from toxic shock after masturbating with frozen
hot dogs. They dedicated the special ed wing in my high
school to her.

Now really seriously, why did you send me this? Don't
people in that backwash state have anything better to do?
Fuck swine or squirrels or whatever it is your kind do on the
farm for amusement?

"I guess I can see how that's a little coarse."

"How could you do this? Do you know how embarrassing this is?"

"Come on." I struggled to find a comeback. "It's not like *you* did it."

"Your friend is a reflection on me. Why are you so perpetually immature?"

"*Me?* Why is it *my* fault? I didn't do it."

"I meant 'you' in the broad sense. You and your 'friends.' Why do you do stuff like this?"

"I don't know." *The better question is how anyone could expect us not to do something like this. Do you think there's a normal twenty-seven-year-old man on the planet who can tolerate sitting in a box writing fucking memos all day?* "It was just a joke."

"Here's a tip. Bestiality isn't a go-to comedy topic for most people. That email went to half a dozen lawyers in the firm's labor department. Now I have to run around and apologize to them. These are *serious* people, and you've made me look like a freak."

"Let me call Bennett. I'll get him to send you an email explaining it was a screwup."

"How?" She had a point there. Offending somebody in an email is a rotten situation. Bennett meant what he wrote. He just didn't mean to send it to the people he was insulting. There's no "I take that back" in email. You can't distance yourself from the words, but you also can't take the brutally honest approach: "Yes, I meant what I wrote. Go fuck yourself." No, you have to *pretend* your comments are just jokes and act contrite about the whole thing. Unless, of course, you're Bennett.

"I'll ask him to send out an apology, Candace." I hung up the phone and dialed Bennett's office.

"Douchebag, you sent that email to a bunch of fucking lawyers."

"What are you talking about?" He acted confused.

"You know."

"No I don't."

"Yes you do. Send a follow-up saying you're sorry."

"No, I won't be doing that." He snapped back, half-laughing. "I said I don't know what you're talking about. Now let us speak of this no more."

"I've seen the email, with your address on it."

"Squirrel-fucker." CLICK. The bastard hung up on me.

I called Candace back. "Look, whatever you want me to say, I'll apologize and claim it was my fault."

"What did your friend say?"

"He wasn't in. But look, the more I read the thing, it was just dark humor. I'm sure, uh—" As I was talking to her, I opened an attachment to an email from Les titled "Dinner is Served!" which started an automatic slideshow on my monitor. "I'm, uh, sure some of the people like dark humor, and . . ." My thoughts started to wander as the images on the computer monopolized my attention.

"You know I like fucked-up jokes, but that was totally misplaced." Candace was still annoyed, but calming by the moment, realizing there was nothing anyone could do to fix the situation, that anyone offended would probably do what we all do in an office setting where someone accidentally speaks honestly: pretend it never happened.

"I'm sorry." I squinted at my computer as the grainy images from a seventies stag film played out on my screen. "I missed what you said there." A woman on my monitor was squatting, squeezing what had to be a foot-long, well-formed turd into the mouth of the same hairy, skeletal man who'd looked so eerily familiar in the pictures Les had sent me earlier. The production of the thing was horrible—probably made in a trailer or a motel, with the shadows of the cameraman visible against the back wall. Real lowball stuff, where you knew everyone involved was paid in coke and had died years ago, and not in their sleep. The focus was still fuzzy, but that was probably a blessing. Any higher definition would have revealed textures, colors and details no human should examine up close. Still, it was clear enough that I could finally make out the face of the male lead.

Gabe Kaplan. It finally hit me. *The guy's a dead ringer for Gabe Kaplan.* I was watching Mr. Kotter eat shit.

"I said I like fucked-up humor," Candace was still talking. "But you have to admit, Bennett's email was pretty offensive."

"I don't know. We might have different definitions of that word."

TIME TO GO INTO CIVIL LAW

The awful thing took place in the bowels of Pennsylvania—
God's country near the middle of the state, hours from
Philadelphia. The courthouse was massive, far more space than
the town needed, and the first floor was swarming with security
personnel.

BEEP. The metal detector went off as I walked through.

"You got all the metal out of your pockets?" A mouth-breathing
farm kid in a police uniform stared at me.

"It's my cuff links. Just frisk me."

"Walk through again, please."

BEEP. When I got to the other side of the machine, I spread
my arms and legs before he could even ask. You had to get used to
the frisking process in those days. The Oklahoma City bombing
was still fresh in everyone's memory. In its wake, courthouses installed high-tech screening devices at the door, turning their en-
trances into airplane check-in lines, with every metal detector set
to the highest sensitivity.

"Can you tell me what floor Judge Trautman is on?"

"Fourth," the guard replied.

"Thanks." And off I went toward the elevators, to go upstairs
and see the sentencing.

Everybody thinks it's exciting to do criminal defense work, and they're right. It's nothing like *Law & Order* would have you believe, but it's far sexier than the average civil case. And the "white-collar" nature of the clients I worked for insulated me from any nasty moral quandaries about representing violent criminals. If criminal law were medicine, white-collar criminal defense would be plastic surgery—well-heeled business clients paying premium rates. And when you're a kid just out of school, representing well-heeled criminal defendants seems as entertaining as a job could be. There's no bigger challenge. The system's stacked in the prosecutor's favor, and if you can't get satisfaction out of helping people fight the state or Uncle Sam, you have no soul.

The only problem is losing, where it suddenly feels like the worst job on the planet. And you never lose once. The first is the actual loss—the conviction. The second is the sentencing. I'd been doing criminal work for a little over a year before I saw a sentencing firsthand. Until then I'd only seen those ugly matters conceptually, from the office, researching sentencing guidelines and preparing memos and briefs to file with the court. This was the first time I was seeing one in the flesh, driving out to the feedlots and silos of rural Pennsylvania to see the wheels of justice grind a client to pulp.

When I got upstairs, the courtroom where they were holding the sentencing was locked, so I stood in the hallway, watching the interested parties pace back and forth, waiting for the convicted prisoner to arrive. The lawyers were there, naturally, and the bailiffs, along with a news reporter or two and various assorted spectators, most of whom looked like bored court employees with nothing better to do.

After about twenty minutes a group of officers brought the prisoner into the hallway in shackles, in the usual prison jumpsuit. I thought I'd have a moment to introduce myself, feeling the need to at least shake the guy's hand, having spoken to him three or four times a week for the last two months. I never got the chance. They dragged him past quickly, like a circus ape, his

wild, wiry hair all that was noticeable through the circle of sur-
rounding uniforms.

When the defendant was seated and the judge had taken the
bench, the lawyers gave statements to the court. The prosecutor
started, describing the enormity of the crime—trafficking hundreds of pounds of cocaine—and its horrific impact on society.
His pitch was economical. There was no reason to grandstand.
He'd already won and the better course at that point was taking
the high road, politely asking for the maximum and letting the
court do the rest.

As the prosecutor slid comfortably into his chair, the defense
lawyer took the floor. After a brief introduction, he went for broke,
giving a balls-out speech on the failure of the "Drug War," then
sliding into the legal bases for the court to grant his client le-
niency. I started daydreaming as he went into the details, until I
heard him say, "I'd call my client a hero, your honor. A patriot."

Did he just say "hero"? "Patriot"? That was pushing the envelope, but I couldn't say I was shocked. The lawyer, Tim Hannily,
had brass balls. He was from Florida and he'd been defending
criminals since the seventies, in the days when money-laundering
defendants in that part of the world paid their lawyers in cash, in
suitcases. Hannily had the knowing grin of a person who'd already seen more strange things than most people did in a lifetime. His tone was respectful, but he was going to say whatever
he liked, and he had the bones to do it, which was obvious from
the quality of his argument. He was forceful, and he sounded hope-
ful even as he knew his client was going down, badly. And why
not say what he wanted? What did the judge care? His was the
last word, and nothing Hannily said could make the sentence any
worse. The judge just sat there, stone-faced in his robe, listening
as Hannily criticized the government's case, the jury's verdict and
any sentence to be imposed. Really, who puts a "patriot" away?

That patriot, Shay Peterson, had been an alleged high-ranking
member of a notorious regional motorcycle gang. My firm had
been enlisted to represent members of Peterson's family. The
prosecution was seeking every piece of Peterson's property that

could conceivably be tied to drug running, no matter how incredible the link, all for deterrence purposes, of course. It was our job to help his family keep it. I'd been sent to watch the sentencing and take notes—see if I heard anything we could use to defend those forfeiture claims.

The story of how Peterson came to this point is complicated. He'd been convicted of working with a career smuggler named Arnold Krass to bring 453 kilograms of cocaine into the country from South America. Krass, recently released from a Canadian prison after serving a sentence for trafficking cocaine to that nation from Colombia, was a confidential informant for the United States Customs Service. He'd done well in the informing business, previously netting $300,000 from Uncle Sam for setting up a 1993 sting of Mexican traffickers looking to purchase $1.3 million worth of cocaine. Krass roped Peterson into the mother of all stings—a plan to hoodwink a Colombian cartel into letting them smuggle into the United States a massive load of cocaine aboard a decrepit cargo vessel called the *Pegasus*. Krass told U.S. Customs agents who were in on the sting about his plan in advance. It's what he didn't tell them, depending on whom you believe, that was the problem.

No organization ships millions in inventory with a service it doesn't know, particularly a cocaine cartel. Prior to securing the *Pegasus* deal, Krass and Peterson had to run shipments of coke from Houston to Baltimore, to make their "bona fides." They were given three shipments to make, two of 100 kilograms, one of 253 kilograms. The first two went smoothly. Drug agents in Texas nailed Krass with the third before he got out of the state. The hub of the alleged conspiracy was Peterson's home in Pennsylvania, so that's where they were prosecuted.

Krass and Peterson claimed Customs gave them authority to do the Houston-to-Baltimore runs, as part of the broader *Pegasus* sting, and that without them, the cartel would never have given them the boat shipment. Krass admitted he'd never received a specific approval from Customs for the Houston-to-Baltimore runs, but that it was obviously implied. The Customs agents claimed they never authorized anything and strictly forbade criminal acts in furtherance of any sting. Never mind that most stings can't exist without some predicate criminal conduct, or the frequent, compelling allegation that law enforcement dodges the issue with a "don't ask, don't tell" policy.

Peterson looked like every caricature of Blackbeard you've ever seen, and Krass was a notorious career smuggler with a lengthy record. The government denied it had a deal with either, or that it would ever enter into such an arrangement. The trial was in farm country, the jury pulled from the sticks of Pennsylvania, and the result was exactly what you'd expect.

Halfway through Peterson's sentencing I knew I wouldn't be staying in the business long enough to see another. I was in a spectators' row, just behind the defendant's seat, and to my right a group of chunky men with buzz cuts sat behind the prosecutor. They wore thick sport coats and white pinpoint collared shirts—the cheap, gauzy variety with the papier-mâché texture. The feet I could see were stuffed into almost orthopedic black lace-ups. Not a loafer in sight, and every suit was deep blue or dark gray. No cuffs in the pants and the ties alternated between rep stripes and miniaturized patterns from Holiday Inn curtains. If the words "drug war" and "cartel" and concepts like "manifest injustice" hadn't been bouncing around us, I'd have sworn I was attending a guidance counselors' convention. Some of them shook their heads as Hannily scorned his client's conviction. This was their moment. They'd brought a menace to justice. Miller Lite and strip steaks for all.

As I watched them all smiling, suddenly the thought of working in civil law seemed a lot more palatable. The players in that world were hired guns, pure mercenaries, and the only thing at risk was money. The Eliot Nesses sitting across from me were true believers, and in this theater, people lost their lives and property.

As I sat there watching the sordid spectacle, I wondered how many other versions of this scene were being played out in other courthouses around the state. The papers had recently been filled with articles about prosecutions and investigations of Peterson's motorcycle gang, all stemming from a pair of Amish cocaine dealers named Jacob Spring Slagel and Jacob Slagel (no relation). The two were busted selling coke to Amish teenagers on "Rumspringa," a one-year period in which Amish kids are allowed to experience power windows, zippers, and television. And, apparently, amphetamines, which the Slagels claimed they bought from bikers.

It wasn't odd that bikers and the Amish would connect. From what I saw and learned in Peterson's case, the outlaw biker stereotype doesn't apply as roundly as most would think. Shay seemed more like a wild variety of "lifestyle criminal" than anything else, a person who simply wanted to live on his own terms. Sure, his idea of freedom was a lot different from that of the Amish, but that central binding concept of the groups was the same. They both wanted to live by their own rules, with the rest of the world and its barbed wire of endless complications at arm's length.

I guess in the end the mistake that clipped Peterson was trusting the government. But you couldn't help thinking *caveat emptor* on some level, that he was marked from the start, that it was his own fault. To live off the grid the way he did, you've got to superficially mesh with it, maintain two identities, one of which can disappear into its air traffic. Peterson was part of something that thumbed its nose at Main Street. He had two strikes against him walking into any courtroom because of what he was—the same Achilles' heel that lands dreadlock-wearing doctors' kids in tie-dyes and Birkenstocks in jail for selling mushrooms at Phish concerts—being identifiable. A biker with a pirate's visage has to be involved in some rotten, illegal shit, right?

Perhaps, but a lot of people get involved in drugs, and a lot of them look nothing like bikers. The retail dope market I'd seen growing up was filled with Republicans, Little League coaches and people who belonged to country clubs and sat in the front pews on Sunday—people identical in many ways to the Buzz-cut Brigade sitting across the aisle from me in that courtroom. The profit in the trade is addictive, with an instant return on risk, the same thing that drives millions of day traders and real estate flippers all over the country. You could say the drug business is one of the last true capitalist ventures left in our economy, the sort of market Adam Smith imagined and Milton Friedman said we ought to legalize. No tax issues to vet, permits to procure or shysters and accountants to hire to guide you through a maze of paperwork to be notarized and filed with all the proper clerks. Just the seller and marketplace.

Wrapping your head around the notion that Peterson was paying for bad business decisions was one thing. Swallowing the government's fiction that there was any larger battle between "right" and "wrong" in the case was another. For practical people who understand drugs as a substance with a simple chemical reaction on the brain, it's near impossible to build any moral totems out of a Baggie of vegetable mass, powder or pills. Peterson wasn't going to jail because he was a villain; he took a risk in a dangerous market and was burned, just like the millions of people who blow up their lives in Vegas or the stock market every year.

Watching the whole scene unfold, I realized something that had been kicking around my head for months: I needed to get out of criminal work and into a full-time civil practice. Part of it was a career decision. I'd been with Sean O'Malley for a little more than a year, and though I'd always known that criminal law wouldn't pay as well as the civil firms, it was becoming increasingly clear that it would take decades to become a player in such a tight niche market. I had friends from law school who were making good money doing civil work, and while I was living decently, I hadn't gotten into a field as irritating as law just to do alright.

But sitting there watching Hannily argue futilely to the judge, I realized that another part of it, the bigger part, was that I didn't have the skin to deal with having people's lives in my hands, or the stomach to tolerate all the "good v. bad" mythology of that universe. I couldn't buy into any of the arguments—the prosecution's moral harrumphing or the defense's "patriot" rhetoric. Who needed to reach those judgments? Right or wrong, Peterson was just living the way he wanted to, and those kinds of people don't do well in courtrooms. Peterson's type was the last extreme point on a continuum of thought I understood, and though I'd never take his chances, I also wasn't going to spend the rest of my career watching those who did crushed under the government's boot. Better to be naïve and think most of them make it, giving up the vice and retiring to the islands, than know what actually happens.

The judge's speech was white noise until he started talking numbers. "Three hundred and sixty months." *Jesus Christ. Thirty fucking years.* They always do it in months, bureaucrat-style. I guess it's just procedure, decorum, hundreds of years of Anglo-Saxon jurisprudence. He'd have been more honest to say, "I sentence you to the rest of your life in jail, and death in a prison infirmary." Peterson was fifty years old.

Hannily passed, wearing the best face he could. Watching a client I only knew by phone get thirty years shook me cold. That creepy comfort of seeing somebody stomped in a bar fight or reading about an execution in the newspaper and thinking, *Thank God that isn't me,* dug into my spine. "Win some, lose some" could never get me through decades of those moments. And whatever does I didn't want to have.

The first thing I did when I got outside was call a friend who worked in civil law. "Hey, I hate to ask for a favor, but can you forward my résumé around your firm?" Criminal law's a place for real lawyers. I belonged in civil work. Besides, I was pushing thirty. It was time to settle down, get on a partnership track, get some stability in my world. Maybe if I got away from the criminals at work, my personal life would slow down a bit.

THE POWER OF PERFECT NIPPLES

Most men self-identify into one of two camps, "ass men" and "breast men," as if those were mutually exclusive endowments. If forced to choose, I'd say I'm an ass man. I'll take a tight ass—the kind that looks like a pair of upright Nerf footballs side by side—over a massive rack any day. And all this, of course, is secondary to the face. No matter how spectacular the uniform, an awful helmet is always a deal breaker (you can't have a decent love life entirely from behind).

But these are just the broad, threshold characteristics that initially draw you in. And I might be a little crass there. What really keeps you with a woman is some special detail—the dimples at the corners of her mouth when she smiles, the pout of her lips when she says "I love you," or maybe the way her hand feels in yours when you walk through the park on a fall afternoon, admiring the change of color in the trees.

Me, I like nipples. Big breasts, small breasts—either's fine. What matters most is what's sitting on their peaks. I am a nipple man. And Lisa had amazing nipples.

Among a few other things.

"So I hear you're fighting over who will be taking me home tonight." Lisa laughed.

"Huh?" It was true. I had been, just moments before. But how in the hell did she know? It happened in the men's room as I was standing at a urinal next to a short drunk who'd been trying to hit on her. He hadn't been directly aggressive, but he was working in that direction, angling closer and closer into the conversation Lisa and I had been having, laughing loudly nearby and trying to find an entrance. When I ran into him in the restroom, he immediately started asking about her.

"So who's the blonde in the fuck-me boots?" he barked from the urinal next to mine. "She's a spicy meatball."

"Interesting analogy."

"Huh?"

"Nothing. I'm working her, dude. She's mine."

"Oh really?" He lurched backward, zippering his pants and bumping into a man passing behind us. "S'cuse me there, brother."

"No problem." The man he'd collided with laughed and made his way to the sink.

"You're pretty confident there." The drunk man turned back to me. "What makes you so sure you're taking her home?"

"I'm not." I zipped up my pants and walked to the sink.

"Really?" He snickered and turned to the hand towel machine, running into the same man he'd bumped into moments before as the man was moving to open the door. "Sorry, dude. Those martinis sneak up on you."

"We'll probably go to her place." I smiled into the mirror.

"Whatever . . ." He laughed at me and pushed open the door.

My bravado was a combination of booze and the fact that I was even getting a shot at a girl like Lisa. She'd been one of the sexiest girls at my college. We hadn't seen each other in five or six years and I had no idea what to expect, but when she stepped into the bar it was clear she still had it. Heads turned in every direction. The fiftyish lawyers with lumpy wives waiting on the other end of train rides home craned their necks and leered, while the female associates from the firms upstairs shot her skeptical glances, wondering what this strange piece of "competition" was doing in the bar. Part of Lisa's surface attraction was style. Knee-level black stiletto boots and a just-short-enough dress will always draw eyes. Part of it was lucky genes—long blond hair, high cheekbones and a dancer's ass. You could see the definition of every muscle in her legs.

I'd heard Lisa moved to Philadelphia from a college buddy. At the time I was still working for Sean O'Malley's office, and every Friday I had drinks with a bunch of friends, including people from college Lisa probably knew. I gave her a call out of the blue and invited her along. She accepted and agreed to meet us at a yuppie bar on Market Street, on the basement floor of one of the big office towers in Center City.

What I'd recalled of Lisa from school was a laid-back party girl, but sweet and unassuming, which was rare for a woman who looked like her. And smart. With all that ammunition, Lisa easily could have been a stuck-up or "high-maintenance" sort, and when I first saw her I almost wondered why she wasn't. I didn't know whether I had a chance when I asked her to come along for drinks, assuming she had to be involved with someone, but I had my fingers crossed. In a worst-case scenario, I figured she'd have hot friends.

And now, less than a half hour into talking with her, having found out she was single, I had to explain why I'd been running my mouth off to a stranger about how I was going to fuck her.

"What are you talking about?" I smiled. She couldn't have known about that exchange. She had to be fucking with me, but how?

"I understand you and another gentleman were discussing who'd be kind enough to see me home tonight."

I took a long drag off a cigarette, to buy some time to think. "That guy next to us seemed interested in you," I whispered in her ear to avoid being overheard. "I didn't think he was your type."

"So you *were* talking about me, then?" She cupped her hand next to her mouth to hide her lips and whispered back as low as she could, mimicking me.

"How'd you know?"

"It's a secret."

"Come on. That will drive me nuts."

"If you insist, *he* told me." Lisa nodded to her left. The man the drunk fellow had twice bumped into in the bathroom was sitting at the edge of the bar, grinning and holding his drink in the air. I toasted him back and smiled. *You're a funny guy. A real fuckin' comedian.*

"I was doing you a favor, you understand."

"Of course." Lisa grinned and sipped her drink. "Thank you so much."

"There were a hundred different ways you could have played that."

"I know."

So many women would have sat on that information, figuring how they'd use it to their advantage. Lisa ran the ball straight up the middle.

"Can you hold this for a second?" She handed me her drink and took off her jacket. I have to assume women either don't care or don't realize what happens when they push out their rib cage taking off a coat. Thrusting a set of breasts in a man's face puts him in an impossible situation. He has to try not to leer, but also not look away so obviously that it makes the moment uncomfortable. In this case, I had no choice. I had a headful of scotch, hadn't been laid in forever, and Lisa wasn't wearing a bra. Her dress was this tight, thin, chocolate-colored thing, she had perky fashion-model breasts, and yes, it was damn cold in that bar.

I must have stared for five seconds—forever in a situation like that—before I realized what I was doing and snapped out of it. How couldn't I? Rock-hard nipples are like fireworks or lightning. It's impossible to stop looking, no matter who they belong to. Every man's had that horrible moment in the dead of July where the air conditioning is on full blast and some sixtyish, two-hundred-pound secretary or 401(k) administrator comes into your office and starts talking about some document you need to review or sign. She's running on about something serious and work-related but all you can think of is those huge udders at the end of the massive, double E torpedos poking through her bra at asymmetric angles, pointing toward the floor. Your mind stays on one repeating message. *Don't look down. Never look down. Stare at the eyes. The eyes, dammit.*

Even more disturbingly, the phenomenon isn't limited to women. A nauseating result of the "corporate casual" movement is the prevalence of ample-bosomed males in pleated dress pants and golf shirts. Four out of five lawyers have "office physiques." Not walrus-like or Michelin Man fat—more sagging, swollen, and flabby in bad places, the sort of people who should never wear anything formfitting. And yet, at least once a day in the summer you'll find yourself talking to a coworker in a tight golf shirt, rolls pouring over his belt, with B-cup man breasts and his high beams on full blast, thinking to yourself, *Jesus, man, have you no shame at all? I'm about to lose my fucking lunch here.*

The only people who seem to be aware of high beams are young women. They walk through the office in the summer with their jackets on or their arms crossed tight over their chests, leading to awkward conversations where both of you pretend not to notice her odd, hunched-over, arms-folded posture. She understands. Nipples are important. Everyone focuses on the size and hang and curve of the breast, but it's the hood ornament on top that makes all the difference. Replace the Flying Lady on a Rolls-Royce with a crucifix, pyramid, or Venus de Milo and you've ruined the car, no matter how amazing the rest of the components are. A bad nipple on a perfect breast works the same way. It's an awful letdown unhinging the bra on a spectacular set only to discover they're topped with tiny, pinpoint nipples. The nipple is crucial, and only a fool or a eunuch would say otherwise. The law knows. It doesn't ban the public display of breasts. It bans *nipples*.

I'm not going to rate every type. That's a matter of taste. There are the brown ones you get with darker-skinned girls and pink ones you get with fairer women. Some are so light they're near indistinguishable from the skin around them. Some are riddled with fleshy little pebbles around the nipple itself, and some are puffed out all around or conelike, as if the areola and nipple were one and the same. Most tend to be circles, but I've seen ovals now and again, particularly on the larger ones, where the areolas tend to appear stretched. Some point up, some down, some 90 degrees dead ahead. I've seen them tilted outward and I've seen them centered. Smaller, pert breasts like Lisa's have always been my favorite. They have these fat knobs that point out sharply, just as hers did in that dress. As I stood there holding her drink as she took off the jacket, the only thought running through my head was, *Christ, you could hang wet towels off those things*. I'd wanted to sleep with Lisa the minute I saw her. Now I needed to.

"You know, you have a terrible poker face for a lawyer."

"What are you talking about?"

"Forget it." She smiled and threw back the last of her drink.

She was right. Everything about the girl made me nervous—in a good way, but still rattled. Talking to Lisa wasn't a game like law school or a job. Women like this didn't come around often. Some people never get a chance like I was being given. This was real life, important. This *mattered*.

At the time, I'd been dabbling in the young professional dating scene, even trying a couple traditional dates. In fact, I had one set up for the following night, with an associate from some satellite office of a law firm just outside the city. She was attractive and I wanted to see what was under her business suit. The problem was the "dinner ritual." A dreadful exercise, so formal and detached, with that ocean of tablecloth between you and all the protocols. It feels like you're on a job interview, volleying filler dialogue back and forth:

"What's your practice like?"

"You know, standard litigation."

"I'm thinking of switching firms. Maybe shifting to the transactional side."

"Really?"

"The partner track at my current firm is too long, and it seems even longer for women. And I don't see them investing in the regulatory law area."

"Regulatory law seems nice. There's always a need for it."

"Are there other areas you're interested in besides litigation?"

"I don't know."

"You have to pick some specialty. It's all about being a specialist these days."

"Yeah, well, we'll see. You want another pinot grigio?"

"Decaf cappuccino, please. Soy milk, with cinnamon, and a touch of nutmeg. I have yoga in the morning. Hot yoga. Have you ever tried hot yoga?"

"Uh, no. No I haven't."

It's during these moments you start thinking, *Jerking off is really underrated.* Hearing this sort of stuff only reminded me of Candace's gibberish about "maturity." So this was "growing up"? Chichi restaurants, shop talk and intentionally "hip" urban hobbies? All these cheap signals broadcasting "highly educated, stable, financially secure mate"? For a lot of people facing thirty, the dating lingo shifts. "Great fuck" and "in love" make space for phrases like "compatibility" and "similar ambitions" angling into the lexicon. Between twenty-two and twenty-seven the scene changes from a world of lust and hookups to what a corporate strategist would probably call a "relationship plan." You walk away from dates feeling as though you'd just pitched a bank for a business loan.

But it was all different with Lisa. We knew each other and had a shared background. There wasn't going to be any compatibility scoring or soft cross-examination of one another. Neither of us gave a shit about what the other did or planned to do. We talked like normal people, like friends.

The only glitch was all the other people with us. I realized about an hour into the "date" that I should have gone out with Lisa alone, rather than as part of crowd, one of whom was Candace. I hadn't expected Candace to come. She'd been on the email invite list for months and usually couldn't make it. This time she did, and she was suddenly interested in giving me relationship advice.

"Are you trying for Lisa?" She pulled my arm as I was getting a drink.

"I don't know."

"She seems to be a really cool chick."

"She is."

"But I know your type. You like brunettes." Candace was clearly on the rocks with her boyfriend at the time, and fairly drunk. I saw where this was going.

"You're a brunette and we fucked around. That doesn't mean brunettes are my type."

Eventually our group crawled to a bar called Cutters, a meat market for lawyers, stockbrokers and gold diggers, one of the best spots in the city to watch the mating dance of the drunk and desperate. We were all well liquored by this point, and Lisa and I quickly broke off from the group, to a spot near the end of the bar, to continue that warm-up chitchat where you talk about some random topic, all the while imagining what you'll be doing to each other in a few hours.

As I leaned on the bar and listened to Lisa, I took in the room in the background, playing like one of those scenes in a Spike Lee movie where to speed up time the main character stands still in the foreground while a flurry of rapid action takes place behind him. Ten feet behind her was a button-nosed blond girl in a blue business suit smiling nervously as a ruddy, pie-faced man in a horizontally striped white-collared shirt barked a joke in her face. This Ted Kennedy character was obviously a partner or manager, taking his minions out for cocktails. Every now and again he would grab his stomach and throw his head back laughing, at which point the underling next to him, as if on cue, would break out in hysterics. Off to the left, almost the exact same scene was playing out with a cute-looking redhead in place of the blonde. In her circle, an older man who looked like Lou Dobbs was holding court.

To my immediate right a thirtyish man in khakis and a blue blazer was hovering over a short woman in a black business suit. He appeared to be laying rap on her, talking close and touching her shoulder, but the only words I could make out were "products liability" and "multinational," which he seemed to use a lot. At one point Lisa turned to order drinks and I listened to a little bit of the conversation.

"So I'll have to use the new laptop at home this weekend."

"Really? Why?"

"They're putting new carpeting on my floor. Beige."

"I like beige."

"This is a really light beige. Nearly cream."

"Cream is nice."

"To be honest, I'd rather if they'd gone with gray. It matches better with black chairs."

"See, I have brown chairs, so beige is perfect for me."

I sucked down the last bits of ice and water in my glass and scanned the rest of the room. Behind me at the bar a weather-beaten "cougar" with colored contact lenses was sucking down a menthol cigarette and making bedroom eyes at a man who looked like a tall Mickey Rooney. Down the line of the bar a dozen men were waving twenty-, fifty-, and hundred-dollar bills over the heads of the people in front of them, yelling "Hey, buddy" at the bartenders. As I turned back to Lisa a train of women in chrome-shiny lip gloss, tanning powder and ambitious push-up bras strutted past, peeling admirers off other conversations in their wake. "Hey yo! Janine!" A spiky-haired man tapped one of the girls on the shoulder as she walked by. "You want a cocktail? Maybe a wine or something? I got a guy at the bar."

I leaned back on the bar and grabbed Lisa's arm. "Bag the drinks. Let's get out of here and get some food. I'm going to hit the restroom. Meet me out front."

I was waiting outside the men's room upstairs, in a line ten people deep, when Candace appeared out of the ladies' room. "Are you coming back to the suburbs?" She brushed something off my lapel. "Some of us are catching a train."

"I don't think so."

"So you're going to fuck Lisa."

"That's up to Lisa."

"You can always come back and fuck me."

"Interesting." The minute I had someone else, Candace was up for a quick screw. All the talk of the past few months about how she couldn't do the casual sex thing because she wanted to fall in love with Mr. Stable at her firm was gone. Just like that. I was tempted to laugh and say, "If you want to get laid, why leave? There are so many great prospects here." I kissed her goodbye instead. "I think I'm going to see how Lisa plays out."

Four or five restaurants and bars later, Lisa and I were at her place. If I had to guess, we might have said maybe a dozen words before throwing *Ritual de lo Habitual* into the stereo, putting "Three Days" on repeat and tearing our clothes off in the hallway. The rest went as you'd expect. And then it went again. And again, and a couple more times, until we were both too raw to continue. On a performance scorecard, Lisa would have been a 9.4, with even the French judge giving her a 9.0.

And yes, her nipples were everything I thought they'd be. Deep brown, just wider than a silver dollar with knobs the size of the tip of your little finger. Seeing them that first night after having been in a drought for all that time was a goddamned religious experience. People live their whole lives never finding those, and there I was, a guy who'd been screwing his hand for the past two months, lucking straight into the holy grail of nipplery. And the best of it was, they weren't a surprise, more like icing.

I left her place in the morning, or maybe it was noon. Time's lost when you're sex-high and grappling with a sea change in circumstances. I'd gone from celibate to two offers, and happily sore, all within eighteen hours. And I had that date with the senior associate set up for that night. If I scored with her (a long shot normally, but not with a hot hand), then talked Candace into a finale on Sunday (I had a sense she'd fuck me as a challenge, or to reclaim her territory), that would be three in three days. I realized this might have been the start of a lucky roll, that "wave" of hook-ups I hadn't experienced in a long time. Once you have the confidence and momentum behind you, all you need to keep it going is women and alcohol in the same place. Yes, I could have tried for a hat trick. Or I could call Lisa back later and see if she was up for a repeat performance.

I argued with myself for five minutes standing in the basement of Lisa's building. *Point: Go for the Threepeat. Counterpoint: No, stick with this girl.* I've never been one for making snap decisions, but I had to call the woman I was supposed to be seeing that night to pick a restaurant for dinner. *Point: You have to try for three in a row. No one can defy the Wave. Counterpoint: Fuck the wave shit. Quantity's a shit substitute for quality.*

I thought about what it would take to get the lawyer chick and Candace into bed back-to-back and what it would actually be like if I pulled it off. I had nothing in common with the associate. We'd probably make some small talk, then have an awkward brunch, trying to think of things to say to each other. And Candace? What would she do afterward? Give me a lecture on why I shouldn't wear loafers with a business suit or that I wasn't putting enough money into my 401(k)?

Suddenly, out of nowhere, a third voice, one of absolute authority, squashed the discussion. *Are you fucking serious? Stop kidding yourself. There's no debate here.* It was right. I don't buy love at first sight or even love at first fuck, but I know this—I was hooked.

I tried to turn on my cell phone outside Lisa's building but the battery was dead. The charger wasn't in my car, so I drove until I saw a pay phone near Rittenhouse Square and called my date for that evening.

"Hi. Yeah, uh. This is P.J." Thankfully I reached her answering machine. "I had something come up. Family thing. I can't do tonight. I'll call you later." CLICK.

My next call was to Lisa. "Hey, you know. I said I was doing something tonight, but that's kind of fallen through, and I was, uh, kind of wondering if, uh—"

"Come by around eight." She laughed. "I need some time to ice myself down a little."

The Crab Orgy

LOST HIPPIES, LOST MESCALINE AND

THE ACCIDENTAL WISDOM OF FOLLOWING

Y ou lost the mescaline?!" Les snapped. "This is a serious problem."

"I understand that."

"What am I supposed to do here? We were all depending on that."

BEEP. "Shit!" The other line on my phone was blinking. "Hold on, Les."

"Hello?"

"Hi, this is Mrs. Woods, New Jersey Bar Association. You called about completing your continuing legal education classes?"

"I'm sorry, can you hold?"

CLICK. "Les?"

"Yes?"

"I gotta deal with some work crap."

"Wait! . . . Wait! . . . Can you get more?"

"Microdots? On five hours' notice?" Mescaline's the Ferrari of psychedelics. None of the jitters of strychnine-laced street acid, far longer than the four-to-five-hour arc of mushrooms and near impossible to find on the East Coast. This was real "vision" stuff—what Indians in the Southwest used to commune with the dead for thousands of years. I had a better chance of getting struck by lightning than finding another ten tablets on a Friday morning in Philadelphia. "Sure. I'll stop by my shaman's office on the way out of town."

"Fuck it. I'll deal with it." CLICK. Les slammed down the phone. He was annoyed. Not at me—just the circumstances. Another facet of his hypercompetitive personality was that Les always got what he wanted. Not overtly—Les wasn't a man of directives. Nor a manipulator. Just the sort who made his desires known, and lobbied others to support them. But this was a simple matter of research and supply and demand. There was no strong-arm solution. Les had five hours to come up with something to get ten people out of their minds for the evening. I figured he had thirty-to-one odds of succeeding, liberally.

CLICK. I flipped to the other telephone line. "Hello, Ms. Woods?"

"Yes."

"I'm so sorry to keep you waiting. I understand I'm woefully behind in my continuing legal education courses and my license has been put on 'inactive' status. I'd like to fix that . . ."

Les called back around noon. "I took care of it."

"You found mescaline?"

"No. I got three ounces of mushrooms."

"Good effort."

"I'm 'The Wolf.'"

"What?"

"'The Wolf'—Harvey Keitel? *Pulp Fiction?* I fix shit people like you fuck up."

Lisa and I got to the summer rental around seven, a standard shore home on the bay in Maryland. Harris, Les, and Bennett were already deep into a bottle of vodka, drinking with a kid wearing cargo shorts, an Allman Brothers T-shirt and cloth bracelets.

"That's the mushroom guy, right?" I pulled Les aside. "What do I owe you?"

"We'll work that out later." Les told me his name, but that's immaterial. For the night we knew him as "Drug Guy," "Mushroom Guy," or sometimes just "That Guy." He had his purpose, and he'd exhausted it the minute he exchanged the bag of fungus for money. For one reason or another, however, he decided to stick around for a few hours, take a free trip on us. And no one seemed to know how to get him to leave. We figured he'd eventually get bored and just disappear, as people on mushrooms tended to do. I've known them to grab random mountain bikes and take off on rides, wander aimlessly into fields, or, as Bennett did once, drive three hundred miles in the middle of the night to the Mall in Washington, D.C., so he could "regain his bearings." I was sure Drug Guy would find something better to do. We were in a resort town full of college students. There had to be a Phish cover band playing somewhere that evening.

I drank quickly to catch up with everyone and we brewed a spaghetti pot of mushroom tea in the kitchen. By nine we were where we wanted to be, except for one nagging annoyance—Drug Guy was still there with us. And worse than that he had the floor, permanently, it seemed.

". . . So where was I? Oh yeah. I got a felony back in '93. I was touring with this family called the Deedles. Really cool old-school NoCal hippies. They lived on a bus. Saw some awesome shows. I think I saw a 'St. Stephen' with them. We were in Denver, right, and I was with this chick and her dad called the cops and I got caught with a scale and some bags and . . . Have you ever been to Denver? The cops are fucking hell there. So anyway, this chick's dad—"

"Hold that thought." I cut him off. "I have to reload this drink."

Les was in the kitchen, making margaritas.

"Where'd you get this guy?" I asked.

"What'd you expect? Someone in a business suit?"

A fair point. Because of my fuckup, Les had no time to pull this thing off. The fact that he even managed to come up with what he had was impressive. Unfortunately, the price was a bit stiff, and I'm not talking about money. There's a code that goes along with buying things like mushrooms or weed, implicit rules and manners strictly observed but never stated out loud. One of them is never asking the person who made the drugs available to leave. It's terrible form to openly recognize the transactional nature of the relationship.

A cynic would say it's just good business—never kill a supply chain. But it's more than that. For a lot of the drug culture—the side buying into the myth that it's a way of life—there's a need to believe that all recreational users are "like minds," that somehow a group of professionals looking to lose their shit for a few hours at the beach are on the same page with an acid-fried tourhead. Generally, you engage in a few minutes of post-delivery chitchat with the courier, just to be polite. Drug Guy, however, had been hanging around for hours, abusing the furthest limits of that hospitality. And there was no sign of him exiting anytime soon.

On a lot of other chemicals a situation like this would have been irritating but tolerable. On something like psilocybin, however, which is strong enough to let you peer into a person's psyche, Drug Guy was unbearable, the sort of chemical casualty you'd see roaming a Dead Show parking lot in a *Cat in the Hat* top hat. He talked like Keanu Reeves with a Jersey accent, sliding "deewwwd" into every other sentence. All about the psychedelic experience and "exploring the mind." Only he had no insights— "spiritual" in the same cheap fashion as your aunt who's into crystals and horoscopes. Thin and derivative, a wannabe hippie born two decades late with no repertoire but the tired road stories you'd hear from any burnout.

"Let me finish making these margaritas. We'll head down to the dock." Les capped the blender and pressed the puree button.

When I got back to the living room, Drug Guy was still going strong.

". . . So this biker dude who was on tour raped a chick who was a friend of the Deedles at a Deer Creek show, right? Well, the Deedles knew this dude who knew 'the Family' . . . The Family's this bunch of chemists who make all the acid these days. It's, like, better than Owsley acid. Anyway, the dude who knew the Family found the biker at a show a month later and 'spun' him with a whole syringe of liquid acid. Just walked up to him, stuck him in the arm and shot a hundred hits into him at once. That biker dude was never the same. They say he walked around Deer Creek for days after everyone left, just talking to himself . . . "

It's impossible to drink enough listening to that gibberish. And he didn't stop. The stories just kept pouring out of him. "Cringeworthy" barely described the scene.

". . . I was living in the Redwood Forest outside San Francisco after the summer tour in 1992 and this old man was there and everybody was saying it was Jim Morrison, but I didn't believe any of that. But then, dude, I shit you not, I ran into him and he knew all the stuff only Morrison could know, like exactly the layout of Morrison's Paris apartment and that the tub in the bathroom where he supposedly died was against the wall, not in the middle of the room the way they have it in the movie. Jim Morrison is living in the Redwood Forest. It sounds nuts, I know, but . . . it's true."

The Morrison bit was all I could take. I like an absurd story as much as anyone else, but there's funny absurd and there's embarrassing absurd. Drug Guy's material wasn't the former. His stuff had the ring of fables, or religious parables, offered not so much to entertain as to advance the notion that the hippie ethos and mythic Deadhead way of life was still alive. I'd heard this routine before, and some of the bits are amusing enough that I could listen and smile, but the Jim-Morrison-is-alive thing was so atrocious I had to leave the room. Did he actually expect anyone to believe that? What was he going to bring out next? Elvis in a row home in Philadelphia?

For a second I considered fucking with him, thinking of things to say in response, something strange enough for him to adopt and run around the country telling other people:

Frank Sinatra date-raped my great-aunt in the thirties, in the Catskills. She was a cabaret singer about to sign a record deal with Warner Brothers, but she went mad afterward, like Syd Barrett. They sent her to the same hospital where they lobotomized that hysterical Kennedy daughter. It was terrible, horrible . . . My grandfather still flies into a rage every time he hears "Summer Wind."

We don't talk much about Gertrude, but I hear she's still alive, a ward of the state somewhere. Denver, I think.

I figured that'd be too much, that I'd lose control and spin a narrative so bizarre he'd know I was fucking with him. I played it safe instead. "You did not meet Jim Morrison in a redwood forest."

"Dude, I know it sounds insane, but he's there. I'm really, really serious."

"If you say so." My mind was revving way too high for the ludicrous proofs that would follow. I grabbed the vodka and headed for the dock. Les and Lisa were there already, standing on the edge, looking into the bay.

"Thanks for getting me, Les."

"I told you I was heading down here."

"I couldn't take another second of That Guy." Lisa was leaning over the edge of the dock and tapping something with her foot.

"Check it out. Those are crabs." Les waved his hand across the bay. Tide was low and it was mating season. What had looked like ripples of water as I walked across the dock were actually thousands of horseshoe crabs. They were each about a foot wide, round and flat, with these long antennae sticking out of their asses. The mass of them appeared to be writhing up and down in the current, but as I looked closer I saw they were all crawling on top of one another in some primordial mating orgy. "The females are the big ones, I think. They lay eggs in the sand and the males grab onto their shells and inseminate them."

"An arachnid circle jerk. Just what I want to see right now." Mushrooms are a visual high. Whatever you think immediately becomes a movie in the mind. I saw an endless horizon of these slimy, Frisbee-like creatures spewing crab semen all over each other.

Lisa pushed one of the crabs with her toe and a whole row of them moved. "It's like they're connected in trains, a female at the front with a bunch of males trailing."

"What was Drug Guy talking about when you left?" Les was unhooking a canoe from the dock, to pull it from atop the crab orgy.

"Meeting Jim Morrison in a redwood forest."

"Fuck you."

"I'm serious. Were you there for that, Lisa?"

"I came down with Les. I couldn't handle the 'Deedles' story. I felt like I was in a Cheech and Chong movie."

"The worst one." Les leaned over the edge of the dock, grasping for a paddle half hanging out of the canoe.

"Which one is that?" I lit a cigarette.

"Good point."

"Do you think he really believes that stuff he was saying?" Lisa asked.

"I don't know if he believes it, but I think he believes *in* it." Les held on to a piling and grasped again for the canoe's tether. "Shit. Can you hold this drink?" He handed his margarita to Lisa.

"He's a 'movement' person." Lisa grabbed the canoe tether Les was handing to her. "They find things to follow."

As I stood on the dock looking over the bay I realized why Drug Guy, even though he was harmless, was so aggravating. In my case, at least, it had a lot more to do with me than him. He reminded me of so many of the lawyers I ran into on the civil cases I handled—the ones who fancied wire-rimmed glasses, adopted their middle names as their primary monikers, and started using their first name as an initial. All the ones who used Latin phrases in conversation or words like "sanguine" instead of "certain." Just standing there, I could visualize so many of them, the way they talked and wrote in their letters:

This is F. Murray Bolemonk, Esquire, counsel to Cucker Toilets and their parent company, Grand Royale Sanitation Ceramics. I am sanguine we can reach an agreement in this

litigation because if not, you have considerable exposure, as
the issue at hand is clearly res judicata in my client's favor.

It wasn't a stretch to imagine Drug Guy in a pin-striped suit, acting the same way. It'd probably take him a few months, maybe a correspondent's course in business law, but he could get the shtick down pretty quick. In a big enough office, a good follower could play lawyer for months before anyone realized he didn't have a degree. ("Did you hire that guy, Alexander?" "I thought you did, Reginald.")

"Why do so many people have to be joiners? You know, like those kids who protest shit all the time or religious nuts. What is that? Is it like a mental illness or something?"

"It makes things easier." Les struggled to pull the canoe onto the dock. "Somebody else has the wheel."

He was right. There's an accidental wisdom in following. Letting something else define you narrows the decisions you have to make. It gives you parameters, a track to follow and a holiday from all the angst that comes with carving your own path. If comfort's the goal, there aren't many better decisions. And that's what pissed me off about Drug Guy so much. It wasn't that he was a walking stereotype, that his kind gave drug use a bad name or that he didn't have an original thought in his head. What bothered me was the crazy bastard actually seemed content in his blind obedience, as if he knew that trying to navigate for yourself would only drive you mad, that "selling out" was wildly underrated. I'd tried that thinking with law school, assuming the career would define me, but found the further I got into it, the more alienated from it I became. If an idiot like him could be so happy, why couldn't I just "join" something, shut off my head and be content?

"So if I gave you the option, Les, you'd rather just follow a template?"

He never had a chance to answer. A horrible cracking noise filled the night air as the piling Les had been holding on to splintered and he tumbled into the bay. "Shit! Shit!" He thrashed in the water and a *BANG! BANG!* sound resonated off the dock as the boat slammed against it. I looked over the edge and saw Les lying in the muck, among hundreds of crabs and the slurry of embryonic fluids and excrement they'd been spewing into the water—the last place anyone in our mind-set wanted to be. "Oh God. I'm soaked in this shit. Fuck! Motherfucker!" He staggered back to the dock, soaked in ooze, kicking the crabs as they scurried around his ankles.

"What happened?" Harris came running down to the dock. "What was that banging?"

"I just fell into a crab orgy." Les walked to the outside shower. "Somebody needs to pour me a *huge* drink. Now."

"Damn. They're awfully randy." Harris looked over the edge. "They might have gotten Les pregnant." He pushed a row of the crabs with one of the splinters from the dock.

"What's the cross between a crab and a human?" Lisa laughed.

"A lobster." I saw Drug Guy coming down from the house out of the corner of my eye. "Soft shell, I think."

"I'd help him deliver the baby." Harris mimicked a doctor spreading a woman's legs to birth an infant. " 'Wider, Les. You're dilating. It looks like twins.' "

"If he keeps it." I picked up the bottle of vodka from the dock and poured myself a glass.

"Oh, I hope he doesn't abort. It's murder!"

"Dude! Dude!" Drug Guy bounced out of the dark a moment later and ran to the end of the dock. "Look at all those things running around on top of one another!" I could sense the gears running in his head. Was he going to quote "Eyes of the World"? Maybe a line from William S. Burroughs? "It's like an evolutionary dance, you know? Instinctual."

"Like sorority girls and disco."

"What?"

"Did I say something?" I realized I was drinking the vodka neat at that point. It didn't bother me, but it probably should have. You have to be careful boozing on a psychedelic. Everything tastes good and none of it affects you until the drug fades and the liquor slams you like a speeding tanker truck T-boning a Prius.

"Dude, they're all running around after each other, like, looking for some connection to latch onto. The dance of life, man."

"I guess. I have to go inside. Get some ice."

Marshal?

Who is Marshal?" My assistant was standing in the doorway, holding one of my time sheets.

"Huh?" I pulled the phone away from my face and scrambled to close the picture of the Latin girl pouring milk across her breasts. The monitor was turned toward me, but I'd learned the hard way that whoever was in the doorway could see what was on my screen in the reflection from the window behind my chair. "Hold on a second, Harris." I held my hand over the telephone.

"I don't remember any 'Marshal' in your cases, but that name is on your time sheets." She'd been entering client code numbers into the sheets for me, what thousands of assistants do every day in law firms across the country. I'd write every task I performed during the day into a tablet, much like a factory worker's time card, with columns for the client name, a description of the work done, and how long it took. That was how I kept the history of my every day in the office, broken down into six-minute increments. When I was done filling one in, I'd give it to my secretary and she'd enter the client numbers. Then it went upstairs, to accounting, to be turned into a "pre-bill." The pre-bill would then come downstairs so the partners who ran my department could review it, edit it, and then turn it into a final invoice.

I was barely a few months into my new job and already I knew, the move was a disaster. My search for a civil litigation gig had taken longer than I expected, and in my haste to be done with it, I signed on with Jensen, Pershing & Quinn, a larger established regional firm. It wasn't a great outfit, not one of the top-tier joints, but it had a decent enough general reputation. My friends in the business, however, had a different view. They warned me I was making a huge mistake by switching from a small shop getting hands-on experience in high-end work to one of the larger "mills."

"It's all about billable hours—just bill, bill, bill. They'll bleed every hour out of your carcass and throw it on the side of the road when they're done with you."

"Whatever," I'd laugh. They said that about every firm. There wasn't one I'd interviewed with or applied to over the prior months that somebody hadn't defined as a "sweatshop" or "hellhole." The people at JP&Q seemed nice enough, I had a friend who worked there, and the firm seemed to be looking for business. At the time I thought I could bring in some clients through a few connections. All things considered, the place seemed like a decent fit, at least for the moment. I was making the switch you were supposed to, aiming for a practice area with a better long-term upside. I couldn't stay in Sean O'Malley's firm any longer, doing criminal work and commercial litigation at the same time. The bigger firms with the rising salaries didn't look at generalists from small shops, assuming you either knew too much or too little, that you wouldn't fit into the culture and that they couldn't pitch you to clients as a "specialist," which justified a high hourly rate. After a slew of unmemorable interviews with various firms, I just wanted to be done with the process. I wasn't impressed with JP&Q, but at the time, getting into any decent civil firm seemed more important than waiting for a perfect fit. When they offered, I accepted.

"Give me a second with this call." I smiled at my secretary. Normally I'd jump when she asked for something. You can never be nice enough to your assistant. If they don't like you, they can sabotage you in thousands of ways. But not this time. It was Friday morning. I didn't feel like doing anything for anyone, and Harris was telling me a story about how he'd been taking photographs of himself and some intern at his job having sex in his office.

"I had her fingering herself on the desk." I heard Harris on the other end of the phone. "The chick was fucking insane." His tale was far too entertaining to pass up.

"I'll come by your desk as soon as I'm done with this," I promised my assistant.

Harris's story was amusing (though not as good as the photos), but it was only half the reason I didn't want to answer my assistant's question. I felt embarrassed about everything having to do with "Marshal." Just thinking about that sordid, cheesy garbage kicked up this awful sense of dread that I'd made a horrible and irreversible career mistake. Just a few months before, I'd taken a call from the *New York Times* regarding a not guilty verdict Sean won in a massive trial followed by the national media. I'd worked against top-shelf prosecutors and been in meetings with CEOs quoted in the *Wall Street Journal.* I'd been in the orbit of some of the best lawyers in the country and working on cases involving staggering amounts of money and wild, scandalous allegations and now here I was, a few dollars richer, roped into lowball chicanery of the dullest order. Just hearing the word "Marshal" made me feel like a creep.

JP&Q hadn't wasted any time living up to the "bill, bill, bill" stereotype painted by my colleagues who'd warned me about the place. I was there maybe a month when Larry Robinson, a pathologically ambitious partner, took over my group. His office was next to mine and we wound up talking a fair amount. Larry was an odd mix—ruthless, but a regular guy. Nothing like the effete, snippy sorts you usually ran into in the litigation business. You could imagine him slurring over Bushmills and Guiness in a pub as easily as you would sipping a cabernet in the Fountain Room at the Four Seasons. He seemed to have no intellectual interest in the field at all. It was just a license, to be liquidated to as much cash as possible. And Larry was brutally honest about the way he viewed the career.

"You want to know how you make money at this?" he told me point-blank a few days after I'd started. "Well, it isn't by being some great fucking lawyer." He had made partner in six years, a meteoric rise almost unheard of in any firm today. They couldn't not make him partner. He brought in more clients than most of the senior partners, enough that the firm had to push an older partner out of my group and give it to him. And everybody knew that was just a stepping-stone. Larry was the sort of animal who'd eventually run the firm. Or start his own. He wasn't working for anybody but himself. "I got ahead because I brought in business," I remember him deadpanning. "That's all that matters."

A lot of lawyers would argue with Larry. They'd say there's still a place at the top for the best legal minds, and in a hypertechnical sense, they would be correct. If you're the Einstein or Mozart of your specialty, there's always space at the summit. For everyone else, however, law's a lace-curtain version of the accounting and consulting industries, a pyramid where the few rainmakers sit at the top and the masses of fungible labor toil underneath, most of them maximizing billable hours for canned, cookie-cutter work, a pack of factory schleps on a French-cuffed assembly line. In that world it isn't about winning or losing. It's about getting paid. Billable hours aren't important—they're everything, which Larry made abundantly clear at every department meeting:

"I want everyone sending regular status update letters to clients. Tell them something about their cases. I know those are small-time entries, but they add up." "Keep your time sheet next to you when you read the mail. Every letter's a '.1' or '.2.' Those '.1s' and '.2s' add up at the end of the month." "Bill every minute you can. Bill the time you were thinking about the case in the shower. Every moment you're thinking about the case is billable time."

Once a week the department would get together and Larry or his lieutenant, Charles Haskell, would analyze the hours billed up to that point in the month. Underperformers got the same speech every week. "We need you to bill as close as you can to two hundred hours a month. If you want a bonus, we expect that effort." If someone complained, the response was always the same—"If you don't like billing your time, go to a plaintiffs' firm."

2,400 hours a year. Sounds innocent enough, right? Those are just numbers to the layman, so let me explain what "2,400 hours" means. Assuming two weeks' vacation, 2,400 hours a year translates to 48 billable hours a week, or 9.6 hours per workday. If you spent 12 hours a day in the office—from 9 A.M. until 9 P.M.—and took one hour for lunch, you would have to actually work—*providing a real billable benefit to your client*—53 minutes of each of the remaining 11 hours. This allows you 7 minutes of every hour to:

1. Surf the Internet
2. Talk to coworkers
3. Use the bathroom
4. Get coffee
5. Take and make personal phone calls
6. Balance your checkbook
7. Check your investments
8. Run to the café downstairs to get a Diet Coke
9. Send and receive personal emails
10. Actually read the lame jokes people send you

If you did what most lawyers do—scan the news online every forty-five minutes and read the legal trade paper for half an hour in the morning—you'd have already wasted close to half of your allotted free time for the day.* At the time, I knew lawyers billing 200–230 hours a *month,* and there were legends circulating about people billing 2,700 to 3,000 hours a year at some firms. I could only assume these were the lawyers who didn't have the Internet on their computers and kept piss pots next to their desks.

Transitioning to this world wasn't easy for me. In criminal defense winning had been everything. Here, perpetuating the

---

*A study juxtaposing a firm's Internet computer logs against lawyers' bills would yield astounding results.

Dance was the goal. It seemed like management's aim was to give an associate 75 percent of the caseload he needed to comfortably reach his billing goals, forcing him to perform every conceivable billable task, necessary or not, in each of the cases in his inventory. It wasn't uncommon for lawyers to run around near the end of the month asking other lawyers for work to make their hourly quotas. My paralegal asked me for busywork all the time.

"Give me something. I need some hours." She'd smile.

"Here." I'd laugh and pull some old transcripts of depositions from a pile of paper on my desk. "Summarize these and write memos to the file."

Everybody fought to be assigned to those huge cases where a lawyer could feast on endless taskwork. Getting control of a case involving financial issues, where you'd have boxes and boxes of accounting or business records to analyze, was striking gold. As one partner confided to me during a firm cocktail party, "There's rarely anything important in those boxes. But you're paid to be sure. You can bill a bunch of hours for reading the stuff and then go play golf. Everybody does that, at every firm."

The system drove me insane at first. Unless you're a congenital cipher, the idea of creating nothing but bills with your days is a hellish proposition. But after a while I couldn't help but look at the situation pragmatically. What else could I do? I told myself I was being immature. Nobody gets paid to have fun, and who was I to demand some existential gratification from my job? If I wanted that I should have become a social worker.

Rationalizations are simple, and what they didn't alleviate was always curable with the usual medications. It's easy to forget the most annoying day after the endorphin rush of an hour at the gym, two stiff Grand Marniers, and a few draws on a joint. And there was one really easy month in the summer when a friend gave me thirty Xanax tablets. That made *all* the aggravation go away. I'd wander through the halls grinning as though I were meandering around the infield at a concert. People would run past, talking about their deadlines, rushing legal papers from office to office and I'd just smile, smile, smile.

Unfortunately, there are only so many sedatives and rationalizations, and even my cynicism had its limits. Where I'd once thought I could do anything for a check, these horrible nagging questions started rolling through my head. Was this going to be my legacy? Piles of pointless paper? After a couple months in the firm, if I were keeping time sheets covering every moment of the work day, they'd have included these entries:

CLIENT CODE	TIME	DESCRIPTION
Prof. Advancement	.9	Research articles regarding alternative careers for lawyers/ stare out window drinking coffee
Family	4	Compare Expedia/Priceline/ Travelocity pkgs. for trip to Miami with girlfriend
Financial Planning	5	Analyze emails from broker friend/ read Yahoo! finance blurbs re: Global Crossing trading price
Prof. Advancement	3	Google search re: sales and marketing opportunities for ex-lawyers
Networking	1.2	Exchange emails with RFD, CHJ, KLZ, MNS, KKT, BWS, NPL re: happy hour/exchange "Art Model" and "Sisters" slide shows with CDS, CFK, RTD, VPL, FKC, ALW, RAA, MFK/cut and paste joke tribute to Hervé Villechaize into email and distribute to YMD, WHG, KLJ, PPL/conversation with BCG re: new paralegal's breasts

CLIENT CODE	TIME	DESCRIPTION
Misc.	3	Discuss impact of the Melvins on modern hard rock with IT manager
Admin.	2	Open "Temporary Internet Files" folder/delete record of all Internet sites visited re: alternative careers for lawyers

Being on the billing treadmill was bad enough, but that wasn't the worst part of the job. The worst part of it was the constant pressure to battle through the weakest cases—the ones any smart business mind would immediately settle—to keep the stream of billable tasks rolling. The first time I considered resigning was when I was forced to try an absolutely hopeless arbitration in which we were suggesting a seventy-year-old grandfather committed or was involved in a conspiracy to commit arson to collect on an insurance policy.

"I can't try this case." I complained. "There's no way I can win that."

"Which case is that?" Larry asked me.

"The one where we're alleging a seventy-year-old man is guilty of arson and he's countersuing. There's no evidence of that anywhere in the case."

"So?"

"He's an old man, and according to the records in the file, he's worth a ton of money. He didn't need to stage a fire. We'll get killed in front of a jury."

"It's in arbitration."

"We'll get killed in arbitration. I can settle it for peanuts if we do it now."

"Yeah, the thing is, we need to look tough. You want to look like you'll go to the wall for these clients. Just avoid getting hit with any punitive damages award."

I tried the case and was beaten like a rented mule. When I accused the elderly man of arson, the panel of arbitrators groaned and shook their heads in disgust. My client wound up paying close to twice what I could have settled for, plus thousands of dollars in legal fees.

After the hearing, the plaintiff's lawyer caught me outside the courthouse. "I know you didn't want to do this," he told me as we stood on the steps. "That was clear."

"Tell the old man it wasn't personal." I laughed. I'd have put my résumé on the market right then and there, but I hadn't been at JP&Q long enough to quit and didn't want to look like a job jumper.

On top of all that, the "Marshal" thing was adding insult to injury, the final reminder that as soon as my year in this place was up, I was gone, like a bullet, to any other job. I was just sitting at my desk one afternoon when Charles appeared in my doorway, wearing his usual Cheshire cat grin.

"We're doing an informal billing seminar in the conference room in an hour. We'd like everyone to go."

"Billing seminar? For what?" I asked.

"To teach everybody what words to use to avoid having clients question invoices."

"Do I really need to do that?"

"Come on. There are a couple of points everyone needs to hear."

He was right about the need for the meeting. Any hourly lawyer will tell you, knowing how to bill is one of the most important skills in modern law, and there's an art to it. Litigation is grossly overpriced and clients have known for years that lawyers pad bills and work cases in the most inefficient manner possible. They don't pay lawyers' invoices the way you or I would a gas bill. Many of them challenge their bills, demanding discounts for every suspect entry. The goal in client billing is maximizing not just hours billed but "realization," the percentage of the bill a client eventually agrees to pay. It's a tricky game of semantics—carefully crafting just the right language and just the right structure of charges in the invoice so a client can't or won't question it.

"I'm kind of busy, Charles."

"It'll only take a couple minutes."

"Fine."

I dragged myself to the meeting late and stood by the door, catching the very end of the presentation:

". . . So break up your tasks as much as possible. Ten small, discrete time entries won't be scrutinized the same way one huge five-hour block with a dozen tasks listed under it will be. And it goes without saying that if you bill in whole-hour increments like 1.0 or 2.0, your time looks estimated, which raises flags. And never use terms like 'compile' or 'organize.' Clients consider that secretary's work and balk at paying lawyer's fees for it."

"What word do you use?" one associate sitting near me asked another.

"Maybe 'categorize,'" the other one answered him.

"How about 'arrange'?"

Jesus Christ. It's come to this? This is why I went to law school? How much seedier was this job going to get? I was tempted to ask if anyone had a pocket thesaurus handy, or suggest we use German, or maybe Portuguese. No client would understand that. *What's Portuguese for "organize"? Anybody?*

Of all the reasons people hate lawyers, this sort of sneakiness is the biggest. At that point in my career, I'd already been involved in defending alleged embezzlers, tax cheats and money launderers, and none of that bothered me. Even the guilty in those situations had some honor. They were taking a risk and if they got away with it there was a capitalist argument to be made that they deserved the fruits of their efforts. Here, the blind spots and loopholes in the system all but guaranteed that no one would ever catch this sort of lowball gamesmanship. It reminded me of those people in college who'd sneak upstairs during parties and take a bunch of your CDs while everyone was too loaded to pay attention.

I never billed the 2,400 hours a year management wanted, but I did manage to crank out more than 180 a month, and I even used the words they wanted me to, which was why my secretary was asking me about "Marshal" that morning.

"Sorry. I had to take that call." I came up behind her at her desk. The image of Harris taking amateur porn shots of some college girl bending over his credenza was still filling my head. "What were you asking before?"

"I asked who 'Marshal' was. It doesn't make any sense."

"That's the wrong question."

"What do you mean?" She sipped her coffee and gave me a puzzled look.

"See this entry right here? '.8 hours—Marshal case citations for brief'? Marshal's a verb."

"I've never heard it used that way before. What does it mean?"

"It means 'to compile,' 'to organize.'"

I didn't like it, but hey, *caveat emptor*. This was the reality of the legal profession. Hours weren't a shitty component of the game—they *were* the game, the only way anyone kept score. This was commerce, not the clergy. Drown the moral pangs at the bar.

The Train Wreck Defense

YOU'LL NEVER KNOW UNLESS YOU TRY

Do you really need that much coffee?" Martin flipped through the papers on his lap.

"I can't think properly without it."

"We've already stopped twice."

"I feel like ass. Those Yuenglings from last night are still with me."

"That's why I don't drink beer, particularly that sweet shit."

"Why is it that I can drink three huge scotches and feel fine, but five beers wreck me?" I threw the car in park in front of the 7-Eleven. "I'm just going to run in and get one more small coffee. This mini-mart stuff doesn't have any fucking caffeine in it."

"Whatever it takes." Martin scratched his chin and stared at the papers.

I blamed the knots in my stomach on the beers, but they were the least of my problems. I was nervous, more than I'd ever been before heading to a court appearance. If you're in law long enough, one of your friends will eventually rope you into doing some kind of legal work for them. Usually it's dry, simple shit—looking over a lease or a will or helping someone push through an insurance claim. Every now and again, though, a friend needs some real help, to get out of a trickier jam.

Representing a buddy's a great deal for him. He gets free services and more personal attention to his case than he'd ever receive from the best hourly hack. For you, however, it's not so good. Losing's always annoying, but in the bigger picture, who really cares if the faceless "Inc." you represent at work gets whacked in court? The firm gets its hourly fees paid either way. And a corporation won't be out with you for drinks every weekend, a constant reminder that when somebody needed you and for once the job actually mattered, you crapped out.

For reasons that now seem like doomed idiocy, at the time I felt the only way to deal with nerves in court was by pouring accelerant onto them. Speed brings clarity, and if you hit that perfect zone where the tongue and the mind are cranking off each other, ratcheting up to higher revolutions with every passing thought, you can string together some amazing arguments. Run into court ripped on forty ounces of black coffee and rattle off at the judge like a Thompson gun. You might not win every court appearance, but at least you'd get off all the points you wanted to make.

And that day, Martin and I needed any help we could get. He had no defense under the law; all I could do was beg and hope there was some quirk in the statutes I'd missed in my research and that a benevolent judge would use it to our advantage.

Martin had gotten popped for a DUI on vacation in Arizona six months before. A total setup—he'd hardly moved his rental car from the front of a bar when the cops nailed him. They'd been watching the place, probably chalking his tires to determine how many hours he'd been there. The police report was filled with the generic "probable cause" justifications for pulling him over—"Vehicle's tire crossed into yellow line" . . . "Driver observed veering from right to left prior to crossing line." Martin got a local lawyer, took care of the hearing a few weeks later, paid a fine and promised the court he'd do an Alcoholics Anonymous program. Other than a spike in his future car insurance rates, he figured the whole thing was behind him.

Then his home state sent him papers saying it was moving to suspend his license for a year.

"What the hell is this?" He called me, upset, one day. "I paid a lawyer. I paid my fine. What the fuck?"

"All the states report that stuff to one another. You get nailed for a DUI anywhere and that state reports it to your home state and your home state does what it would have done if you'd gotten busted there."

"What are the defenses?"

"I don't think there are any."

"This is bullshit. I need to use my car. I can't commute on the train. My lease still has half a year on it . . . I can't afford to move closer to the office and pay for two places at the same time. What the hell do I do?"

"We start stalling."

I asked for as many continuances of his hearing as I could and tried to massage the prosecutor over the course of a few phone calls. "This guy's not a bad egg." I painted Martin as the usual harmless kid who'd had one too many whiskeys on holiday. "He was letting off some steam on vacation. He's got no record. Nothing."

"My hands are tied. It's a mandatory penalty." The prosecutor was cool about the whole thing. "But so you know, I'm not going to press hard. I don't have to. Your guy pled no contest in Arizona, so he automatically loses his license here. I don't have to say anything at the hearing except 'Your honor, here's the law.'"

I couldn't ask for more out of the prosecutor. We could have wound up with a Boy Scout, the sort who'd vow to throw the book at Martin and scold me about the "severity of the crime." Over the years, I've worked with a handful of prosecutors. Some are pragmatic sorts, quick to offer a plea to avoid work. Others are hyper-competitive or politically ambitious. They'll play hard and scare you, but in the end they'll usually offer a plea to protect their win-loss record. Every once in a while, however, you'd stumble into a zealot, the kind who could turn an easy little court appearance into the Scopes Monkey Trial—a vigilante who'd grandstand with abandon and vilify your client for the sheer glee of hearing himself roar. Thankfully, most are too drained by the bureaucracy of the public sphere to care much about a rinky-dink hearing like ours.

"I'm probably going to say a lot of strange shit today. We're fishing here. I have to see if the judge can do something for us that I don't know about." I was rambling to Martin, thinking out loud and pouring the coffee down my throat. "Just follow my lead, okay?"

"That's the strategy? That sounds like a train wreck."

"Exactly." That was the plan—slam a bunch of points into a judge's head and see what happens.

Making a "train wreck" argument sounds easy but it's actually a nuanced thing, with dozens of constantly moving parts. On one hand it's vaudeville, a sloppy shuck-and-jive act—arguing your client's impossible position, charming the court, and praying it proposes a compromise that exists in common practice but nowhere in the law books. On the other hand, it's surgery, measuring the absurdity of your arguments to ensure you're showing just the right amount of passion to gain sympathy from the judge without insulting the process. If you can pull off those first two elements, all you have to do is dance through the shrapnel of the senseless debate you've created and grab the best settlement offer when it comes. You'll never "win" with the strategy, but in these conditions, success isn't about winning; it's about minimizing the degree of loss. Breaking even is a home run.

The hardest part is actually standing in court and delivering a futile argument to an often merciless judge. It's one thing to submit hopeless papers. Lawyers do that every day. Pitching that garbage in a courtroom involves a much deeper level of risk and probable public shame. The process is a lot like hitting on an attractive woman in a bar, getting over the threshold fear of rejection that keeps so many of us standing in the corner, drinking and talking about how much we'd like to meet some cute girl ten feet away, but never mustering the guts to make a move on her.

And if I had to guess where I first learned the "train wreck" strategy, it would be a bar, and a scene a lot like that, before I'd even become a lawyer. It was New York City, New Year's Eve, 1995. I was with Bennett and Harris. We were supposed to be at a club some college buddies had rented for a private party, as some group of our friends seemed to do every year. Unfortunately, this one turned out to be a scam. A couple of grifters had tricked the organizer into renting a place that didn't exist. All the people who'd bought tickets and went to the address of the "nightclub" found an empty warehouse. The crowd of victims pulling up in cabs was angry and the temperature outside was in the single digits. Everyone quickly piled into an already cramped tavern a block away, packing the place with bodies.

Luckily, Harris, Bennett and I had pre-binged, knocking off a bottle of Beam's Choice at Bennett's apartment before we headed out for the evening. You could never drink enough before going to one of those New Year's parties. With all the pushing and shoving required just to reach the bar, you needed to be loaded before you even stepped out for the night. Bennett got himself so drunk in advance that he fell down when the subway train braked at the first stop, flailing backward and almost taking out a pile of people standing behind him like a row of dominoes. By the time we got into the bar we were freezing, thirsty, and desperate. Running out of liquor on the upswing of a fresh whiskey drunk might as well be a terminal illness in the moment.

"Those idiots. I can't believe they got taken like that," Bennett complained about the organizers of the party.

"They didn't get taken." I threw back a shooter of Maker's Mark. "We did. It was our money."

"We need more booze. These aren't going to do it." Harris was shaking his head over a collection of empty shot glasses on the tiny bar table between us.

"I'm not going back for more." I'd gotten the first round and the trips back-and-forth through the crowd to bring back all those drinks from the bar had been exhausting. On the last one somebody pushed me and I spilled Guinness on a brown-haired girl in an evening dress standing next to our table.

"Sorry about that. Somebody shoved me."

"Have enough drinks there?" She glared at me.

"What a bitch," I snapped to Bennett, who'd watched the exchange.

"Excuse me?" She turned back.

"I didn't say anything."

"Asshole," I heard her sneer as I turned back to Bennett.

"I need some action." Harris thrust his hips back and forth, bumping into the table and spilling some of our liquor. "I'm really worked up—"

"Hey! Hey! Careful with the drinks." Bennett grabbed the table to stop it from shaking.

"I can't help it," Harris barked across the table. "I'm so horny. I've been watching so much tard porn lately."

"Tell me that exists," I reached for a napkin to wipe off the liquor he'd caused me to spit into my hand.

"It's like snuff films. You can't buy it at a regular store. I have a friend who gets it for me."

"Fuck. Now I have the hiccups." Bennett choked trying to laugh and exhale from his cigarette.

"I'm serious," Harris deadpanned.

"I'm still into the elderly stuff," I said, the whiskey I'd coughed up still burning my nose.

"Oh, tard porn is much better. They get so randy." Harris stuck out his tongue, bit it and started thrusting his hips again, slamming into the table. "It gets me excited just thinking about it. You guys want to make a circle around me so I can work one out here?"

"Aim for Bennett's glass. He likes White Russians."

"Here, give me it." Harris leaned in to grab Bennett's glass, pretending to unbuckle his pants at the same time.

"Careful!" As his arm toppled drinks across the table, I jumped backward, smack into the same brown-haired girl again.

"Can you watch where you're walking?" She glared.

"Sorry." I coughed. "I really am."

"We need a glass of Jägermeister. You could make a 'Smoker's

Phlegm' with the money shot,"* Martin barked in the background as the girl stared knives at me.

"My aim's terrible," Harris went on. "I have a deviated urethra."

"Hollywood-style?" Bennett asked. "Shooting too much coke into your dick?"

"It's genetic. My grandmother had one."

After what felt like forever, the girl finally blinked. "Tell your friends to keep the jokes coming. Hysterical stuff, really. Retard sex . . . jerking off . . . Hysterical!"

"Did anyone ask you to listen?"

"I can't help it. I'm drawn to your amazing wit."

Things went on like this for an hour or so. We'd throw back shots and joke and every now and again Harris, Bennett or I would bump into someone in the group of girls next to us and a short exchange of insults would erupt.

Sometime around 1 A.M. I went to the bar to pick up a round. The brown-haired girl appeared to my right, unraveling a handful of bills to order drinks for her friends. "Oh great," she snarled when we made eye contact.

"What's your problem?"

"My problem? I have a low threshold for dickheads."

"Let's start this over, okay? It's New Year's Eve and—" *Wait.* I thought to myself. *Why talk?* There was no point in speaking to her. She was one of those people who used language as a wall, with no responses but cheap snark. Bitter, probably burned in a relationship and still working through the man-hating phase. Hand on her hip, lips pursed, and her eyes rolling—every one of the girl's outward indicators screamed contempt. *Whatever.* I was loaded, she was good-looking enough and it was Manhattan, one hour into the new year. I grabbed the girl's shoulders, pulled her against me and started kissing her. Half of me was bracing for a slap, maybe some shouting and a bouncer grabbing

---

*"Smoker's Phlegm"—One shot of chilled Jägermeister topped with the contents of one single-serve packet of mayonnaise. Or Miracle Whip.

my collar. It never came, and she made no effort to break off the embrace.

"I guess you like dickheads after all."

"Don't."

"What?"

"Just don't."

"You want to go somewhere?"

"Yes, before I change my mind."

I walked back to the table and placed the drinks we'd ordered in front of Bennett. "I'm leaving."

"With *her*?" he whispered in my ear.

"Might as well see where it goes. I can't figure it out either." And I still can't. If we'd kept talking she'd have probably thrown a drink on me, but there was something about physically getting in her face that made all the difference.

And years later, that's exactly what Martin and I were going to do in court to make his hopeless defense. We didn't have to make an oral argument that morning. We could have let the judge decide the issue on the papers. He would have read them, and without the benefit of seeing Martin and hearing our position, he'd feel nothing and just follow the law. But there, with us in front of him, the person who'd suffer the punishment staring him in the eye, maybe he'd find some way to do us a favor. The only issue was how we'd ask for it. Begging in court's a lot more than just saying "please."

There are two methods to arguing in court. You can tell the judge what to think or you can wait for him to speak first and try to align your argument with his views. And if you haven't been in front of him before, you don't know which to use until the moment he's sitting above you. Some like to take control and frame the issues, asking questions. Some don't read anything and want to be spoon-fed all the facts and law. By formal training and native disposition, I'm defense-oriented. Nothing makes me happier than hearing a judge say, "I've read your arguments and have a few questions," at the outset of a hearing. It's easy to react to a judge's lead and give him what he wants to hear.

In Martin's hearing I was the ignorant party, or at least I hoped that was the case. The issue was simple and the judge had to have seen it before. My job was to draw him into a conversation and give him some reason to take mercy on Martin. No judge decides a certain type of claim exactly the same way every time. They always have some leeway, even with a mandatory sentence. I just had to get him into a sympathetic frame of mind.

"Sympathy, sympathy, sympathy . . . What would get us sympathy?" I was talking to myself, the way I always did before hearings.

"Sympathy? What are you saying?"

"You might have to pretend you're an alcoholic, getting treatment."

"What?"

"Maybe just a really bad binge drinker."

"Why?"

"We need people to like you."

"How is that supposed to—"

"Wait. Hold that thought. I like this song." I turned up an old Dead bootleg playing on the stereo. "This tune has always confused me. You think it's about the Bible, you know? 'Greatest Story Ever Told'? But the chorus makes no sense."

"What the fuck are you talking about?" Martin stared at me.

"You know the chorus, where Bobby sings, 'The one thing we need is a left-handed monkey wrench'? What does that have to do with the rest of the song? What the hell is a left-handed monkey wrench?"

"You just sang to me."

"I needed to give you the melody."

I had no doubt Martin was running over train schedules in his mind, contemplating how he'd commute to work after I made an ass out of both of us and the judge yanked his license. And possibly mine, on principle.

There was no explaining the mechanisms in my head. Our approach was scattershot on the surface and my mind was all over the place, but there was a design to all of it. Have you ever wished that every important test or interview could be held on the fly? That instead of having to prepare and think about the thing and psych yourself out, somebody would just grab you by surprise and throw you in the process with nothing to rely on but your wits? That sudden chaotic demands and having to think in the moment are miles more comfortable than plotting and planning to execute as though you're working off a playbook? That it's all so much easier when you're off the cuff and *loose*?

"Dammit." I hooked the truck sideways across a median.

"What are you doing?"

"That was the courthouse, behind us. I missed it."

"Have you been in this court before?"

"They're all the same. It'll be full of lots of wooden banisters and seats. You've seen *To Kill a Mockingbird*? Like the courtroom in that movie."

"I'm not sure that's the best description."

"Well, there probably won't be any people in seersucker here."

"Right . . . And that would make me who, Boo Riley?"

"*Radley*. Boo *Radley*. And no. You'd be the sharecropper who gets acquitted. Can you hand me my cell?"

"Is it necessary for me to be in the room with you?"

"Hold this for a second." I handed him the coffee and flipped open my cell phone. "I can't steer with my knee. This suit's so slippery."

"I'd rather not talk when we're in there. Can you work that?"

"Of course. I'll do all the talk— Hold on a second, Martin. Janet? Janet? Yeah, hi. You know I won't be in today, right? Good. Good. Just checking. Oh, thank you. I'll be fine. See you tomorrow."

"Who'll be fine?"

"I told my secretary I was getting a root canal." Technically, I wasn't supposed to practice any law outside what I was doing for JP&Q at the time. Something about them being liable for any malpractice I committed. It was probably bullshit, a tactic to force associates to give the firm a cut of any clients they cultivated. "Where were we?"

"You were saying how I wouldn't have to answer questions."

"Well, the judge might ask you a question, but you won't have to *testify*."

"What's the difference?"

"The 'oath' thing. But you can't lie anyway. You already pled yourself into a hole. We're making an equity argument."

"Equity? I thought you said we didn't have an argument?"

"Equity's what you argue when you don't have anything else, crying for mercy." I noticed the courthouse passing on my left. "Shit, I missed the entrance again." We pulled a three-point turn in a driveway and drove back up the street.

"Are you okay?" Martin turned down the stereo.

"I'm fine." The coffee was catching up with me and creating that horrible pressure anyone familiar with caffeine's effect on the intestines understands. "I just need a men's room, quickly."

"So equity can overrule the law?"

"Sure." If the judge and the opponents don't understand the issues, sometimes the court will rule totally contrary to the law. And if nobody appeals, no one ever knows.

"So the court could hook us up somehow? I just need a few months."

"Happens all the time. You just have to get lucky. You can get amazing results if you get a really dumb judge." I thought I was comforting him, but Martin was too smart for that. He understood "roulette odds," and that in a forum where you could win with a doomed argument, there was just as much of a chance you could get slammed with a draconian penalty. But I didn't know any other way to explain the court process. You lose so many cases where you should win and win so many you had no business bringing. What was I supposed to say? "Some elected politician is going to hear your case. Let's hope he's in a good mood and understands the 'zest for living' that causes a nice white-bread kid to point a rented Mustang onto a main drag in Phoenix with a 1.8 blood alcohol level"?

"You'll be all right, dude." I slapped Martin on the shoulder, turned off the truck and darted across the lot for the courthouse.

"But I *really* have to get inside. You know where to go, right? If you don't, just say the judge's name. Somebody will tell you." I sprinted through the security checkpoint, wincing "hello" as people passed, smiling. "Which way to Judge Beckett's courtroom?"

The hall was long and the run was agonizing, but I wanted to make sure I checked in early with the judge's clerk. I figured the court would be handling a bunch of arguments en masse on a first come, first served basis. "Hello, I'm representing Mr. Lennart. *State v. Lennart?*"

"Oh, great. You're here." A man in a gray suit to my left held out his hand. "James Clausen. From the District Attorney's office."

"Of course." We shook hands. "Pleasure to meet you." By this time I was straining to keep my composure. It was hot and humid, the suit was stifling and the pressure of the toxic sludge of last night's beers and quesadillas and the morning's coffees was spreading my colon tighter than a sausage wrapper in a microwave. "How long's the wait?"

"None." James smiled. "The judge is waiting for us."

"Oh . . . Great. Great." I felt beads of sweat running out of my hairline and into my sideburns. "Just let me, uh, get my client."

I darted down the hallway to the men's room. It was an ancient courthouse, with tight small bathrooms done in yellow block tile. The doors to the stalls were rickety, the locks didn't work and the coat hooks had long ago succumbed to vandals or rust. Not the worst I'd seen, but hardly dignified. I held the door shut with one hand, struggling to hold my jacket with the other while keeping my balance and of course, just as everything was set and I was as comfortable as I was going to get, somebody came in and started walking around. He didn't use the urinal. He didn't run the water. He didn't even pull out hand towels to blow his nose. The prick was checking his hair, I knew it. I sat and waited. And waited. All of it in horrible pain, and then, finally, after what felt like days I heard the soles of the man's shoes turn on the tile and the door open and shut behind him. Finally, privacy.

By that point the perspiration was coming out of every pore

in my body. And you'd think nature would be kind after that torture and gift me with easy dispatch,—a clean, quick christening of a perfect chocolate submarine. Wrong. I won't disgust you with anything descriptive beyond this—"Carvel soft-serve ice cream." The "A" section of the *New York Times* uses less paper than I did wiping myself in that stall. Ten minutes later, five pounds lighter, and understanding the "burning" referred to in Preparation H commercials, I ran back down the hall, scarlet-faced, breathless, and pretending to be looking for Martin.

"Sorry for the delay. I'm having trouble finding my client."

"He's in the courtroom." The judge's clerk smiled.

"Isn't that crazy?" I wiped sweat from my brow.

"Where were you?" Martin asked when he saw me come into the room.

"I had some serious ass issues." I pulled him aside and guided him down the center aisle. "Sit here and just follow along." I pointed to the first spectators' row.

"I don't sit next to you?"

"Not unless you want to be asked questions. Just sit up straight and look remorseful." Luckily, Martin wore the All-American Kid look—blue blazer, rep tie, and khaki pants—as though he'd been born in the outfit. The jacket and shirt weren't a size too big or cheap-looking, as though a lawyer had sent him to buy the outfit for a court appearance. Aesthetically, you couldn't have a better client.

"What's remorseful look like?"

"Like you're at a wake."

He looked downward and let his face drop. "How's this?"

"Perk it up a little, like it's a wake for someone you only knew from work."

I slid into the defense counsel chair and arranged my papers on the table. "You know, I was thinking in the bathroom—"

"You're not going to say I need rehab, are you? They could make me go if you say that."

"Is there even such a thing as a left-handed monkey wrench?"

"Turn around." Martin sneered through his teeth.

"The Honorable Barclay Beckett presiding," the bailiff shouted as the judge walked to the bench and everyone stood.

The judge was fiftyish, neatly composed and well spoken, and he cut straight to the action. "I understand the issue here. But I'd like to hear the state first, so I can get a little more background."

The prosecutor was quick, reciting the law and how the license suspension was mandatory. The judge smiled and listened though he'd heard it a million times before. "Your honor, it's just the law. Loss of license for one year."

"Thank you, counsel." The judge turned to me. "Now we'll hear from the defense."

"Good morning, your honor. At the outset, I have to admit, we can't dispute what the prosecutor said. There was a plea, but my client requires his car for his job and without it he won't be able to work, which would be an unfair penalty. I understand the state's interest here, but the fact is, my client has already suffered punishment in Arizona and now he finds himself subject to punishment again here. That's twice. Being punished initially, then again. Once there, once here. Two times, for the same crime. It's really, really redundant. Almost double jeopardy."

"But not." The judge smiled.

"True."

"I tend to get that one right." The judge looked Martin up and down and adjusted his microphone. "I understand your position, but what can I do? The applicable statute is clear."

"Your honor, if my client loses his employment, that would kick off a downward spiral of problems, and I can't understand what benefit anyone realizes from forcing a person who is trying to get back on track and overcome his demons to lose his job and spiral further down." I took a deep breath and turned to look at Martin. He shot me a glance of confusion. Getting his life back on track? Demons? He was loaded on vacation. I had more "demons" than he did. "It doesn't do him any good as far as his alcohol problems go if he can't work and he gets caught in the downward spiral of the job loss and certainly the state doesn't want to send its residents into those spirals." When I looked back again, Martin had his face in hands.

I was fumbling, confused, spraying furious verbiage all over the room. A little stumbling's okay when you're looking for mercy. Makes you look earnest. Nobody's in a hurry to do favors for a razor-tongued operator, but even with that leeway I was too disjointed. The argument I wanted to make wasn't coming out clearly because in my head it seemed too "perfect" and impossibly convenient.

There's a bias every advocate has to overcome in a presentation or argument—that the audience comes to material from the same background as you do. Your perception is not objective reality. What sounds ludicrous in your head might sound entirely normal to the person hearing it. Some people actually like Nickelback, love LeRoy Neiman, or believe they'll be "raptured" to heaven. Some think 9/11 was an inside job. Some people still wear briefs or have basic cable.

Law professors and career coaches offer all sorts of techniques on how to give convincing arguments you don't believe in. They say things like "Make good eye contact," "Don't pause between phrases and say 'um' a lot," and "Gesture with your hands to emphasize a point." That's all stagecraft, for people who need it. The best bullshitters are born with the ability. It's second nature and they know the simple central tenet of the skill: Stop Thinking and Just Say It.

Harris was the king of this "suspend disbelief" approach. In college he used to make up rumors—warped vignettes really—that people would circulate as fact. Coming from anyone else, these tales would have been discounted as baseless fantasy, but when Harris told them, people completely bought the stories. The reason was twofold. First, his delivery. Harris pitched the stuff with a dead straight face, never coming out of character. Second, the narrative always straddled that fine line between believable and ridiculous, where the listener would be thinking to himself, *No one could—or would—make that up.* The material was so well manufactured that people wanted to buy the stories no matter how suspicious they sounded. Anything that perfectly twisted *deserved* belief, regardless of its merits.

I once watched Harris tell a story about two lacrosse players who lived in his girlfriend's dorm. The thing flowed out of his mouth seamlessly, not a moment of hesitation as he free-formed it on the fly:

Last night, I was walking into Melissa's building at about 3 A.M. and saw Chad and Mark sitting on the floor of the TV lounge, both shirtless. Chad had his shirt tied around his eyes and Mark was tracing pictures or symbols on Chad's back with his finger and Chad was trying to guess what Mark was drawing. Both of them were giggling.

I never asked where he came up with that one. I didn't want to know. Two weeks later I overheard a gossip next door relaying Harris's tale almost word for word to a gaggle of sorority pledges.

"[A]nd Mark was, like, running his fingers all over Chad's back and massaging him . . ."

"Oh. My. God. What a shame. Chad is such a babe."

"Totally. Chad's on-fire hot. Such a waste."

Once I learned Harris's tricks, I could spot his work moments into hearing a story through the grapevine:

"Tim Scully and Jon Patterson double-teamed Katie Berman without condoms. And then, like a half hour later, she hooked up with Ted Hechtor, and he ate her out. How gross is that?"

"Kevin Taylor was a hermaphrodite when he was born and had years of hormone therapy. That's why he has those women's hips."

"I heard Jon Casper and his sister had this deal in high school, where if either of them didn't hook up with someone when they went out, they'd have sex with each other."

I didn't have a fraction of Harris's acting skill, and I'd usually shy away from arguing wildly, but Martin was a friend and there was only one course to follow.

"Your honor, my client lives in a rural area, and if he has no license, he won't be able to drive to any alcohol rehabilitation classes. He'll be breaking a promise and his problems will all but assuredly spiral out of control. And besides all that, I personally vouch for this man. I've known him for a decade and he is of the highest character." *In all the right ways. You'd want him with you in a foxhole. Even more on a weekend in Vegas.*

The judge leaned over the bench. "I can't lessen the penalty. The law says he loses his license for a year. But what I can do is suspend the start of the suspension."

"That, Judge, would be fine with us."

"Well, that's what I'll do." Does the State have any objection?"

The prosecutor stood up. "No, your honor."

"Fine then. We'll delay the license suspension for a period of six months. That should be long enough for him to do whatever he needs to do."

"Thank you, your honor." I stood in the well of the court as the judge exited, wondering what he'd been thinking. The idea that Martin would be attending AA meetings seemed ludicrous in our world. Would he ever really go, even if they made him? But then, what did that matter anyway? We weren't the court or prosecutor here. Who knew what was plausible in their minds? They could be teetotalers or recovering boozehounds. Living as Martin and I did, it's easy to forget that a lot of people view the surface systems around us as serious reality, or at a minimum, far more than just a source of occasional "lifestyle interferences."

I'd like to think the judge and prosecutor were just doing me a favor, saying, "Here, you deserve something, kid"—a little professional courtesy. But I'll never be sure. You never really know why anything happens in a courtroom.

"Let's clear out of here before someone changes their mind." I shoved our legal papers in my bag and headed for the door with Martin.

"Fine with me. I feel dizzy."

"Dizzy? That worked out as well as it could."

"You had me spiraling more than a fucking ballerina."

"I'm so sorry you didn't like my argument." I held up my

watch. "Look. It's almost noon. Presbyterian drinking hours. Let's stop at a bar and celebrate. Then you can drive home."

"Fuck you."

"And it's 'pirouette,' by the way."

"What's 'pirouette'?"

"Dancers don't spiral. They *pirouette*."

THE ART OF BALANCE

(LESSONS FROM THE FLASHLIGHT ROOM)

Somebody, please, kill me. I sat at my desk sweating, the pulse in my temples pounding, staring at the crumpled receipts from the weekend spread across my desk, struggling to read the numbers and the names of the places I'd been. Three hundred dollars in cash withdrawal slips? Three hundred dollars in cab invoices, liquor store receipts and bar bills? The balance in my account showed I'd spent a thousand dollars on Saturday night, but how? I hadn't gone to dinner or hit any expensive clubs, at least that I knew of. What the hell had happened?

I chugged coffee and tried to jog my memory, but concentrating on any one thought was impossible. My brain was jelly, every part of me hurt, and being in an office only put a serrated edge on the pain. Straining the mind even slightly gave me this intense headache, like someone was jabbing an ice pick into my sinuses.

Nothing's worse than a Monday morning hangover, that tail end of an extended sickness starting Sunday afternoon, caused by what you did over the previous thirty-six hours. You sleep away most of Sunday, figuring the worst of it's gone, but then that wretched alarm goes off on Monday at seven-thirty and it all kicks in again. Anyone who gets his money's worth out of a weekend knows: The real pain comes the morning after the morning after. You sit at the desk cursing yourself, swearing you'll never do it again, knowing that's the biggest lie in the world.

As I pored over the receipts, memories of the weekend came back, but it was all garbled, playing like a bad acid trip—blurs of color, figures and sounds impossible to put in any narrative except to know that it all had been *wrong,* in every carnal sense. The only way to piece it together was to start at the end and work backward, like a crime investigation.

The first thing I recalled was the phone ringing early Sunday morning, at one of those obscene hours when you're sure the voice on the other end is going to tell you a relative died or they found your car burning in a west side ghetto. "Hello? This is Tom Roth from the Courtyard Suites Hotel."

"Who?"

"Tom Roth, Courtyard Suites Hotel, Philadelphia. We have a room in your name. Can you please come over?"

"Now? I'm in bed." It hurt just to speak, and all I could taste were acrid whiskey fumes pouring out of my mouth. "Just put it on my bill."

"That's the thing. We've had an incident in the room. We'd like to see you as soon as possible, please."

"An incident? What happened?"

"Can you please come over?"

I threw on some clothes, stumbled to the living room couch and shook Les awake. "Get your stuff together. We have to go to the hotel."

I called Bennett from the cab. "What the hell is going on?"

"The people across the hall stole a half ounce of weed."

"And a cell phone! They stole my fucking cell phone!" I could hear Jerry, some work friend of Harris's, screaming in the background.

"Yeah, yeah. Got it." CLICK. The conversation was giving me a migraine.

"I knew this was a terrible idea. We should have just gotten a car service and gone to Atlantic City."

"I had a good time." Les snickered.

"Good. You want to field this meeting with the manager for me?"

"I would, but I have, uh, jai alai practice in an hour."

"Of course."

"My serve's been shit lately."

We got to the hotel, slipped through the lobby and walked upstairs to survey the room. Drapes were pulled from a window and the carpet and sofa were soaked in whiskey and Coca-Cola. Cigarette butts and crushed beer cans littered the floor and random articles of clothing were strewn about. Nothing amazing, but a little angrier than usual. Furniture and the carpeting are assumed casualties, but I couldn't help wondering, *What kind of sick mind attacks drapery?*

"Dude!" Jerry grabbed me in the hall. "I need my fucking phone. These cocksuckers across the hall stole it."

"Can't you buy another one?"

"That's not the fucking point." His voice was nails on a blackboard. "It's got chicks' numbers in it and shit like that."

"Look, I'll see what I can do." I headed downstairs to the lobby.

"Have a seat over here." The manager ushered me to a couch. "I want you to know that we take these matters very seriously, particularly racial incidents like this."

"Racial incident?" I felt the enamel on my molars cracking as I clenched my jaw. "What are you talking about?"

Nothing good can ever come out of a "racial incident." The words are repellent on the surface, like "date rape" or "sexual abuse," conjuring up all sorts of rotten images. We'd violated a pile of laws over the last twenty-four hours, but the Civil Rights Act? What the hell had happened here?

"There was an altercation between the people in your room and some people across the hall. One of your guests claims they stole something, but he didn't tell us what."

"How's that a 'racial incident'?"

"The people in the other room were black."

"That's 'racial'? Do you know what 'racial incident' sounds like? It's eight-thirty. I don't need that."

"Nine-thirty. It's nine-thirty."

"My watch is slow. It never runs right in daylight saving time."

"I see . . . Well, uh, look. We know people get out of hand with strippers in the room, and—"

"Not the people in my room. They're gentlemen."

"The concierge noted several liberally attired women heading to your floor. But that's no matter. What I'm looking for here is just a statement from you of what was allegedly stolen."

"Yes, well, I won't be doing that right now. First I'd like to go up and talk to the people across the hall."

"I can't let you go up there. Security reasons, you understand."

"I was just up there."

"We didn't know who you were."

"If I can't talk to those people, how am I supposed to know what was stolen?"

"You want to find out what was stolen by asking the people who stole it?"

"Trust me on this. I'm a lawyer."

"I'm sorry, sir, we can't do that."

"I'll just take the check. That'll be fine."

I understood the repair costs and taxes on the bill, but the slew of identical duplicate charges—"$10.99," "$10.99," "$10.99"—made no sense. Bartering it down was the proper course, but I didn't have the stomach for the discussion.

"Did you get my phone?" Jerry caught up with me as I tried to sneak out of the hotel. "I'm not letting those assholes get away with my phone."

"They're looking into it for me. I dropped a few legal threats on them. But now I really have to get back." I patted him on the shoulder and staggered out of the hotel, feeling like I'd just been had. Was it possibly all a scam? I remembered the kids from across the hall the night before. They looked a little young, high school-ish sorts in "gangsta" do rags and baggy pants. And the manager was wrong—there were white kids in the room, with spiky hair and chains. Were the hoods in some conspiracy with him? He'd give them skeleton keys, they'd steal from drunks and then he'd scare off the victims with some horror tale about a "racial incident"? So much ugliness and paranoia spinning through my head, but why? The night had begun so innocently . . .

"I can pucker it in time with the music." The skinny girl's sphincter was keeping perfect rhythm with a Madonna mash-up playing from a portable stereo.

"Where'd you learn to do that?"

"I trained with a mirror on the floor. It's tricky."

"I can imagine."

"Does anybody want anything else?" she whispered in my ear.

"I'm all right, but he really likes golden showers." I pointed across the room to Bennett.

"I can't do that." She gauged my eyes to see if I was kidding.

"Performance anxiety, I understand. Have some more liquor." I'd have said anything to cause amusement at that point. The group of us were supposed to be in Atlantic City, for a "guys' night," but for one reason or another, mostly poor planning, things never gelled. So there we were, stuck in Philadelphia, in a hotel, ordering strippers from the phone book.

"I'm not peeing on him, but I'll do something else." The short one fellated her finger. "Fifty dollars."

"Why are you asking me? Ask him."

"You ordered us, didn't you?" I had. You always have to do the ordering when you're the lawyer. Everybody assumes you can negotiate. They give you the phone, then bitch about the goods when they arrive.

"I didn't ask for a fat Rosie Lopez!"

"This girl has tracks on her arm and tits like an Aborigine."

"My wife's hotter!"

You never get what you want with strippers. Unless you're in Vegas and rolling in cash you barely get what you need. It was my policy to ask for the impossible—"Skinny. Blond. No cottage cheese. We'll pay." That'd get you a pair of chain-smoking coke monkeys, which was as good as it got in the world of "delivery dancers."

All things considered, these two weren't bad. One was short and a little plump, the other tall and skinny and strung out.

"How high are you guys?" the skinny one asked as she spread her legs in my face. "X is as good as money."

"Yeah, well, there's none of that." The only substances moving around the room were joints, bottles of Maker's Mark and what seemed like hundreds of cigarettes, filling the space with thick gray clouds of smoke.

"When's the girl-on-girl action?" Bennett yelled.

"Excuse us for a second." The skinny one dragged the short one into the bedroom and closed the door. The short one popped back out a second later.

"Can you get this guy out of here?" She pointed to a body lying sideways across the bed, mouth open, snoring.

"The Corpse," as we referred to him that night, was a high school friend of Les's. All I knew of the guy was he walked into the hotel, downed ten bourbon shots, smoked a joint, and passed out before the sun had even set.

"He's out cold. Don't worry," I assured the girl, wondering why a woman who'd just lip-synched with her anus suddenly needed privacy.

I heard Harris arriving a minute later. "Hey guys! I couldn't find butcher's smocks. But I got some carving knives and a tarp. Where are the girls?"

"What did he just say?" The skinny girl glared at me.

"I didn't hear anything."

"The butcher knife shit." She darted out of the room. "You think that's fucking funny?"

"He's harmless—just a joke." I pulled her back into the bedroom. "The important issue is the girl-on-girl thing."

"She won't do it." The skinny one pointed at the short one.

"I'll give blow jobs." The short one sniffed. "Isn't that better?"

"You'd think, but no."

"What's going on in here?" Martin came into the bedroom, poking his finger through the aluminum foil on the top of a red and white pill bottle. "You want a Mini-Thin? You'll dance better." He held out a handful of round white tablets.

"What is that?" The short one grimaced.

"You've never had ephedrine? It's good. Helps you lose weight. Not that you need to lose weight or anything." The girl stared at him, not saying a word. "Fine, more for me." He threw the tablets in his mouth and chased them with his drink.

Things would only go downhill from there. Ephedrine's a brutal, unforgiving high—a bronchodilator that floods the body with adrenaline, causing your scalp to tingle like your hair's on fire, your hands to go numb, and your penis to shrink back into your bladder. "Mini-Thins," "White Crosses" or "Two-Ways," whatever the brand name, every one's a vicious, shitty buzz. Three to five hours of nail biting, nervous chatter and an unnerving desire to take huge, deep breaths. I'd once seen Harris eat thirty Mini-Thins. He lost his mind for the better part of a day, stumbling around, saucer-eyed with crusted drool forming at the corners of his mouth, asking people to light his cigarette over and over. "I can't feel my legs. You think that's a bad sign?" Ephedrine is no one's friend. In half an hour, Martin would be impossible to control, and short of using a tranquilizer gun on him, there wasn't much we could do about it.

"Come on. I have three hundred dollars here." I pulled out a stack of bills. "Just licking."

"No lesbian stuff." The little one wouldn't budge.

"But you'll give hummers?" Strippers are native pragmatists. It's kind of a job qualification. We'd somehow stumbled into the one-in-a-thousand irrational idealist.

"How much to watch?" Bennett appeared to my right.

"You want to watch a blow job?" the short one barked.

"I'm a fan of technique."

"I have the best." She smiled.

"Can you blow him back from the dead?" Bennett pointed to the Corpse.

"Two hundred dollars."

I counted off the bills and handed them to her. "Let me get a hit off the joint first." She darted to the living room with the skinny one in tow. Bennett promptly ran to the closet, opened one of the double doors, and got inside. "Quick. Get in." He pushed open the adjacent door. My initial thought was *No,* but then I figured, *Why not?* What else was I going to do? Sit in the living room drinking myself into a coma?

The short one came back into the room a minute later and dragged the Corpse to a seated position on the edge of the bed, facing the television cabinet. "Hey, don't you want to get up? You're missing the party."

"Whaaadaya . . . Who are uh yyyyyoouu?" He rubbed his eyes as she tried to find his zipper. "Shhhh. Just sit still." She put a finger on his lips.

"Pssst. Hey. Watch this." Bennett whispered from the other side of the closet, waving a remote control with one hand and cracking the door open a tiny bit with the other. CLICK. The hotel guest services guide came onto the screen. CLICK. A movie selection appeared. CLICK. A listing of local restaurants popped up in its place.

"What are you doing?" I whispered to him.

"Shit. I think I just ordered a movie." He stared at the remote control. "The TV menu is really confusing." CLICK. A local newscast was on the tube.

"Whysuh, uh, the channel changing?" the Corpse slurred.

"Stay still." The skinny girl was still struggling to unzip his pants.

"You're real pretty." He teetered sideways. "Your hair is so shiny."

"Stay up, baby." She grabbed his shoulders as he fell forward. CLICK. The Home Shopping Network shot onto the screen. "And if you act now, we'll throw in the matching tea-kettle and dog bowls—all for $79.99! A thirty percent discount!"

"Whuz that?" The Corpse pointed at the television.

"What?" She turned to check the screen. "I don't see anything."

As soon as she turned her head back to the Corpse, Bennett aimed the remote at the television. CLICK—"Wheel! Of! Fortune!"

"Whuthefuck?" The Corpse leaned toward the television and lost his balance, falling forward onto the floor and knocking the stripper backward into the television cabinet. CLICK. Bennett switched back to the Home Shopping Network. "And we'll also include the oven mitt holders. Genuine Belgian ceramics! Folks, you're NEVER going to see a deal like this again!"

"Fuck this!" She crawled out from under the Corpse, leaving him on the floor, crumpled in a fetal position, moaning into the carpet. "Pam Anderson couldn't get him hard!" She flipped open the bedroom door and stomped out of the room. "I'm *sohhh sorry.*" The Corpse groaned and clawed at our heels as Bennett and I stepped over him on our way out. "Come back . . ."

Back in the living room, Martin was under the coffee table, rummaging around on all fours. "Have you seen my shoes? I have to go and I need my shoes!"

"Go where?" Bennett asked.

"I just have to go!" His eyes were wild and darting all around the room. "Now!"

The room was at a tipping point of sorts. Every binge has a crossroads moment where you make a conscious decision to kick in the second wind and keep going or give up, let the booze take over and pass out drooling on the sofa. Liquor's the first ledge on the mountain. It only gets you so far, and that gets dull quick. No euphoria, just a "different" stage as common and predictable as sobriety. Where did we go from there? What was the next level?

I didn't know the answer. All I knew was we couldn't stop. This wasn't a random nihilist romp through a Saturday night. It was a statement—an exhibition of a way of life on one hand, a reaction to a way of life on another. It probably didn't stand for anything deep, meaningful or right or wrong, but I knew on some basic level it was important, about restoring a sense of balance.

To a lot of lawyers facing thirty, the tyranny of the time sheet is total and terminal. The pressure to give up, make the work your life and sprout roots from your ass into the swivel chair is overwhelming. When you're a kid, the idea of becoming a worka-holic seems ludicrous, something out of a Monty Python skit. Then you start working in a field like law and realize how, even if you're consciously trying to avoid it, you can become exactly that. Your every minute of the day becomes a possible billing event, and the more time you trade away, the more you assume you'll get paid. It's such a shit-simple business model you start thinking, *Well, I'll just work around the clock and then I'll get rich!* And it's not just a law thing. They might not be kept in a tablet like a lawyer's but in any job the hours pile up quickly if you let them. Once you buy into the notion that your time belongs to someone else, the game's over. You'll be on the merry-go-round for years before you even realize you're there, running in circles.

Some of us, however, react differently. We're slaves to the time sheet like everyone else, but not in the ordinary sense, indentured instead to something I'd call the "3-to-1 Ratio." The first time I considered the ratio had been months earlier, 2:00 A.M. EST to be exact. Alex called me drunk off his ass from San Francisco, where his firm had temporarily reassigned him to work on some big case.

"Do you know what time it is in the East?" I yawned, won-dering why I'd been stupid enough to pick up the phone at that hour.

"I've been standing outside a bar waiting for a cab for forty-five minutes. You were the first person dumb enough to answer my call."

"You're fucking lit."

"Oh yes. Yes I am. Some lawyer out here told me about this strip club called the Mitchell Brothers Theater. I spent the last three hours in this thing called the 'Flashlight Room' where these dancers fuck each other with those huge wands they use to guide aircraft on the runways. It's mesmerizing. The sword fights look like something out of *Star Wars*."

"So you're enjoying the Left Coast. Good for you."

"The job sucks, but the per diem isn't bad, and I will say this: You forget a lot of shit watching chicks screw each other with lightsabers. One hour of that erases three at work."

It was drunken gibberish, but the wisdom of the ratio struck me immediately. Three-to-one—it represented a perfect balance in our situations. If you had to give away sixty hours a week, the only way to keep things even in your life was to max out each of the twenty or so you had on the weekend, making every one a "superhour" worth three of the ones lost in the office.

Hearing the "3-to-1" concept articulated wasn't really an epiphany. Alex hadn't stumbled into a new mantra or mission statement. I'd been a slave to the ratio for years and didn't even know it. It explained all the lost weekends and Monday morning hangovers. It explained why I could never sit still for even a moment on a Saturday afternoon and felt guilty if I wasn't out of my mind or engaging in something hyperstimulating every second of my free time. It explained why Martin was running around the suite looking for his shoes so he could take off on a quest for something he couldn't even describe. The ratio distilled a simple concept we all understood. At our age, in our stations, you could never get high enough to be truly, completely free, back to that ignorant optimism you had from eighteen to twenty-three, where the world seemed open in every conceivable regard. But that wasn't a reason not to try.

"Goddammit. I can't believe I lost those fucking shoes!"

"Have a shot, Martin. You need to calm down." Bennett spanked the short girl, who was bogarting a joint. "I have good lungs." She slapped her breasts on his cheeks and blew smoke in his face.

"Fuck it." Martin slammed his fist on the coffee table. "I don't need them."

"You can't go anywhere barefoot!" I screamed, but it was too late. The door slammed behind him and I heard the elevator bell ring in the hallway.

"That's it! I'm getting new strippers." Jerry grabbed the phone book and started flipping through the escort listings. I'd only met the guy that day, but I already knew one thing about Jerry: he hadn't been laid in a damn long time. Jerry was a strip-club, steak-and-cigars kind of guy, the sort of "man's man" who seems to materialize out of thin air at any of these sausage parties. I like strippers as much as the next guy, but more as party ornaments than anything else. Jerry was the kind of guy who really dug that scene—got a "control" high from telling a naked ex-cheerleader what to do. All the guy talked about were topless bars he'd been to from Tampa to Toronto, and how he wasn't pleased with the entertainment so far.

"Come with me." I grabbed Bennett and took off. I figured we'd run into Martin in the lobby, but he was nowhere to be found. We hailed a cab and five minutes later we were in my apartment.

"What are you doing back here?" Lisa came home from a dinner with friends a few minutes after we arrived.

"I had to pick something up." I smiled and tapped my nose.

"Sweetie, do you really need that stuff now?"

" 'Need' is such a fluid concept."

"Why didn't you just take it with you?"

"Coke around strippers? It'd get killed in five minutes."

"You could hide in the bathroom."

"Not with strippers around." Bennett laughed. "Everything's open territory. You should come back with us, Lisa. See it all first-hand, a live male bonding ritual."

"I just might." Lisa popped a bottle of champagne from the refrigerator.

"I don't need champagne." Bennett protested.

" 'No' isn't an option." I handed him a flute. "Once the bottle's open, it's got to be finished."

By the time we got back to the hotel room, things had fallen apart. The door was wide open, "Runnin' with the Devil" was blasting out of a clock radio and Les and Jerry were standing in the middle of the room, furiously dialing cell phones.

"You must be Jade." Jerry clicked his phone off and put his arm around Lisa.

"My name is Lisa."

" 'Lisa.' I like that. That's fine." He started pulling money from his pocket.

"I'm not a stripper."

"I know, it's 'dancer.' I'm sorry."

"I'm not that, either. I'm P.J.'s girlfriend." She laughed.

"Fuck." Jerry's face fell. "Jade was supposed to be here fifteen minutes ago!"

Les grabbed my arm. "I can't reach Martin and he's been gone a long time."

"He can't get far barefoot. He's in a bar nearby." We quickly decided on a search plan and headed outside. Bennett went east, I went west, Les headed north and Lisa walked south. Twenty minutes later we were back in front of the hotel. No luck.

Jerry was closing the door when we got back upstairs. "Fuck this. Jade's not going to show. We're going downstairs to the bar." Harris was passed out facedown on the couch.

"Get up!" I screamed in his ear, but he didn't move, so Bennett and I pulled his legs until he fell sideways onto the floor. "I have the spins! Leave me alone!"

"Here. This will make you feel better." I handed him the Baggie, he tapped a line onto the glass, rolled up a dollar bill from his pocket and snorted it.

"Okay. I'm up. Now what?"

"We find Martin."

"I'm not doing that. He could be anywhere."

"Ingrate. We don't need you anyway. I think I know where to go."

"Wait!" Harris grabbed me. "I need another. You got me up. You're obligated."

"Interesting logic." I handed him the Baggie. "You ready to go, Bennett?"

"You know, I've been thinking, I should probably watch the bar downstairs with Harris. In case Martin goes there. Two sets of eyes are better than one."

"Yes. Of course. We'll need both of you there."

"And I should hold this." He grabbed the Baggie from Harris. "You shouldn't run around with that stuff."

"Thanks so much. What would I do without you?"

Les, Lisa and I jumped in a cab out front. "Delaware Avenue, please. The strip club, down near the Wal-Mart."

Show 'N Tel was a full-nude BYO strip club across town. I figured Martin might have gone there since we'd talked about it earlier. Walking through a filth-ridden hellhole like that barefoot was insane, but then, man's basically a Neanderthal on ephedrine. When we got to the place, crowds of drunken college students, middle-aged virgins and probable serial killers were milling around the entrance, half of them dragging coolers of cheap light beer into the building. Les and I paid covers and split up inside. He went right, toward the stage. I went left, toward the private film booths.

"Can I help you?" A wrinkled redhead in a halter top and acid-washed jean shorts stopped me in the hallway, poking her finger into my chest.

"Just looking for a friend."

"I'm a friend."

"Good to know." *Are you serious? I wouldn't shake your hand with a ski glove.* I turned and darted into the racks of porn tapes, almost slamming into a balding potbellied man with long hair and a Frank Zappa mustache, clearly stepping out of a booth, adjusting his belt. "Excuse me, sir."

"You're right, excuse you."

I ran around the aisles, but there was no Martin to be found, so I headed back to locate Les. Onstage in the main room, I could see two pasty girls pouring beer on a drunk, shirtless man tied to a chair, drooling vomit on his chest. "Bad, bad!" They whipped the poor bastard with his soaking wet shirt as his friends laughed. To my left a thin Latin girl was spread-eagled in front of a gallery of white trash in trucker hats, guzzling cans of beer from a Styrofoam cooler on the floor. They whooped and howled, crumpling up dollars and firing them at her with full windup motions. Balled-up bills bounced off her thighs, landing in a pile at her feet.

Les came walking up to me, shaking his head. "No Martin." The punch of the drugs was fading and the scene was accelerating the comedown. "I have to get out of here."

"Agreed." Les threw his beer. "Back to the room?"

"Fuck Martin. If he's jailed, we'll get a call." Les and I met up with Lisa at the door and the three of us got a cab back to my place, where we eventually passed out.

Other than the morning meeting with the hotel manager, Sunday was spent in bed. On Monday morning the alarm clock startled me awake, out of one of those deep REM slumbers where the first twenty minutes feel like you're walking through gelatin. *Fuck. Is it a workday again already? Make it a bad dream, please.*

Martin called about a half hour after I'd gotten into the office. "Hey, I heard you were all worried about me. That's sweet. I love you too."

"Where the fuck were you?"

"I walked for a while, I guess. I came out of a blackout up around Broad and Spring Garden. My feet were all cut up, so I got a cab back. Next thing I knew, I was hanging out with these guys from across the hall. I must've walked into the wrong room."

"Did you get into a fight with those guys?"

"Hell no. We got baked, then I took them to our suite, to get some bourbon. Some stripper was in there, asking for that Jerry guy."

"Let me guess. Jade?"

"Could be. I have her number somewhere."

"Then who the hell was fighting?"

"I don't know. That was late. I was back in the bedroom trying to fall asleep, watching TV. All I heard was Jerry screaming at someone in the living room. Sounded like he was all wired up or something. I locked the door and stayed in the room."

"Who stole the half ounce?"

"You know, I think we might have smoked a lot of that. Or maybe the Corpse left with it."

"When did he leave?"

"No one knows. We woke up in the morning and he was just gone."

"So you were in the hotel the whole time?"

"Except for when I was walking."

The second line on my office phone started lighting up. I waited for my secretary to pick it up, but she was off getting coffee. "Fuck. Hold on, Martin."

"I have to go anyway, but—"

"Just one second."

"No. I really have to go. But before I forget, when you get a chance, let me know what I owe you for the movies."

"Movies?"

"The pay-per-view thing on the TV in the bedroom was real confusing. I kept hitting 'Enter' over and over. I think I bought a bunch of movies."

I clicked over to the other line. "Hello?"

"Hi. P.J.? Yeah, it's Jerry. Harris's friend . . ."

"Yes, I remember."

"Did you have any luck getting my cell phone back?"

"It's eight-thirty on a fucking Monday morning."

"Nine-thirty. It's nine-thirty."

Meet the New Boss

Hey. Come here." Patrick was standing in my doorway, signaling me to follow him.

"What? I'm busy." I didn't need his silliness at that moment. It was late, and I was finishing a brief that was supposed to be in days ago.

"You've got to see this. Before the cleaning people go through." Patrick was insistent.

"All right, but make it quick. I want to get out of here."

"This'll just take a second." He snickered.

Patrick was always dragging me into his office to spill some sordid story about last night's carnal adventure. He'd recently been divorced and reliving his adolescence, one fuck to the next. And he'd caught an impressive wave of luck with the ladies. When we first started working together Patrick was striking out with every woman he talked to, but then one day he snared a drunk paralegal at a happy hour, got his confidence, and things rolled from there. In a few short weeks, he went from hopeless to fearless, walking up to any woman in any bar, laying on a charm offensive and not giving a damn if she blew him off. When he was rejected, he just moved on to the next girl, using exactly the same rap over and over again until it worked, making up for years of marital monogamy at blinding speed.

"Follow me." Patrick walked down the hall to Charles's office, looked around to see if anyone was watching, then darted inside. "Check this out." He flipped on the lights and pointed to the window.

"I don't see anything."

"Exactly. Now, watch this." He clicked off the lights and pointed to the window, a wall of plate glass across one side of the office. "Stand over there." I moved a chair out of the way and positioned myself alongside the window, as though I were facing a television from the side, at that 10-to-20-degree angle where the picture becomes distorted.

"Okay. What am I supposed to see?"

"Look closely at the glass."

"All I can see is people in the apartment building." Our building faced a massive residential complex across the street. Looking through the window, I saw people milling about through their kitchens and living rooms, making dinner, watching television, or talking. Patrick walked up to the glass and pointed to two spots on it. "See the handprints?"

I angled my head and looked closely. The same way those smears you leave on the inside of your windshield wiping condensation from it with your bare hand are only apparent at night, the clear outline of hands pressed flat against the glass suddenly became apparent. They were high, over six feet up and spread far apart as though someone were splayed against the pane, face forward and arms extended outward and upward. "See the face?" Patrick laughed, pointing to a blob of smears below and between the handprints. "And the marks from her knees?"

"Are you saying what I think you're saying?"

"I was too drunk to drive home last night so I brought a chick here. She was dirty. So dirty. My office is filled with research for that marketing stuff I'm working on. I needed a place to fuck and Charles's office seemed perfect."

"You can get a hard-on in this place?"

"I didn't have a choice."

"You sure the people across the street didn't see you? That'd be hard to explain to management if someone complained."

"Are you kidding? That was the whole idea. She got off thinking somebody could be watching. I got her right here too, over the desk."

"You should have boned her on the conference room table upstairs, the one with those huge overhead lights."

"Maybe tonight. I'm meeting her at the Devon for drinks."

"You could also go to her place, like a human."

"Are you kidding me? I was working here until two last night after she left."

"I thought you were too drunk to drive."

"That doesn't mean I can't work. It sobers me up."

"Sacrilege."

"What?"

"Wasting a buzz like that."

"There's no option. I might as well have a bed installed in my office. I'm here all day and night." That wasn't hyperbole. When he wasn't fucking, Patrick was working. He'd been going around the clock for weeks, writing some huge marketing proposal to roll out an environmental law practice Larry had been building. He toiled on it night and day while billing an ungodly number of hours on cases as well, all of them honest. Patrick didn't fluff his time sheets or play political games to get ahead. He was solid middle-class and bought into the belief that if he just worked really hard they'd make him partner, pay him a load of money and he'd have a nice cheesecake life.

"When this group starts rolling, things are going to be sweet," I remember him saying a lot in those days. He seemed to think Larry was going to make him a player in the new department. "I can't wait to take this marketing pitch on the road to clients. The numbers will be huge." I used to listen to Patrick and wonder if the late nights of working and later nights of drinking had severed his link to reality. Larry, not Patrick, was soliciting the clients for the new practice group, and he would be the face of it. The prospective clients were Larry's leads, from his connections. And from what I knew of Larry, he didn't share the spotlight. Even if Patrick were eventually made partner for his efforts, he'd just be a "service partner," one of those yeomen paid barely more than a senior associate, toiling in the trenches for the "rainmakers" who soaked up all the profit for bringing in the work.

"Service partner" isn't a bad slot if you're looking for lower stress and willing to put your ambition on ice, but that wasn't Patrick at all. He wanted to be a rock star, and had invested everything, including a load of his life savings, into the career. And that's what made his gullibility so confusing. Patrick *lived* the job, knew the firm and the industry from top to bottom and still, somehow, he never seemed to grasp a central cardinal rule of the profession—that you could never, ever, blindly trust a partner. I started recognizing that reality after just a few months at JP&Q, and the more it crystallized for me, the more it seemed so inescapably obvious. How could Patrick and so many other associates like him buy into the myths about how we were all parts of a team, working together? As good as management could treat you on any given day, unless you brought in business, you were just labor.

Despite that glaring reality, Patrick never comprehended, or simply refused to believe, that he was just a set of hands. When he complained about being overworked and underappreciated by Larry, I gave him the only advice I knew: "Get tight with a client. That's the only way you get leverage over him."

"I wrote the guts of the marketing proposal," he'd respond. "Larry needs me for the environmental law group. He's fucked without me." When I heard that, I knew Patrick was living in a completely fictitious world.

As it always does, reality set in a few months later, when Larry took Patrick's marketing proposal—all those months of intense research and analysis—and pitched it to clients by himself. Patrick felt he'd been passed over, that Larry was "plagiarizing" him in some way. That wasn't the case, of course. Patrick got a paycheck for what he did, and that was all Larry was obligated to give him.

"This is such bullshit. I worked my ass off and all Larry tells me is I'm not working hard enough. He even gave me a shit bonus," Patrick bitched and moaned. Every time I listened to him I had to stop myself from grabbing his collar and saying what needed to be said:

Don't you get it? It's Larry's department. He owns you until you do something to free yourself. You have three options. One, fuck him. Steal his leads and go to a competitor with your knowledge. Two, quit. Call his bluff and see if he really needs you. Three, shut up and take it. Complaining isn't going to get you anywhere.

But I never said that out loud. Patrick had to emerge from the "Hard Work Alone = Partnership = $$$ and Happiness" fantasy on his own, and I couldn't really blame him for hanging on to it. I was just snapping out of it myself, and it wasn't a pleasant education. You feel like a mark, a hopeless silly rube—like a pack of partners were laughing at you somewhere, thinking about how you paid tens of thousands of dollars for the privilege of being their indentured servant. The easier course was just to bite my tongue, nod at Patrick's complaints and steer the conversation to a fuck story.

"Did you really get busted by security sucking a chick's tits in your office?"

"It wasn't security. It was Tim Winston, from the appellate group. He was cool about the whole thing—just opened the door, met eyes with me, and then immediately shut it. I saw him in the hall the next day and he laughed."

"I'm not surprised, considering he's fucking one of his associates."

"I wish I knew that at the time. I was shit scared he was going to rat me to Larry."

Patrick eventually got smart and put his résumé on the market, and he got lucky almost immediately. A huge national firm in town had been hemorrhaging lawyers to dot-com companies promising huge stock option packages. They needed bodies to fill the empty desks, which had been multiplying exponentially, as every ambitious associate was racing to leave the law firm world for the quick riches of the tech boom. The firm quickly scooped up Patrick, offering him a fat raise and bonus package to fly around the country trying product liability cases. And, of course, he had a blast resigning, leaving Larry without a major chunk of the brains behind the new practice group he was selling and the nasty realization he'd lost one of his best employees by overestimating his leverage.

I was thrilled for Patrick when I heard about his good fortune. It couldn't have happened to a nicer, more decent guy. We went out for drinks and celebrated a lot during his final days at JP&Q, but even in that revelry, it was bittersweet talking to him. On one hand, he was getting paid a lot and had reached the highest prestige level an associate could in Philadelphia. On the other, he was still a lost believer, double-fisting the Kool-Aid.

"So I'm exclusively trying these cases for Huge Company, Inc. They get sued all over the place and I represent them in trials all over the country. I stay in sweet hotels and get a fat bonus for hitting two thousand hours."

"You only work for one client?"

"Yep. I tell you, man, it's fun. I had dinner at the managing partner's house last week and this guy's the shit. He really seems to want to take care of the associates. We had a few bottles of Opus One at this sweet pad he has in the suburbs. I'm really psyched. This is where I'm sticking it out."

They say the definition of insanity is doing the same thing over and over and expecting a different result. Under that standard, Patrick was certifiable. Here he was, gushing about his new firm exactly the same way he'd talked about his future with Larry while he was at JP&Q, transferring the same naïveté from one firm to another.

"You're just going to keep trying these cases? That's it?"

"The trials are all cookie-cutter. The same issues over and over. I'll do this for a while and shoot for partner. That's serious fucking cash. But I'm still going to try cases no matter what happens. Die in court, that's how I want to go out."

I don't know too much about running a business. I was drunk through most of Management and Marketing 101 and wound up getting C's in both classes. But one thing I did recall was the professor talking a lot about how dangerous it was for any business to depend on one client for most of its revenue. If Wal-Mart's buying 70 percent of your product and it suddenly decides it can get it elsewhere for 25 percent less, you're in Chapter 11 pretty quick. Patrick serviced one client, and that was just the problem from the business side. His belief that the managing partner of the firm "really want[ed] to take care of associates" was the bigger concern. That was just a lie. Well, let me add a caveat there—a "lawyer's lie." He'd "take care of" Patrick, that was true. Just not the way he expected. But there was no explaining that to Patrick. He was riding high, for however long it would last, and it was nice to see the guy so happy when I ran into him at the usual after-hours haunts.

"So how are the ladies treating you?"

"Let me tell you about last weekend. I started drinking with these two chicks in the Four Seasons and we ran up this ridiculous tab. We were wasted. I mean, really trashed. They offered me a ride home but then they drove me over the bridge and I wound up in this condo in Cherry Hill. It was insane. All we did was fuck and get screwed up for like twelve hours. They were eating each other out, finger-fucking . . . One of them had this huge double-sided dildo. It was crazy."

Normally I'd call bullshit on a story like this, but I'd seen Patrick at the beach that summer ordering rounds for an entire group of women at a yuppie meat market. He was throwing cash around like a hedge fund manager and talking about getting a car to Atlantic City later that night to gamble. "Come on. We'll hit a casino. I know a guy up there who'll hook us up with anything we need."

A gravy train like that always ends badly, and Patrick's was no exception. One morning I opened the *Wall Street Journal* and saw that his only client, Huge Company, Inc., had filed for bankruptcy. I knew as soon as I started the article that Patrick's luck had run out. When a company files for bankruptcy protection, all litigation pending against it—the cases Patrick defended—is immediately stayed, then usually liquidated in the bankruptcy court. A month later, that managing partner Patrick had such an affinity for "took care of him," with the usual pleasantries, no doubt. "Sorry. Just business. Nothing for you to do now."

Patrick got a job at another firm a week later, but it was lower pay, a lesser firm, and desk work again—laboring as he'd done for Larry. No trials. No bottomless expense accounts. A generous paycheck, but an utterly vanilla gig, doing the grunt work for somebody else taking the credit.

A mutual friend who worked with Patrick at his new firm called me a few months after Patrick had taken the position.

"Hey, have you seen Patrick?"

"Not in months."

"Have you talked to him?"

"No. Why?"

"He disappeared. He hasn't come into work in a week and he's not taking calls."

"I haven't see the guy. He probably ran off for the coast with some eighteen-year-old." Patrick's fortunes weren't at the forefront of my concerns. I was busy interviewing to get myself out of JP&Q, and that was more than enough to think about.

A couple of weeks after that call, I was sitting in the office when a number I didn't recognize came across my cell phone. It was Patrick, calling out of the blue to ask if he could borrow $300.

"Long time, no speak." I met him in the lobby and we walked to a cash machine around the corner. "Where have you been?"

"Oh fuck. What a pain in the ass. The new job was for shit. I was going to have to get a goddamned cash advance to pay for a date tonight. The landlord has me over a barrel because I'm moving out of my place and breaking the lease. Everything's upside down. I'm totally out of walking-around money until next week." I didn't ask him what he'd done with the tens of thousands of dollars he should have had in the bank, figuring that would only embarrass him.

"People are looking for you, you know." I handed him the cash.

"Yeah." He smiled. "I know. Thanks. I really appreciate this."

"Don't sweat it."

"We have to do drinks sometime."

"Yeah, give me a ring." I knew I'd never hear from Patrick again, and it wasn't because he'd owe me money. Getting burned as he'd been put the zap on his mind. I could see it in his eyes that last day we talked. He looked lost, out of sorts, and my guess is he must've felt like a fool, being used and thrown away like that. Practicing law in a desperate, cash-starved place like Phila-delphia is working in a shark tank. The closest allegiance a lawyer has in those straits is a temporary ally. Everyone's his opponent at some point on some level, even his partners. Trusting any lawyer who wasn't a close personal friend the way Patrick trusted Larry or the managing partner at his new firm was like being a cancer researcher and chain-smoking. As one seasoned litigator at JP&Q used to remind me about promises or agreements, "If it isn't on paper, it never happened."

But I couldn't really blame Patrick for hanging on to the myths. Nobody wants to think he's just being used, that hard work alone isn't near enough to earn a corner office. Nobody wants to think the business is just that mercenary, or realize in hindsight his biggest mistake was being gullible enough to walk from one bait-and-switch straight into another.

That was the last time I saw Patrick. After hitting up one other friend for a loan, he vanished from the face of the earth. No one heard from him, ran into him on the street or saw him at any of the bars where he used to hold court. His phone numbers were disconnected and he didn't respond to any emails. People told me he opened a small personal injury firm for a while, but then he quit that and opened a nonlegal business somewhere on the Main Line.

I like to think Patrick did well, wherever he went. He was

good people and a quality freak, but he'll always be a dark memory. I was getting more and more jaded by the day. Patrick was supposed to prove me wrong, and all he did was validate that cynicism. But the real shame of it was Patrick truly loved the career, and he'd have been a damn successful lawyer . . . if he'd just learned to stop trusting his colleagues.

The Costanza Method:

Part I

The Costanza Method: To succeed in life by saying exactly the opposite of what conventional wisdom dictates one should in any given situation. This practice is based on a famous Seinfeld episode known as "Opposite George," wherein George Costanza receives a series of promotions and dates with gorgeous women by stating exactly what his instincts tell him he shouldn't. A variation of the Costanza Method may be applied in the law firm context, where one can succeed, at least for a short time, by simply making obvious yet always unspoken observations or criticisms about one's office, opponents, and career.

Never give up!" "Never say die!" "Fight to the last drop of blood!" From the pep talks of my Little League coach to every company retreat I've suffered through, people have been beating me over the head with those mantras since I was old enough to listen. They're just cheap platitudes, of course, but if you think about it, they only make sense. How else are you supposed to succeed? Nobody rallies troops into surrender or shrugs against the dying of the light. That's craven, cowardly, an affront to everything it means to be an American.

And that's a shame, because giving up is underrated.

In an inside-out backward universe like law, giving up can be a fast track to the top, or at least a new pay scale. When you give up, you let your guard down, and when you let your guard down you say what you're actually thinking. And when you say what

you're actually thinking, which is the last thing you're ever supposed to say, you suddenly find you start getting what you want
(or at least a lot more of what you need).

The turn of the millennium was a lousy time to be a litigator. Unless you were bringing class actions on behalf of hedge funds,
there was no money in lawsuits. Everybody and his brother was
rich or getting there off the tech boom, and if you weren't you
were something to be pitied. Working in a "long-track" field like
law was a short bus for suckers and chickenshits. Internet Capital
Group was the new Berkshire Hathaway, Global Crossing was
splitting shares once a month, and every decent business lawyer
was fleeing to an Internet company drowning in venture capital
money. Every day you'd hear about a friend of a friend cashing out
his options and quitting the workforce before he'd even really
started.

Litigators were useless instruments in that economy. Fucking
around in the court system was horse-and-buggy bullshit for
people too dim or gutless to find a job on the new gravy train.
Reading the *Wall Street Journal* in the morning was like having
your nose rubbed in shit. If law weren't an annoying enough job
to begin with, now you were faced with an overwhelming sense
of dread that you were going down with a sinking profession.
People and businesses don't sue each other when they're flush,
and in those days, even as some of the market data was pointing
to an implosion of the tech bubble, the flood of cash still seemed
endless.

It was a week or so before Memorial Day, 2000, at the tail end
of that boom, when I learned that the partners I worked for at
JP&Q were secretly planning to leave the firm at the end of the
summer. The knowledge came by accident. I was drinking on a
Friday afternoon with an old college buddy named Graham who
happened to be the brother-in-law of Charles, one of the seceding
partners. In a vodka-and-tonic-induced lapse, Graham asked if I
was leaving with my department, as though I should have known
of the plot all along.

"So, are you going with Charles and the group when they leave?"

"What?"

"Your department, when they take off this fall."

"What are you talking about?"

"Your group, you know . . . The partners leaving the firm."

"You're kidding me."

"You didn't know? Shit, I have to stay off this stuff." Graham laughed and held up his vodka. "Don't tell anyone I told you."

"Deal." I smiled and tapped my glass on his. "But tell me the whole story."

"I guess they just got sick of being dicked by management and wanted more cash. Why else, right? From what I hear, they're gone by September."

"A toast to their new firm!" For a moment, as I raised my glass to Graham, I thought the smirk on my face was going to remain permanent. I couldn't say I was shocked. Larry and Charles brought in loads of business, and if they stayed, dozens of other partners would continue to feed on their spoils. And if I'd learned anything up to that point, it was that loyalty to anyone but yourself in the legal business was grossly misplaced. Still, it was a surprise, even if it validated a lot of suspicions I'd had, seeing partners in the group holding meetings behind closed doors, whispering in the halls, and asking associates for lists of all the cases we were handling out of the blue.

"Giddy" generally doesn't describe the mood of a twenty-nine-year-old man, but as I processed the information, it was all I could do not to run around the bar kissing everyone like Jimmy Stewart at the end of *It's a Wonderful Life*. I had the summer off. Graham had just given me a three-month vacation. I couldn't literally skip the next ninety days of work, of course, but if any of the partners in my group gave me any kind of shit, I had the ultimate get-out-of-jail card.

The first thing I did was confirm the story with Charles the following Monday. "Hey Charles, I have a question." I closed his office door as though I were about to dish some gossip. "Why are the partners meeting and asking for lists of all of the associates' cases?" Charles was a good guy, but the consummate shrewdie, always plotting and suspicious of everyone's motives, and he knew I drank with his brother-in-law. He'd read between the lines of my questions.

"We're just trying to get a grip on the files, you know?"

"Of course."

"Trying to figure out who's best to handle certain cases and, uh, you're a good associate and, uh, we'd like to put you on some serious stuff." Charles couldn't come right out and admit anything. The best he could do was grin and dodge the questions, which he knew was exactly the answer I was expecting. He also knew he had a terrible poker face. "If anything's going on, you're okay. Trust me."

"I understand. Just curious, that's all." There wasn't any use in pressing him further at the moment. I figured that was as close as Charles could come to inviting me along. He probably assumed I didn't trust him, but that on some level I'd be excited by the possibility of bolting for a better opportunity.

He was wrong. I trusted Charles. But I had other plans.

When I got back to my office, I called a headhunter to line up some job interviews. There was no way I was leaving with my department. Whatever they were doing, wherever they were going, it would still be a billing-treadmill, and I'd had more than my share of that time-sheet slavery.

"I'm leaving early." I smiled to my secretary.

"Where are you going?"

"Stuff to do. I'll see you tomorrow." I'd usually make up an excuse, but now, why bother? As I passed people on my way to the elevator, I thought about what the firm would do with everyone left behind when the people in charge of my group bolted, those Bronze Age secretaries waiting out retirement, the drama-queen paralegals and the service partners in their rumpled oxfords. Who'd be promoted to fill the void? Who'd be fired? The suspense could drive a person mad. . . . A person with a houseful of cats and a stamp collection. I hit the elevator button for the lobby and called Lisa.

"I'm coming home a little early." The next stop was the liquor store down the block, then a cab ride home. For at least the rest of the summer, I was on holiday.

The next two months were a blur. I started buying bottles of Stolichnaya and champagne the way most people buy milk or orange juice, and Harris and Martin all but moved into my apartment. Most of it was standard fun, like college, only with somebody paying me to go to class half in the bag. For the first time, I even started tinkering with the boundaries between work life and reality. In the past, I'd tried to limit my vices to binges, avoiding daily, sustained consumption of anything. The thinking was, if you did something every day, it'd get dull and routine, like work. I mean, without a low, where's the high? But that summer I had nothing to lose. Why not break my rule, see if there wasn't some way to make the next job a little more tolerable?

There are a million different "office highs" people use to cope with the workday. Some people go to the gym before work or jog in the afternoon to get an endorphin rush. Some people drink at lunch or pop pain pills. I've known people who ran home to grab a quickie at lunch, one who claimed to masturbate in a seldom-used men's room in a remote part of his building and one who would pop the top off half a dozen industrial markers, seal them in a ziplock Baggie in his desk for a few hours and sniff the built-up fumes when he needed a quick escape.

Sadly, for me the "office high" was not a successful experiment. Sure, Ativan or the Grand Marnier latte will get you through the morning, but they're exceptions, and they only cover a few hours of the day. Red wine at lunch brings a painful afternoon (listening to some opponent bark into your phone on a merlot buzz is like having your ear stabbed with a rusty corkscrew) and beer's a cruel tease. Two's never enough, but three means four, and four means more, which equals you sitting behind the desk, bitter and annoyed, hiding, waiting out what feels like an endless death march to five o'clock.

But of all these ideas, the worst was the "wake and bake." Les and Martin had been fans of the technique, and when either one of them would see me out, guzzling bourbons and bitching about how much I hated being in the office, it was always the same proselytizing.

"You're way too stressed. You need to bake before you go in. It makes the mundane shit interesting. The work becomes a game." To me it seemed a horrible idea and terrible waste of dope. I couldn't blast Traffic or Zeppelin in my office or swap favorite scenes from *Rushmore* with my secretary. And what if a partner roped me into some awful meeting? "Uh, P.J., can you sit in on a strategy session in the Klepnik case? You know, the one where the guy claims he was scalped by an improperly installed ceiling fan. We got some new photos from the scene and want a fresh set of eyes to evaluate them." The cost-benefit ratio seemed terrible. Yes, the "wake and bake" did work, and yes, it could make the morning amusing. But when it failed, it made an already irritating situation fifty times worse.

"Hey, can you do me a favor and write a reply to this motion?" Janet, a partner down the hall I worked with, appeared in my doorway a little after nine-thirty one morning. "I'm busy getting ready for an arbitration and it needs to be done ASAP."

"Huh?" It was a random Tuesday in the middle of the summer. I'd just been settling in, flipping through the newspaper and scanning the Internet. I wasn't Cheech-and-Chong-stoned or anything like that. Just comfortable, happy—in that placid zone where the idea of getting up to take a piss seemed like too much work to bother. *Oh please, please, let this be a joke*, I almost cried when I saw her shuffling legal papers in her hands.

"It's pretty simple, self-explanatory." Janet laid the papers on my desk. "Thanks. I really appreciate this."

I read the words on the pages, but none of it made sense. The text was a pile of geometric black designs on a white background, a slop of long words and meandering arguments. *Why now? Why does every day here have to be torture?*

Staring at the motion, I immediately flashed back to Business Law 101, a college course I'd taken close to a decade before. For one reason or another, a friend and I decided to smoke a splif before writing a presentation we were to deliver the next morning. I remembered how typing the damned thing seemed to take forever, and how awful its text had been. I remembered standing in the front of the auditorium the next morning, struggling to deliver it to the class, stumbling through all the typos, run-on sentences, and pointless, incomplete phrases, looking at the professor's frown and thinking, *Shit, I'm going to have to beg this guy for the "Gentleman's C."**

Some people can write just fine when they're stoned. Some better than they can sober. These are people who've smoked enough that they can do just about anything in that condition, from taking LSATs to skeet shooting to giving a best man's speech at a wedding. A roommate of mine in college used to rip bong hits before exams, explaining that he needed "to be in [his] natural state to do well." Normally I'd say these people are mad, but dope's different from any other drug. Nobody admits it, but there are people who can all but perform surgery baked out of their trees. For some people it just seems to regulate the mind, like a sort of black-market Prozac.

I am not one of these people. There was no way I could punch through a legal argument with a stitch of clarity in that condition. Still, however, as a matter of general decency, I couldn't leave Janet with nothing when she needed a hand. Of all the lawyers on the floor, she was easily the nicest and most decent of the bunch. So I chugged a coffee and whipped together the best argument I could. It might have been coherent, or it might have been gibberish. It might have been both or none or a lot of other things, but I'll never know because I didn't stick around to find out. As soon as it was done I got the hell out of the building, to avoid having to run into her again. And she never followed up with me, which I took as a Gentleman's C.

---

*It was a well-known fact that some professors would convert a D or F to C if you groveled hard enough and promised it would never happen again. You usually had to be a senior and demonstrate that anything under a C would imperil your career prospects, but I'd heard of it working for sophomores and juniors.

Note to self—no more wake and bake.

There were a lot of rough mornings in those days, but the odd thing was, I never felt better. I could say it was simply physical, that when you have minimal stress and endless hours to go to the gym and sleep in, the body will take anything. But it was more than that. For the first time in a long time I felt as stupid and reckless as I'd been at eighteen, and all it took was a summer off. William Blake was nuts—the road of excess doesn't lead to the palace of wisdom. It does, however, lead to a very happy place, at least temporarily. If done right, yes, through sheer vice you can recapture a sense of those moments you knew as a young fool, where all that seemed to matter was the next fuck.

The only problem is, once you start reopening those channels in the mind, like a dam springing leaks, what flows out of them starts eroding the wall between your professional and actual personalities. The "filter" that keeps your mouth in check at work starts faltering. You don't fumble or spout off uncontrollably like some Tourette's victim. It's more a giving-up sort of thing, realizing how silly all the workday doublespeak sounds. You start asking yourself, *Why all the acting and deference to procedure? Why not just be myself?*

The first time I noticed the wall beginning to crack was in something called "motion court." Almost every morning, at least one local court would hear motions in cases pending before it, little arguments over procedural matters on which the adversaries couldn't agree and needed a ruling from the judge. I tried to go to every one of those arguments I could. When I didn't have any motions to argue in my own cases, I'd volunteer to argue them for other partners or associates. The way I saw it, no matter how annoying the argument might have been, it beat sitting in the office. And it was great for racking up billable time. You could bill huge hours reading newspapers or magazines waiting for the judge to hear your argument, and if you had two motions in different cases scheduled for the same day, you had twice the time.

One day that summer, I volunteered to argue another lawyer's motion in defense of some cookie-cutter negligence case, against a plaintiff's lawyer I'd seen in court a few times before. He was short, forceful, and animated, the sort of person you knew never listened to anything because all he could think of was his next comment. The man seemed to have something to prove, always getting in the last word, annoying the judge by asking for things he knew or should have known the court couldn't give him. On this motion, he was seeking volumes of corporate records in a simple negligence case involving a defective walkway he claimed caused an accident.

"Your honor, I require all documents regarding the lease agreement between Aegean Real Estate, Inc., and Yasry Land Development relative to this property because the crux of my case is that . . . wah, wah, wah-wah, wah, wah-wah, wah-wah, wah . . . Under the rules my client has the right to explore . . . wah, wah, wah-wah, wah, wah-wah, wah-wah, wah . . ." I tried to follow him at first, but his voice quickly morphed into a fast, nasal variety of that gibberish the producers used for the voices of adults in Charlie Brown specials. Thankfully, paying close attention wasn't all that important. It wasn't my case and I didn't know negligence law, but the nails-on-blackboard quality of his delivery was all you needed to hear to know the judge would do all he could to rule against the guy.

"Can you give him what he wants?" The judge raised his hand and addressed me, cutting off my opponent.

"Your honor, that would take weeks, maybe months. He'd request a continuance of trial and this case would go on forever. This isn't a huge claim. He just keeps asking for everything imaginable, to try to irritate my client into settling." I looked over at the lawyer. "You don't want any of the stuff for real, do you?"

"Please speak to the court, not counsel."

"Sorry, your honor."

Inside the four walls of the litigation game, it's not a defense to nakedly say the other side's request would drag the case out or accuse him of using exactly the cynical tricks everyone knows plaintiffs' lawyers employ to leverage settlements out of people. The judge can't rule in your favor on those bases. Under the rules of court, if a party is technically entitled to certain documents, he's supposed to get them. But that's the litigation reality. Outside that box, in the world of an overburdened court system, there's nothing more important to judges than getting cases finished and off the docket, particularly the thousands of frivolous negligence claims filed every year. I'd basically turned to the judge as Mel Brooks or Woody Allen would address the audience in their films and said, "Your honor, this guy's going to make so much work for all of us. Please don't let him drive us nuts."

"Counsel, I'm going to deny the motion." The judge marked the order and handed it to his bailiff. "I don't see the relevance here."

I remember being amazed by the argument. Not by the result, but by the total disconnect between the people involved in the thing. There was my opponent in one world and the judge and, luckily, me in the other. My adversary and I had stood ten feet apart, and it might as well have been ten thousand miles. Leaving court, I thought about all the motions I'd lost and wondered how many times I'd beaten myself up for no good reason, thinking I hadn't mastered the merits of my argument when in fact the real problem had been that I was arguing in the wrong reality.

The second time I noticed the wall failing was interviewing for a new job. Over the summer I'd talked with a bunch of firms—a string of awful, awkward meet-and-greets. I listened to a middle-aged spinster mutter about her firm's zoning practice over a Caesar salad in a strip mall Applebee's, endured a managing partner with a Borat mustache barking about how he'd "work [my] fucking ass off" for the "obscene salaries" young lawyers were getting and faced hiring committees of slope-shouldered men named "Irving," "Marvin," and "Eugene" quizzing me on my knowledge of "creditor's rights" law, every one of them filled with the same canned questions:

"How has your experience at JP&Q been?"

Excellent. I love it, which is why I'm here interviewing with you.

"Your writing looks good. Do you enjoy the research part?"

Yes, I also enjoy surgery and dental appointments.

"We're very meticulous here. Can you handle that?"

That depends on the size of the check you're giving me.

It's hard dancing for suits. The process wears out the saccharine glands in your tongue. Saying things like "Law school was grueling at times, but rewarding" almost trips the gag reflex, and by the time you're done coughing up pap like "I really get a charge out of researching cases," you feel creepy, soiled, like your grandmother just caught you jacking off. And no matter how many different ways I tried to gloss it over, it was obvious I didn't want any of the jobs. I was there strictly for the money, but the only honest answer—"It's a job, and it sucks, but if you pay me a fuckload, I'll deliver"—would have gotten me blackballed as soon as the syllables left my tongue, even if that's exactly the bargain under which almost every person in a law firm is operating. Playing the Man in the Gray Flannel Suit is a lot harder than you'd think. My acting skills were decent, but there was no doubt, I was still very much an amateur.

Not surprisingly, I didn't receive any offers. And frankly, I was kind of relieved. It was a good thing, I figured—an efficient marketplace weeding out a misfit lacking the sense to leave on his own. In August I started talking to a career consultant about transitioning out of law. Maybe find a way to cash in on one of those Internet jobs before the tech boom completely collapsed.

Then I got a call from a lawyer named Dennis Levin, the head of litigation at a firm called Dorsey Fishman. "Strange" was the only way to describe my interview with the firm. Dennis spoke slowly, methodically, measuring his words and dragging them out like some movie caricature of an egghead professor. And every now and again, without warning, the guy would stop what he was saying midphrase and look up at the ceiling in these awkward silences that seemed to take forever. A couple of times he made long, disturbing eye contact with me, not saying a word. I could hear the seconds tick off on my watch as I sat there smiling, looking for any hint of what was going through his head. *Do*

I have a huge whitehead on my nose? A festering cold sore crawling over my lip? Does he want to fuck me? Kill me? Maybe both, and not in that order?

The managing partner, Jonathon Dorsey, was a nice guy, but he scared the living shit out of me. He was far too chipper for the setting, with an almost *High School Musical* excitement about the law. "The thing with us is you'll get the very best training. We're committed to being the very best and nothing less. Some firms claim to train associates, but we really train people to be the very finest lawyers." He chirped along like a wired elf in a Japanimation cartoon, laughing for no reason every three or four phrases. "Top-notch training! Nothing short of it." *Christ, they're all crazy here. This one's ripped on diet pills. That or he honestly gets off on this shit, the sick bastard.*

"Well, we're on the same page. I could use some good training." *Which one of you will be taking me out to shit in the park at lunch?*

When they finally got around to asking me why I was leaving JP&Q, I said what every career coach would tell you not to. "I hate the place. Time sheets this, time sheets that. You feel like you're on an assembly line. All they care about is hours." And eventually, as it always does, the obligatory "What would you say is your biggest weakness?" question came around.

"My biggest weakness? I don't know. Who really knows until he's in the job? You're always bad at something."

"Okay. Do you have any questions for us?"

Where's Chuck Barris? Somebody gong me out of this mess.

Dennis called a few days later and asked me to come by for a meeting, which I knew meant he was going to make me a job offer. "I don't think I can do this, Dennis. I just don't think it's a good fit. I don't want to just jump at an offer here."

"I think you should reconsider," Dennis responded. "It's a good move for you."

"Can I call you back?" *Reconsider?* His response baffled me. Firms had their pick of bodies to fill associate slots. None of them asked you to "reconsider" when you turned them down, particularly an associate like me, who'd barely been doing full-time civil work for two years.

I sat back in my chair and processed the discovery. *The more you act like you really want the job, the more you fail, but when you give up and stop acting like you want it, you get it? And when you get it and reject it, they want you more?* So basically law firms were like sorority girls? What a fool I'd been. How didn't I see that? My problem in those other interviews had been trying when I should have just followed that old cynical advice about fickle women: "Treat them like shit and they'll love you for it."

"Hello, Dennis?" I called him back a day later, to avoid looking like I cared too much. "Yeah, I've reconsidered, and I think I can take the offer. I'll come by this afternoon."

Giving my two weeks' notice at JP&Q was orgasmic. Actually, that's unfair. Quitting *any* law firm is orgasmic. There aren't many feelings better than looking at the piles of paper in your office and thinking, *That's somebody else's bag of shit now.* One of the few nice perks of being a lawyer these days is you're expected to serially switch jobs. Every twelve to twenty-four months you can take a two-month vacation (factoring in the two weeks' notice, weeks of pure time off in between jobs and four weeks of "learning curve" time where you do nothing at the new place).

If the antics of the previous months had been a sort of personal Woodstock, what followed now was Altamont. The weeks after I'd given notice were a carnival of senseless abuse and gluttony, almost impossible to describe in any coherent or organized sense—an awful kaleidoscope of slurring and shouting, video games, bed spins, bong hits, cheap champagne, and wretched shaky mornings, all sprinkled with those terrible moments of lucidity, the kind where you look in the mirror and realize you're smoking the filter through the tobacco.

In the sleep-deprived corner of a Saturday or Sunday morning around three or four, I'd look at the calendar on the refrigerator and think, *Shit, this is going to end soon.* Sometimes I'd stare out the window and talk to myself. *Why not just keep going? Catch a plane to some Third World island with nothing but credit card bills for cash advances and blown deadlines in your wake?* Be Gone, in every sense of the word, naked on a Third World beach so pristine and isolated the notion of going back to a concrete box in a place like Philadelphia could never permeate the brain. Leave the bastards back home nothing but an email:

Re: Gone

By the time you read this I'll be in the air. Some of you will think I've lost my mind, which is fine. Tomorrow, only one of us will be wearing pants.

If only I hadn't fallen for Lisa. She'd never go. Sober, at least. And really, though I desperately wanted to believe otherwise, neither would I. As much as I'd traded dozens of emails with Alex over the years, discussing how a man could live like a king for a year in Costa Rica on $10,000, the grand escape was just a dream, or hallucination. Dropping off the grid was losing, and losing wasn't an option, no matter how much I hated the game.

Eventually I'd start the new job and perform as I always had. My hands would always be on the wheel, a prisoner of some irrational sense of responsibility I couldn't seem to shake. It had always been that way. I was never the guy who "blew up." Never failed a class, been arrested, wrecked the car drunk, knocked up some chick when I was blacked out or burned the house down while my folks were away. Getting caught or letting something spin out of control always seemed an amateur's play. The fun was finding the edge and playing around it, not falling off the thing.

The Costanza Method:

Part II

The last day at JP&Q was a bloody end. It started the day before, of course, in a restaurant on Walnut Street, drinking with Bennett. He'd been around for a few days, wasting time at a conference, eating, boozing, and complaining.

"I don't know how you live here."

"Do I need to hear this again?"

"You can't even buy liquor and beer in the same store."

"I like ruts."

"There's got to be something to do."

"Like what? What do you want to do?"

"I don't know." He stared out the window. "Do you still have that nitrous cracker?"

"Plastic, brass, or aluminum?" I laughed, hoping he was kidding.

"Do you have any cartridges?"

"You're serious?"

"Why not? What else are we going to do?"

The next stop was Wonderland, a head shop in Center City that sits above a sex-toy and porn store called the Pleasure Chest. One-stop shopping for bongs, nitrous, dildos and every legal variety of filth, all within a 1,000-square-foot space. It was one of the best "people-watching" spots in town. You had the Bondage queens milling about the leather lingerie racks, the David Berkowitz look-alikes in Members Only jackets scurrying around with copies of *Ass Masters IX* and *Cum Dumpsters III* videotapes in their hands, and of course, the stoners—stumbling around, flipping through the whips, chains and clamps, giggling to one another . . . A perfect snapshot of how wrong life can go when you smoke too much dope or don't learn how to talk to women.

As childish a high as it might have been, I wasn't shocked that Bennett wanted laughing gas. Everyone loves nitrous oxide. It's a short trip, but you get a hell of a bang out of it while it's working. And as far as I know, it's the only drug you can actually feel destroying your brain matter as you inhale it, which gives you an idea of the intensity of the high. Even the process of using the stuff is entertaining. "Sssss," the gas leaves the balloon and enters your lungs, then suddenly, "Oh . . . yessss," your voice drops to a thick sludge bass somewhere between Louis Armstrong and the cross-dressing serial killer from *The Silence of the Lambs* and everything in your mind

just

stops

dead.

After three balloons your limbs are rubbery. After six everything in the room is *Penthouse*-airbrushed with a gauzy film and a reverb echo is running through your head, as though someone's boxing your ears. After a dozen you're legally retarded. Attempts at witty rejoinders come off like crackhead ramblings, and finding "pizza" in the phone book is impossible. You pick your face up from your hands and meet eyes with your cat, sitting in judgment, shaking his head in disgust. Suddenly the couch is your only friend.

"How about a Stonewall Jackson?" Bennett laughed as he pulled a bottle of bourbon out of the freezer back at my place.

"Actually, I have a tube." Martin had given me a blue glass

bong with a white skull at the base a few weeks before when he upgraded to a better model.

"Let's do it up." That was easy for Bennett to say. Happy hour was just a warm-up for him. When Bennett was on his A-game, he seemed impervious to the effects of mind-altering substances, the sort of person who could easily finish a bottle of whiskey by himself, which I've actually seen him do. Most of my friends envied his obscene tolerance, like it was a sign of grit. It always seemed a curse to me. What was the point if you didn't get high?

And high is what a Stonewall Jackson would get you. It's a common cocktail, known by a million different names depending on where you went to high school or college. A simple but lethal recipe:

1. One bong hit
2. One bourbon shot
3. Exhale

Stonewall Jacksons were traditionally performed among a group of four people, until a fifth of whiskey was finished. I'm not certain of its derivation, but the name seems to fit. Jackson was a notoriously unpredictable Confederate general who disobeyed Robert E. Lee, often issued bizarre and incoherent orders, and was accidentally shot to death by his own soldiers. Not a far cry from the possibilities that might befall you after a handful of SJs.

Most think dope's the reason you make an ass out of yourself in the throes of a Stonewall Jackson stupor. It's actually the bourbon. Scotch will make you charming, vodka's liquid Percocet, and beer a fount of oafish non sequiturs and flatulence. Red wine will put you to bed, white's piss, and tequila's vomit fuel. But bourbon, well, bourbon is the cocaine of alcohol, amplifying every aggressive angle of your personality and dragging all the rotten suppressed thoughts to the surface. A bourbon drunk is what you'd be in the jungle. It's a simple fact to anyone who knows the stuff: You're more your actual self on bourbon than you are dead sober. Bourbon is liberation, but only for those embracing their inner baboons.

By the third SJ, I was a wheezing, spitting fool, which is about when the nitrous moved into the mix. Bong hit, balloon, shot—a "Stonewall Oxide." The combination only made sense when you think about it, a "three great tastes that taste great together" sort of thing. And under those circumstances, it was probably inevitable. It's a rare drink or drug that wouldn't be a lot better with another, or at least that's the thinking when you're in the position to be making those decisions.

After a couple of Stonewall Oxides, you know how a case of the bends feels. When you first suck up the gas, your heart races a bit, then your head feels featherlight, then the room stretches out, as if viewed through a fish-eye lens. A vise-like pressure clamps down on the temples, everything goes two-dimensional and the music turns tinny, the sort of sound you'd get from an old transistor radio. Weezer's *Pinkerton* was on the stereo, "El Scorcho" was bouncing off the walls and at the time it sounded like the greatest song I'd ever heard. "I'm a lot like you, so please / Hello, I'm here, I'm waiting / I think I'd be good for you / And you'd be good for me . . ."

"How do we get a cab?" Bennett was waving the phone like a dagger.

"We're going somewhere?"

"Get up. Stop petting the carpet and give me the number for a car."

"Give me the phone." I dialed zero and the Jamaican doorman, an imposing six-foot-five figure with a deep baritone like Baron Samedi, the constantly laughing villian from *Live and Let Die,* answered in his usual exaggerated accent. "Good eeevening, sir."

"I'll need a cab, please."

"Ah, yes." He laughed. "And where will you be going, sir?"

"Apartment 920."

"That's where you are, sir. Where are you going?"

"Undecided."

"Ah hah. A fine location, sir." He snickered. "It weel be here momentarily."

"All right, Bennett. We should go to the lobby."

The next memorable "peak" of the evening was a cute redhead slapping me in the middle of a bar in Olde City.

"Why did you do that?" I was shocked when she hit me.

"You know why I did that."

"What are you talking about?"

"You grabbed me."

"No I didn't."

Her boyfriend, a spiky-haired man in a black T-shirt, jumped to her aid. "Did you just check her fucking oil?" I couldn't help laughing, making a mental note to remember the phrase. *"Check her oil." Classic.* It was a short moment of levity. As he was angling to get in my face, I noticed a bouncer plowing toward me through the crowd. *Shit.* I started toward the door but the bouncer moved faster, and I was certain, though I couldn't see him, that the angry boyfriend was still trailing me. Ugliness was bearing down on me from every direction. *So this is how the night ends, pummeled to hamburger by a bunch of mooks? Well, I can't say it wasn't coming, and why not? Get the full Philly experience.*

"Come on, you're outta here." The bouncer dragged me forward.

"I'm leaving anyway." I yanked away from his grip as he pushed me through the doors.

Bennett was standing on the sidewalk, holding a cab. "Sorry about that. She had a great ass."

"You dick. Some gel-head almost attacked me for that."

"Shut up and get in." He hopped into a cab and opened the window between the driver and the backseat and barked at the cabbie, "Take us to Rose Petals."

"Rose Petals?" the cabbie answered back in a confused Middle Eastern accent.

"That's what it's called, right?" Bennett turned to me.

"Massage parlor." I leaned over the seat. "Asian girls, in Center City." I knew from experience you didn't have to give much more direction than that. It seemed every single male within two hundred miles of Philadelphia had heard of the place.

"Oh yes." The cabbie put the car in drive and smiled into the rearview mirror. "Thank you."

Going to a "washy-washy" joint was a waste of time for me. I didn't pay for it, and even if I did, I wouldn't have paid for a "happy ending." If you can't give yourself the best handjob available, you're doomed. It's okay to be a failure in a lot of things—dancing, hitting fairway woods or driving a stick transmission in traffic. But when you fail at masturbation, God's telling you something. Jumping off that bridge might not be such a bad idea.

Rose Petals was off a side street in the middle of town. No advertisements outside, for obvious reasons, just a door that opened to a flight of stairs with a waiting room at the top. The "lobby," if you could call it that, was an assortment of office chairs semicircled around the perimeter of the space, facing a hallway entrance to the massage rooms hidden by a blind covered in Japanese artwork. The clientele in the place were exactly what you'd expect—paunchy divorced guys, pear-shaped office clerks and wasted out-of-town businessmen stopping by after a night at Delilah's or Cheerleaders, the high-end strip clubs on Delaware Avenue. In one corner a doughy cubicle mole was riding an exercise bike in boxers and brown dress socks, his man breasts rolling up and down as he pedaled.* In another, an acned kid in a Flyers jersey waited for what was, hopefully, his first time.

"You wan showa?" A fortyish woman in a robe suddenly appeared.

"No. Talk to him." I pointed to Bennett.

"Massage, yes?" The woman kept pressing.

"No. Thank you, I've got to, uh—" There was only one response. I turned and bolted down the steps. Television's taught me honor and pride in workmanship are sacred matters in Asian society, and I didn't want to find myself declining a weepy immigrant masseuse. "No, really, you've got the most beautiful hands. But my girlfriend has this thing about me and hook—I mean, 'massage

---

*Why did a hand-job joint have an exercise bike? I can only assume to bolster the fiction that it was some sort of "health club."

professionals.'" At that point I'd had too much of everything. I wanted home, bed, and sleep. It felt like I'd been up for days, and I was suffering that awful irrational fear the first rays of the rising sun would be creeping down the pavement outside.

The door swung open, thankfully into a pitch-black sky. *Jesus still loves me.* I staggered down the alleyway, half humming, half singing like some homeless drunken wretch. "I'm a lot like you, so please, hello . . ."

The next morning was beyond bleak. "Fuck her in the ass! . . . Eat a little *pusssseee!* . . . *yeeeahh yeaaahh,* you motherfuckers!" The alarm on the stereo cued up a bootleg of Jimi Hendrix, Buddy Miles and Jim Morrison jamming at some New York nightclub in 1969. Hendrix and Miles were struggling through "Tomorrow Never Knows" while Morrison screamed profanities at the audience. The disc has no musical value, strictly a novelty item. I couldn't recall fishing it out of the CD rack or putting it on the stereo the night before, which seemed about right. Nobody remembers choosing music like that. When I walked into the living room I encountered a war zone—nitrous canisters strewn about the floor like spent shell casings, half-drunk Amstels on every surface, busted rubber balloons scattered about and a dusting of ashes across the coffee table. Everything reeked of stale smoke and skunked beer. Or maybe that was me—my breath or the toxins emanating from my pores.

"Getting sober" is impossible. I've tried hitting the gym, cold showers, steam rooms, mass-dosing with B-12, and drinking a gallon of water before going to sleep. None of it erases the pain of a body struggling to pump out pints of innard-rotting poison. Brush your teeth, wash your hair and slap on a bottle of cologne, all you'll affect is a fresh-smelling drunk. I brushed my teeth three times and gargled over and over with half a bottle of Scope, but nothing killed that awful metallic taste of laughing gas in my mouth, which seemed to be the only thing my tongue or nose could register. It wasn't until I'd coated myself in what I thought was cologne that I realized I'd been using an old women's perfume Lisa had left on the bathroom shelf. *Fuck it. Who cares? It's your last day. What do you have to do? Hand in security passes? Clean out your desk?*

The message on my voice mail when I got to the office was confusing. Somebody from the HR department was calling about an appointment. "Margaret will call you regarding the exit interview." I played it twice to make sure I heard it right. *Exit interview? Why?*

Margaret was in charge of associate management and development, a forty-fiveish woman who spoke with a Mary Poppins lilt and favored bright clothes and huge pieces of jewelry. The few times we'd met she was outfitted in a red jacket, with a gold and jewel-encrusted broach stapled above one of her breasts, looking like a female version of the British General Cornwallis from a painting in an art book I had at home. I guess Margaret had a reason to be noticeable. She was one of the head bureaucrats in the HR department, those people who acted as witnesses whenever anyone was fired, to make sure all policies were followed.

Policy's a big thing in the human resources world. In fact, it's the only thing. Wherever you're working, be it a factory, school, Kmart or law firm, HR departments are always the same: queer, creepy universes all to themselves, disconnected from the rest of the organization, almost like an internal affairs unit inside a police department. The hierarchy's always the same—one or two managers at the top, with a collection of windup toys underneath, the sorts who can check two hundred boxes on a government form in a minute. The kind who never deviate from order unless something gets in the way, at which point they keep banging up against the issue with one constant refrain—"The handbook says this isn't supposed to happen."

In addition to all the usual HR management duties which, apparently, included conducting exit interviews, the only other job I knew Margaret handled was sending out occasional emails about new associates:

Melvyn Thunkle is a 1999 graduate of Villanova Law School, with an impressive résumé. He's an ambitious young lawyer with a distinguished background and comes to us highly recommended by Professor Clarence Sneedmer, a foremost speaker on Pennsylvania appellate procedure.

While a student, Melvyn edited the *Horticultural Law Quarterly* and authored the well-received article "Leichtenstein: Two Hundred Years Under the Boot of Swiss Tyranny" for his school's *International Law Review.*

Lovely. Can't wait to meet him.

I met Margaret in a conference room on the eighteenth floor. It was far too small and far too bright for my state of mind. She was wearing red lipstick, and, in the brutal fluorescence, for a moment it felt like I was being interrogated by a rodeo clown. The room was listing slightly, as though I were on a boat. I was sweating, my hands were clammy, and every time I turned my head too quickly, these little swirls or pinwheels (which I've since been told are caused by some imbalance in the fluid of the eyes attendant to severe dehydration) appeared in my plane of vision. For a moment I felt like crying, just folding up on the floor in a fetal position, sucking my thumb and drooling—a full-on breakdown.

"So why are you leaving?" She smiled. My eyes darted around the walls for a second as I struggled to cough up an answer, a crush of thoughts logjamming between my eyes. The hungover mind is a terrible place. You've still got some of the insight of the drunk, but none of the smoothness. Where you'd have been as slick as Dean Martin in your cups, now your lips quiver, and the mind questions whether the syllables the brain is streaming to the tongue are brilliance or a dog's breakfast of incoherent slop. The responses always seem to turn out the same—clipped, half-muttered answers, best taken as cryptic, at worst, the nervous sputterings of an imbecile. That, or you develop diarrhea of the mouth, starting a thought, then falling almost immediately into a run of asides until you can't even recall the point you were trying to make.

Then, out of nowhere, through all the confusion in my head, it struck me—I could say anything. I was free. There was no need for me to keep up the fiction that I believed in the firm or the career or pay any deference to the myths they pushed as reality inside the place.

"I'm leaving because I'm dead if I stay here. I'm a litigator. I can't go in-house and I don't think this firm will last." *Damn, that felt good. Say some more.* "There's no business to be had in this city, and I'm on such a treadmill I couldn't go out and get it even if there were. I see a bunch of partners siphoning the profits off the top and waiting out retirement. They know this industry is getting less and less profitable every day, so they just try to beat more hours out of the kids. I'm an indentured servant here."

"What do you mean?"

"What I said." I wondered if she thought "indentured" was a term of art. "There's no future here."

"In what regard? I think a lot of people think they have a future here."

"Everybody kills themselves to make what? Two hundred thousand, maybe two hundred fifty a year when they're in their fifties? You'd do better on a dollar-per-hour and quality-of-life basis as a plumber. And this city's economic future isn't getting any better."

"Wait a minute." Margaret stood and walked to the door. "I want you to talk to someone." Twenty minutes later a partner named Terrance McKenna was sitting across from me. Terrance was the head of some important committee in the firm, a fiftyish business and employment litigator known for his directness and honesty, one of those rare lawyers who was actually a true straight-shooter. He didn't "massage" anything he said. You knew exactly what the man thought, or at least that was his reputation in the firm. Terrance was highly respected, almost at the top of the management pyramid, and sitting across from him, I couldn't help wondering what a heavy hitter was doing meeting with a fungible billing unit like me. In fact, I had no idea why any of them were meeting with me. I was *leaving.*

"Can you tell Terrance what you told me?" Margaret asked.

I gave him a similar rant.

"You're right." He smiled. "Philadelphia is a terrible market. But there will always be a place for good lawyers."

"A good lawyer is a lawyer with clients. And how do you get

that here?" I was getting tired at this point and could feel beads of sweat pouring from under my arms and down the sides of my torso. My armpits and shirt were soaked and the mix of deodorant and Lisa's awful perfume were beginning to run. *Jesus, you smell like a cosmetics department.*

"I don't know. The competition is extremely difficult. The business in Philadelphia is all networked." I understood what he meant. There's no industry coming to the city because it's old and cancered with plaintiff's lawyers, onerous regulations, and high taxes. What's left is in the hands of maybe a hundred lawyers with high-end connections, and the more people and businesses run from the city, the smaller the pie gets. The only firms immune to the market shrinkage are the true national outfits that service Fortune 100 clients, and the legions of personal injury lawyers who shake down insurance companies and hospitals that can't leave the city.

"But even if you have business, clients are shopping by price." I said. "We're going to be like accountants in fifteen years."

"I don't agree," he said, pausing to emphasize the value of his words. "Clients will always pay a premium for good service. You're being cynical there."

Of course I was being cynical. Law's an openly cynical business, and the process of wringing profits out of young lawyers is one of the most cynical labor exploitation systems ever invented. First, seek dependable workers—talented but risk-averse, the sort of mind comfortable in a rigid hierarchy. Hungry, bright believers who'll work like dogs and consciously avoid asking the questions that would drive a seer to leave or manipulate the system to his advantage. Second, maximize the talent pool's output. Correctly utilized, over an eight-year career at a firm, an associate can pump out 16,000 to 18,000 billable hours. At a rate of anywhere from $175 to $400 per hour, depending on the type of firm and the associate's experience, that's a nice return on the salary and benefits invested. Third, aggressively cap costs on the pricey overhead. When a senior associate wants prestige, knight him a "non-equity partner." If after a few years he complains about that, give him a modest raise, tell him he doesn't have a shot at equity partnership, and label him "of counsel." If he still complains, do nothing. He'll seek a better deal elsewhere, just as he was reaching maximum operating cost.

"How can't I be cynical?" I laughed. "This job's like being on a merry-go-round that just keeps going faster. Nobody stops to think about anything because everybody's trying to bill every second of every day. We have meetings devoted to finding ways to bill more time. Meetings about how to create invoices. Is that insane or is it me?"

The truth of it is, practicing law for anything less than the boy-band money a few top rainmakers and the class-action pirates pull down is simply irrational. The billable-hour business model is exactly what that old industry cliche describes—"a pie-eating contest, where the prize is more pie." Unless you're the kind of sick fuck who enjoys figuring out ways to write down 180 to 200 hours in a tablet every month, it's a shit sandwich. And don't think it gets better with age. I've ridden the morning train into Philadelphia. I've seen the sixtyish service partner hunched over in his beige raincoat, reading deposition transcripts and correcting legal memoranda, squeezing every last billable moment out of his day. I've watched him park his car and trudge through the rain in his suit, seeking out a colleague waiting on the platform.

"Hey Bob, how's that case you have with Phil Pressler's firm going?"

"Good, good. Judge gave us a favorable ruling on the motions to keep out some of their damages expert's testimony."

"Great. That's Judge Schanker, right?"

"Yep, yep. Schanker."

"Good judge. Good judge."

"What's in the briefcase today?"

"Time sheets. Lotsa time sheets."

"Oh yeah. End of the month again. Good luck with that."

Repeat every twenty-four hours, five days a week, for forty years.

The old bastards probably convinced themselves long ago that they actually enjoyed pushing paper. That or there was no other career option available, so thinking about whether it was fulfilling would only dredge up frustrations better left stifled. Maybe that's the only way to live through the deadening repetition. I'll always wonder if that tactic's innate or learned, and if it really holds through life or just works like a tax deferment strategy. If in their twilight years those old codgers look back on a legacy of procedural arguments and boxes of time sheets and suddenly one morning, when they're eighty-three, it hits them like a lightning bolt: *Shit. I fucked up. I want a do-over.* What's the old saying, "Nobody ever died wishing he'd spent more time in the office"?

Terrance fiddled with his glasses and stared me in the eye. "How would you like to work in my department?"

"I've already accepted a position elsewhere."

"The offer involves a twenty-five-thousand-dollar raise."

You have to be fucking kidding me. I'd slaved all those thousands of hours for the firm and done everything I was supposed to, exactly what any career guide would tell you: "Act positive and professional," "Be a team player," "Don't complain." Nonsense. It's only when they know you know it's all just a game that they respect you.

The only problem with the counteroffer Terrance had made was it was too late. Once you've told them you know what's behind the curtain, you're ruined for the institution. As much as they respect you, they can't trust you, and you can't trust them. So while I desperately wanted that money, the only thing I could do was turn it down.

When the meeting was over I bolted for the elevators to get out of the building as soon as possible. I was sweating, tired and worn, and I didn't want to waste a moment more than I needed to in the place. It was summer and Harris would be drinking somewhere in an hour, which is where I desperately needed to be.

The elevator doors opened and I slipped between two young secretaries and stood at the back of the car, leaning against the wall. "Are you wearing Obsession?" One turned to the other. "What?" the friend snapped back. "Are you kidding? Is it, like, 1995 again?"

"It's Chanel." I passed them as I got off on the ground floor. "Old school."

I put on my sunglasses and stood on the sidewalk, processing the situation. *Play your part and get treated like a copying machine. Lob tomatoes at the stage and get offered a $25K raise.* It wasn't an earth-shattering epiphany, but there are a lot worse discoveries a person can make at twenty-nine. I had the next ten days off, months of pretending to work as I learned the ropes at a new firm after that, and for some utterly baffling reason, people seemed to want to pay me more than I had any business receiving. All things considered, this was the best hangover I'd had in a long time.

Sudden Asshole Syndrome

IN PRAISE OF HEMLOCK

sobered up a few days into my new job and the reality of what I'd done hit me. *You turned down a $25K raise? You idiot.* I even went as far as calling JP&Q back to see if the position was still open.

"Sorry," they told me. "It's since been offered to someone else."

It wasn't the money that made me feel stupid so much as the immediate realization that working at Dorsey Fishman was a horrible mistake, the sort that could only end badly. I had no concrete proof of it initially, just a feeling based on what I'd seen early on—the sort of sharp gut reaction I was learning to trust.

For starters, the firm was too small. Where I'd been one of so many before, now I was one of a dozen. There was nowhere to escape the way you could in a big office, no way to get lost in the shuffle when you needed to or close your door and sweat out the previous night's poisoning with no one noticing. No ducking assignments, sliding in at ten or phoning in the work. And the place was so organized, so stifling. I couldn't help feeling that I was being watched, rated, and evaluated every second of the day. The office manager had even set up my computer with the screen facing the doorway, so I couldn't hide what I was looking at from a partner walking into my office. It was painfully, brutally clear: these people were going to scrutinize and micromanage me, and there was no way I could get away from them.

The lawyers at Dorsey Fishman were serious types, efficient, sober, and stoic, as far from my "kind" as anyone could possibly be. I realized that the first time I met with them, before I'd even started at the firm. It was a party at Jonathon Fishman's home on a Saturday afternoon. I'd entertained friends at my apartment the night before and was suffering the aftereffects of vodka, cigarettes, mushrooms and sleep deprivation from playing cards into the early morning. *What was I thinking?* I remember walking into Jonathon's still feeling a little squirrelly, cursing the Camel Lights for that awful "cigarette hangover." My tongue felt like wool and my head was still filled with gin strategies, mixed up with a pile of random mushroom memories, a mess of strange images I wasn't sure were dreams or reality or a combination of the two. The only thing I knew for sure was I'd be slow and stupid until I got a drink. Coffee wouldn't fix this; I had to get back on the horse. Kill the sweats and fidgeting, calm the stomach and get into a zone where I could properly form sentences. These were my new coworkers, my new bosses. Coherence was a must, or at least something close to it. Twitching and barking "The ace is not a face card!" at the first person to say hello wouldn't be a proper start.

"Hello, P.J." Dennis met me at the door and introduced me around the house, to all the partners and associates and their spouses, running me through the whole gauntlet, sans cocktail. Jonathon was the last person we ran into, downstairs, just inside the sliding doors opening to the pool. He was fiddling with a stereo that looked like it was from 1976, one of those ancient relics with a record player on the top and a dual cassette deck. On the floor nearby was a pile of old vinyl albums, some yellowed and frayed, like they'd been there collecting dust since the Summer of Love. I felt like I'd gone back in time—slipped through a wormhole, out of reality into one of the pool scenes from *The Graduate*. It wasn't hard to imagine Jonathon walking toward me, putting his arm around my shoulder and saying, *P.J., I want to say one word to you. Just one word. "Plastics."*

"Hello. Good to see you could make it." Jonathon shook my hand. "Would you like something to drink?"

"I thought you'd never ask." Ten more minutes without one and I might have started crying.

"There's Coke, Diet Coke, I think, and iced tea out by the pool. Oh, and if you'd like, there's some light beer in the cooler. I think there's some Snapple in there also."

"Great. Thanks." *What kind of person doesn't have liquor on hand for a party?* It was cruel and wrong, downright un-American. You don't do that to guests. It's like having a cash bar at a wedding or serving fruit punch at a football tailgate. Liquor's a necessity for dealing with coworkers in a social setting, everyone knows that. I darted over to the cooler and threw back three Miller Lites in short succession, to kill the growing fear running through my head. I didn't mind teetotalers. Hell, they probably had it right. Who knew how far I might have gone if I'd abstained a little? But anyone this clean and straight gave me the shakes. *Snapple?* How would we ever understand each other?

I tried talking a little bit about golf and skiing, the usual sorts of icebreakers. Jonathon responded with a story about how he sold his vacation home because he found himself working all weekend while he was there. It was obvious I was stepping into a huge cultural disconnect. These people clearly lived for the work. This wasn't going to be a "fun," "light," or "enjoyable" job in any regard.

Still, I could've gotten past that, and past the size of the firm and everything else that creeped me out about the place. If I'd learned one thing in my short career, it was to face a day in the office like a prisoner doing solitary confinement. Go in, do the work, talk as little as possible and leave. It's a usually a foolproof strategy. Unfortunately, my boss, Dennis, wasn't the sort to let a man do his time in peace. He ran more of a hard-labor joint, like the chain gang in *Cool Hand Luke,* and yes, just as the oft-quoted line from the movie goes, Dennis and I had a serious "failure to communicate."

The first sign of trouble with Dennis popped up two months after I started. I was sitting at my desk one morning when he walked in and dropped a book of Pennsylvania court rules in front of me. "I want you to read these in your off time."

"Why?"

"You clearly don't have any facility with them." He was wrong. I understood them. I just couldn't recite one on a moment's notice the day before when Dennis showed up unexpectedly in my office, peppering me with rapid-fire questions. At ten in the morning I barely knew my name, let alone the exact page where the rules explained how many days we had to respond to some opponent's motion.

"I don't know the name of any streets in Philadelphia off the top of my head, but I knew how to get here this morning, didn't I?" I wasn't kidding about that. When I used to run around Manhattan delivering packages as a summer job, I drove by memory, eyeballing landmarks that told me where to turn, not even thinking about the street names. Hell, I barely know the names of any of the streets around my house today.

"That's not the point."

"No, that is the point. You ask me questions like I'm a computer, ready to pop off a complex answer the moment you want it. Nobody can do that."

"You need to be fluent in the court rules."

"I am, if you give me a chance to look it up without standing here, watching me and asking follow-up questions."

"You should be able to find it quickly and answer. That's your job. That's what lawyers do."

Let me explain the court rules. We're talking about hundreds of pages of directives dictating when, where, how and in what form certain legal papers may be filed. And below each rule, two or three pages of commentary on when it was first written, each time it was amended, how it was amended, and why. Saltpeter for the mind—duller than the manual for your microwave. Reading that dreck in my off time would be something along the lines of collecting and arranging all the dead insects in a mosquito lamp by size.

And where did Dennis think I was going to find the "off time" in which to peruse those rules? Jonathon told me I was required to bill somewhere in the area of 2,200 hours a year. Unless Dennis had a secret stash of crystal meth he planned to feed me, even if I was silly enough to actually try, there was no way I could ever follow his absurd directive.

I sat speechless for a moment, pondering whether to tell Dennis to fuck himself. On a personal level, I didn't dislike the guy. When he wasn't giving me the Torquemada treatment, he could be funny, droll, and darkly sarcastic. We'd talk about political candidates, Dylan records, and college basketball. He was well read and curious and engaging on so many topics it was obvious something as pedestrian as litigation wasn't or shouldn't have been his chosen trade. On that level I understood him, even sympathized with the guy.

But that wasn't what stopped me from saying, "Are you fucking kidding me?" when he put that book on my desk. Lisa was in graduate school at the time. I was paying most of our bills and I needed a pile of money to buy an engagement ring I was planning to give her. She hadn't asked for one and would have killed me if she knew what I was spending, but getting hitched isn't one of those things you can half-ass. Lisa had put up with me for thirty-six months, and in my view that earned the biggest rock I could afford. Dennis was the source of that money, so when he put that book in front of me, I sucked up my pride and bit my lip, repeating over and over in my head, *Get the ring . . . Get the ring . . . Get the ring.*

A lot of partners seem to think they get respect from associates because of their intelligence, the title or the fact that they've achieved an equity stake in the firm. Of all their delusions, these are the biggest. The only reason any associate takes a partner's abuse is because the partner controls that associate's salary. Dennis wasn't much more than a human cash machine to me. If I hadn't needed the money, I'd have laughed when he dropped the book on my desk, and if he'd gotten in my face about it, I'd have been hard pressed not to scatter his teeth around the room, which I'm pretty sure he knew.

And that lack of respect was clearly one of the reasons Dennis picked on me. He knew I wasn't really interested in the job and was merely tolerating him for a paycheck. Immediately that was a problem because he needed to be able to trust my work. On another level, however, I think it annoyed him to have someone around whose attitude was an affront to everything about the profession he held sacred. The less I seemed to care about little mistakes—typos or forgetting to put a document's page numbers in the same font as the text—the more he made it his goal to make sure I did. "Law is a jealous mistress," the "lifers" of the field like to say. If Dennis believed that, what kind of comment was I making about his choices by treating "the law" like a hooker?

Telling me to read hundreds of pages of rules in my free time was just the beginning. From that day forward, the terminal tension between Dennis and me manifested itself in grueling, almost daily Socratic attacks. He'd come into my office in the morning, start off friendly with a little chitchat about something in the news, then slowly segue into a case I'd been assigned:

"Have you looked into the rule regarding economic damages in the Wormer matter? Suppose the plaintiff changes their claim? Can they still say they have the same losses?" "Have you considered the argument on the joint liability of the defendants in the Neidermeyer case? Conceptually, shouldn't that be the thrust of our brief? What do the cases on the issue say?"

Sometimes he'd walk in with an opponent's motion I hadn't even seen yet and start quizzing me about its contents, as though I should have been prepared to address the arguments in it.

"I didn't know the thing had even been filed until you brought it in here," I'd protest.

"It's not raising issues you didn't already know about," he'd respond. "How are you going to address them? How much time do we have to reply under the rules?"

"What about this?" "What about that?" "Suppose that . . ." The questions were ceaseless, all of them barbed, aimed at proving me a slacker or an idiot when the reality was I just didn't care. Suddenly I was back in law school, surrounded by gunners forcing everyone to entertain their hypotheticals. The Socratic method has its place, but anything beyond bare minimum exposure to the technique gives you an understanding of why its first notable practitioner was forced to drink a pint of hemlock. It's the conversational equivalent of poking someone, a backhanded form of passive-aggressive irritation any socially astute person avoids.

And in a work setting, the irony of Socratic annoyance is that the more you flog an employee with it, the more it produces exactly the opposite of its intended result. I'm certain on some level Dennis figured he was toughening me up, mentoring me into a better lawyer. But all he did was validate my decision to leave the firm as soon as I could, and clarify why he hadn't been able to keep his previous associates.

When I'd complain that he was being ridiculous in his criticism, Dennis would flip the papers at me and spout off this high-handed phrase, "We are lawyers, are we not?" When I heard that, I knew it was time to give up, just sigh, "Yes, understood," "I'll fix that," or "Got it"—anything to placate him. Working for Dennis was the closest I'd come to being defeated by a job. There's no pain like playing the submissive for a man three quarters your size. It feels wrong in every regard, a reversal of natural law, but that was my reality. I was Dennis's gimp, his permanent fraternity pledge.

And the torture wasn't even the worst part of it. What really drove me mad was knowing it was never going to stop. Dennis was a creature of the conventional law firm hierarchy, following the old industry fallacy that you can torment the best work out of an associate. The truth is, premium performance in any field only comes from people who *care*, and nobody really *cares* about a job in something like litigation. I knew Dennis understood that, but I also knew he was a hopeless traditionalist, and rejecting the system that had created him begged a question he didn't want to ask. It was just easier to do as he'd been done—drive the thumb-nails into me for as long as I could tolerate it.

I spoke to Alex constantly during the time I worked for Dennis. He'd switched jobs a few times since law school and was going through a lot of the same annoyances. We tried to give each other useful advice, but that never seemed to happen. The conversations always degraded to discussions of *Simpsons* episodes or whether the Stooges were better than MC5. Often it was just venting, or a layman's anthropology lesson, dissecting the species of office life around us, hoping to find some way to handle them short of naked, brutal violence. Sometimes it was both.

"I can't take this fucking job anymore." I remember calling him one particularly grim morning. "This guy I work for seems to get off on fucking with me. It's like his hobby or something. I'm going to punch the son of a bitch. I'm serious."

"I figured you were just whining the past couple months." Alex laughed. "The guy must be a serious dick."

"I wish he were a dick. In fact, it's his nondickishness that makes him so fucking irritating. Does that make any sense?"

"Totally. You always know where dicks are coming from. If you've got to be fucked with, being fucked with by a dick is a luxury."

"Exactly. You can fight with a dick. It's all out in the open. This guy's passive-aggressive. Nitpicking, needling, it's all back-handed, nonconfrontational shit."

"Sounds like a douchebag."

"Nah. Not enough ego. He's just always giving me the fifth degree. Out of the blue, he'll just start cross-examining me."

"Better you than me. I'd have already killed an asshole like that."

"He's not an asshole, though. It's more a personal thing, just directed at me."

"How's that not an asshole?"

"Assholes are dicks to everyone, 'universal douchebags.'"

"You mean 'universal dicks.'"

"What's a 'universal dick'?"

"An asshole."

"Yeah, but like I said, you can't really call him an asshole."

"I'm not. You just said assholes are universal douchebags, but you meant universal dicks. 'Universal douchebag' is redundant. It's like 'white Caucasian.' Hold on a second. I have to grab this call real quick."

As Alex clicked over to his other line, Dennis walked past my office, looking in for a moment, then turning and continuing on toward the reception area. Thank God I was on the phone. It offended Dennis, I think, to compete with anything else for my attention, even for the second it took me to hang up or tell him I'd find him when the call was over.

"Sorry about that." Alex clicked back onto the line.

"Hey, if I suddenly start throwing around litigation terms or say 'Okay. Fine, then,' and hang up, it means the prick is outside my doorway."

"What does this guy look like? Is he effeminate?"

"I wouldn't say he's a lumberjack. What does that matter?"

"Pricks tend to be fancy." As Alex was talking, Dennis glanced into my doorway again, saw I was still on the phone and continued on toward his office. I knew that when he got back to his office he'd call me and ask me to come down to discuss something. "Sort of like male bitches."

"What's a male cunt?"

"A scumbag."

"A cunt and scumbag are not the same thing."

"Have you ever called a woman a scumbag? No. Nobody says, 'You're a real scumbag, Mary.' When a chick does something sleazy and vicious, she's a cunt."

"Or a bitch."

"A 'bitch' is emotional, irrational. A cunt's cold, like a scumbag, doing something shitty on purpose."

"Even under the British usage?"

"It's pretty much the same meaning. Unless your boss dicks you on a bonus or lies about something, he can't be a British cunt."

"No. The guy's real honest. It's just like, every time I talk to him, I never know whether he's going to be friendly or suddenly start fucking with me."

"There's some bipolar chick on the other side of my floor like that. They put her on pills. Now she just stares a lot."

"No, he's generally predictable. He'll show up in my office and start asking me all kinds of shit, and if I don't answer he suddenly erupts into an asshole, asking me about other cases and pointing out how I'm not managing them properly. It's like a 'sudden asshole disease,' or something like that."

"Syndrome."

"What?"

" 'Sudden Asshole *Syndrome*.' That's better."

"Hold on a second." The red light went off on my phone. "Hello?"

"Can you please come down to my office?" It was Dennis.

"Yes, just give me one second. I'm finishing up a call."

"On a case?"

"Yes."

"Which one?"

"It's some research I'm getting from a friend, in the, uh, Stratton case."

"What issue?"

"Several. Let me get back on with him. He's waiting."

"I'd like to know where we stand on the Kroger motion. I haven't seen your draft of the brief yet. I'd like you to bring that with you." He just kept talking, as though my other call didn't matter.

"Got it."

"I have to take a conference call and I don't have much time, so I'd prefer we talk shortly."

"Yeah, I got it. I'll be down in a couple minutes." *Shit. Here we go again.* Dennis would read over my initial draft and start picking apart the language. I'd tell him it was still a raw document, that I hadn't known he wanted to see it that day and was still working out the kinks. He'd gloss over that excuse by claiming there was some fundamental flaw in it, far beyond the remedy of any touch-ups or reorganization, flip the papers in my direction and chide me for wasting his time. On the way out I'd remind Dennis he'd called me into his office, not the other way around. He'd just stare at me in response, as though he'd suddenly suffered brain damage and lost his every power of comprehension.

"So what's the cure for Sudden Asshole Syndrome?" I clicked back over to Alex. "I'm about to run into a case of it."

"I don't deal with assholes, dude. Wait a second, though . . . Oh yeah, here it is. Sudden Asshole Syndrome . . . First diagnosed by Norse anthropologist Aldridge von Hufnagel. Characterized by uncontrollable urges to insult dim subordinates. Oh shit . . . WebMD says it's terminal."

"You're useless."

"It's my fault you can't work for a douchebag like everybody else?"

I never found a cure for Dennis's malady, but I treated the symptoms the usual way: quitting and getting another job. I waited out just enough time at Dorsey Fishman to buy Lisa an engagement ring and avoid looking like a serial job jumper. A headhunter I'd spoken to a few times called one afternoon and asked if I could interview on short notice with a firm called Miller Graham, a notoriously aggressive litigation outfit across town. "They need an associate with your experience level, like, yesterday."

Two days later I was sitting across from Evan Miller, the managing partner of the firm. He reminded me of my first boss, Sean O'Malley, a larger-than-life personality—smart but informal, with a blunt, irreverent sense of humor. I liked the guy immediately.

"So why do you want to leave your old firm?"

"I'm bored. I'm sitting in an office 24/7 being micromanaged and there's no juice to any of it. It's not fun. They tell me this place has an aggressive practice and I need to do something interesting or I'm going to lose my mind." That was far more honest than I should have been, but the guy seemed like a straight shooter.

Evan was as direct with me as I'd been with him. No games, Socratic horseshit, or needling. He just leveled with me. "I don't want hours, or face time, or any of that. I just need people who can win." If I had to pick someone he reminded me of it would be Al Davis, the Raiders' owner. He didn't talk about billable hours once during the interview, just winning his cases. Normally I'd think that was just lawyer posturing, but he had this infectious confidence. If he was bullshitting, I didn't want to know it. I'd walked in cynical about the job, and for the first time in years he made me think I just might be able to enjoy a career in law. Evan didn't cure my skepticism about the industry, but when he said, "Our aim is to have a firm that doesn't suck as much as most of them do," I was sold.

A week later the headhunter called and said Evan was making me an offer, along with some cautionary advice. "This firm is an intense environment, you understand that. People who can handle stress like that seem to really enjoy the place, but it can be very high-pressure. The associate training is trial by fire."

Stress beats boredom any day. I immediately accepted the offer.

Evan needed me to start working on a highly contentious case as soon as possible, so I gave Dennis my two weeks' notice as quickly as I could.

"I like you personally, but workwise, we weren't a good fit." I didn't expect any disagreement from Dennis on that point, and I didn't get any.

"Do you plan to do this long-term?" Dennis smiled.

"What do you mean?"

"Be a lawyer. I don't think you really want to be a lawyer."

"There isn't something you'd rather do?" I gave him an opening to confess what I already knew: that a big part of the reason he'd mercilessly cross-examined me was his own frustration. Dennis couldn't afford to talk to me like a normal person. He had to bill every minute he could, processing and responding to arguments ceaselessly and racing at repetitive tasks to cover the overhead. Dennis could have admitted all that right then and there, but he didn't. He'd been doing the job for decades, and it was far too late for him to start getting introspective. Instead he replied with his usual—a question.

"You don't get any satisfaction out of working behind a desk, do you?"

"That's rhetorical, right?" I smiled, replaying his words in my head as I spoke. After so many interrogations I couldn't help assuming his every question was the tip of a Socratic inquisition. "I mean, really, does anybody?"

Everything Went Pink

BETTER ADVOCACY THROUGH CHEMICALS

I won for Evan, and quickly. But I'm not sure I took the right lesson away from the experience.

The whole thing started at a wedding along the Hudson River on a late fall afternoon. My first drink of the day had been Red Bull and Maker's Mark. From there it branched into Jägermeister, tequila shots, scotch, espresso, and this terrible, shitty dope the waiters had been smoking behind the bandstand. The last thing I recall of the evening was slugging from a bottle of champagne somewhere in the early hours of the morning. It was cheap and sweet and tasted like Asti Spumante, but it was free, and I couldn't tell my hands from my feet, let alone good booze from bad. At that point I was walking unconscious, plastered to the point where I could barely put one foot in front of the other and everything in my plane of vision was doubled. I remember stumbling around the remnants of the reception and having people grab me by the shoulders, asking if I was okay.

"Are you all right?" A man exiting the bungalow next door stopped me from tripping into a flower garden as I fumbled on the steps to my room, searching to find the key so I could pass out inside.

"I'm fine. Juzzz tired . . . You know." I finally managed to pull the key out of my pocket. "Success!"

"Do me a favor." The man grabbed my shoulder. "Don't sleep on your back."

"What?" I knew I was loaded, but was I really that much of a wreck? Enough that somebody had to warn me against choking on vomit in my sleep? Was I in John Bonham territory? I immediately felt shamed, embarrassed, and frightened, certain I'd made a spectacle of myself at some point during the night—that I'd face a lecture the next morning about how I'd knocked over a waitress carrying a tray of drinks or told a filthy sex story to somebody's fundamentalist uncle.

"Not on your back, all right?" The man was insistent. "Sleep on your side."

Who was this guy? I wondered. *Some fucking teetotaler? He'd never seen a drunk with bed spins before?*

"Yeah, yeah. Thanks." I stumbled into the bungalow, flipped on the lights and looked in the mirror. *Do I really look that bad?* Yes. Yes I did. "Ghastly" was the first word that came to mind. My eyes were bloodshot slits in my face, my cheeks were bloated, and I wasn't wearing my clothes so much as allowing them to hang off my frame. My hair was in my eyes, my shirttails were out of my pants, the knot in my tie was down around my sternum and I was listing back and forth, barely holding myself erect. Standing in a suit in front of the mirror, I looked like a cross between the country-club booze bag and something off the Stones' '77 tour jet.

I slept on my side and, yes, I survived the night. When I got out of bed the next morning, however, I wished I hadn't. The pain was merciless, excruciating, and it only seemed to worsen with every moment that passed. There are hangovers that come on strong and leave after you vomit. There are hangovers that creep in slowly and catch you in the late afternoon. And there are hangovers, always involving champagne, that make you pray for death.

Every system in my body was in shock. I couldn't breathe from the cigarettes or hear from the ringing in my ears. The room was still spinning, my heart was pounding from withdrawal or dehydration and I had to struggle to hold down the can of ginger ale I'd had for breakfast. Eating was out of the question.

The mere concept of entering a crowded restaurant on a Sunday morning, with waitresses clanging plates and children darting about squealing, chased by flustered soccer moms barking, "Get back here *right now!*" gave me chest pains.

In a history of binges beginning when David Lee Roth was still a legitimate rock star, this was the worst Day After I'd known. I was facing certain physical breakdown, paralysis, and probable organ failure. The chills and nausea were ceaseless, and the worst of it was that we had a three-hour ride home. I'd never make it, I was sure. Somewhere along the road I'd lose my mind, open the door and leap into passing traffic, just to end the pain. Sitting in a chair outside the bungalow as Lisa packed the car, I could barely keep myself from crying. Prayer seemed rational for a moment.

"I'm going to die," I mumbled, holding my head in my hands. "My body feels like it's toxic, like I'm more polluted than not."

"That's possible." Lisa downed her coffee.

"You survived." I heard the voice of the man from our neighboring bungalow, the one who'd kept me from falling into the flower garden.

"Oh, this is the guy." His wife laughed.

"Thanks for the sleeping tip," I moaned in response. Just thinking about the previous night caused a sharp pain in my temples.

"You went to high school with the bride, right?" Lisa came outside and made small talk with the man's wife as I sat on the stoop, staring at the gravel around my feet, stanching the occasional fit of dry heaves. "The band was incredible." "They were fantastic." "Everything was fantastic." "I loved the bridesmaids' dresses. So chic and understated." "So you're in from Washington? That's such a long ride." "Where are you headed?" I listened as the women did the usual morning-after-the-wedding recap.

"Well, we're hoping to get back to Philadelphia, if he lives." When I heard that, I knew Lisa was looking at me, but I couldn't raise my head.

"I might be able to cure that." I heard the man walk to his car and open the trunk.

"So was the bridal gown Vera Wang?" the women went on. "I thought it was Badgley Mischka."

A moment later I noticed a shadow in front of me. "Dude, take one of these." A hand appeared in front of my face with three or four huge pills in its palm.

"What is it?"

"Properazine."

"Pro-chlor-perazine," the man's wife corrected him in the background.

"Whatever. It's an anti-anxiety pill mixed with a muscle relaxant. My brother gets it for migraines."

"It's an 'anti-psychotic.'" The wife laughed.

"Best thing for nausea on the planet. They give it to terminally ill patients so they can eat."

"I'm not much of a painkiller guy." I stared at the pills in my hand. I knew "anti-psychotic" was just a medical term that sounded a lot stranger than it was, but I still couldn't help wondering, *Were these people giving me some heavy-grade brain-freezing agent? Generic lithium? Thorazine? Was this the medication of some dangerous schizophrenic who'd gone off her regimen?*

"Trust me. This stuff's great."

"Thanks." I cracked open another ginger ale to chase down one of the pills.

"You're going to want to eat something with that," his wife jumped in again. "It's not weak stuff."

"I can't." I cracked one of the horse pills in half and put it in my mouth, figuring a smaller dose corrected for the lack of food in my system.

The guy wasn't lying. The drug was simply amazing. A half hour later I was eating a McDonald's cheeseburger from a roadside drive-thru, something I usually couldn't stomach sober. By the time we reached Philadelphia, I was well enough to go running. The anxiety, stomach knots and spins, all of it was gone. The drug was almost too effective, like I'd cheated nature. I remember feeling guilty about going to the gym that afternoon, like I should have been upstairs in bed, lying in pain, learning my lesson.

I put the rest of the pills in a little tan "Pillbox" in my under-wear drawer where I stored random drugs people gave me or left around the house. I figured it was better to save them than use the stuff as "associate's little helpers," to kill boredom and angst at the office, the way I would Xanax or Ativan tablets people gave me from time to time. These were a different class of pill, too strong to be spent like that. This was the sort of thing you only used in emergencies, against those really atrocious Sunday mornings coming down.

A week later, on a Monday morning, I received this email from my new boss:

From: Miller, Evan
Re: Carter Motion for Turnover

I am in Kentucky through Friday. You have to handle the turnover motion in Carter.

The Carter case was the reason I'd been hired, the conten-tious lawsuit Evan had needed a lawyer to start preparing for trial immediately. It was a standard contract dispute between busi-ness partners that had somehow escalated into a scorched-earth war—more brutal than any piece of business litigation I'd seen before. The primary adversaries couldn't sit in the same room with each other and nobody even bothered to ask about the pos-sibility of settlement. The parties filed countless motions against each other, alleging every imaginable violation of the court rules and taking every available cheap shot at one another. I'd told Evan I wanted to work on something ugly and aggressive. He said he had what I wanted and promptly threw me into the Carter matter. And now here I was, barely three months into the new job, just learning the ropes, about to handle a motion seeking turn-over of $250,000 of our client's money.

Trial was months away, but the most aggressive of the other side's lawyers was so sure he'd win he filed papers seeking to have my client's money turned over to his in advance. The motion was nasty, a long-winded, overblown narrative of my client's alleged nefarious behavior, dripping with vitriol and that faux judgmental disgust lawyers throw at opponents for emotional effect. Writing the response to the damn thing alone had taken days. Now I'd have to argue it.

Normally a motion like this wouldn't have been a huge deal. Possession's nine-tenths of the law, and if the court ordered the money turned over, the other side would still have to force it from my client's hands. I could file an appeal and tie up that process for months. But in this case, due to the circumstances of the dispute, the money was lying in a bank account the other side had access to, and had only been prevented from taking by a court order freezing it pending the outcome of the trial. If the court granted this motion, the money was gone, and like I said, possession's nine-tenths of the law. Even if we won at trial, good luck ever getting that money back. Losing wasn't an option.

Many young lawyers would brag about being given that level of responsibility. Some would kill for that kind of recognition. "My mentor really thinks I'm up to the task! I won't let the firm and client down!" I am not one of those lawyers. Validation never meant much to me. As far as motions went, I got off on the endorphin rush of winning, and that was all I chased. Hearing the judge rule in your favor was a high, like sex or that first Red Bull and vodka of the night. It was immediate gratification and it made the job fun. The problem with this motion was the judge hated my client and was totally biased. At every turn in the case he'd ruled against us, often unfairly, and though the motion was garbage, it was easy to see the judge granting it.

That was what concerned me. The kick of winning a motion is great, but the pain of losing is just as intense. Having to congratulate the winner, wait for the elevator, then trudge out of the courthouse, the whole time analyzing why you failed, is a terrible low. This motion was losable, very much so, and I had no intention of taking that walk of shame with $250,000 on the line.

Don't get me wrong, I was nervous, but I was also psyched for the fight. Grandstanding and running your mouth off for an audience is a gas, and motions are the best place to put those skills to use. Sure, trials can be fun, but they require a lot of organization and run on for days or weeks. That gets old in a hurry, unless there's a chance you're going to win an ungodly sum at the end. Motions are just the right size—one issue, one argument, and you're doing all the talking.

Motion arguments are like acting class, a place where a young lawyer can find his voice, experiment with tone, delivery, and technique, or, when you've got a dead-lock winner, just ham it up for shits and giggles. I'd used a lot of voices over the years, my favorite being "Southern gentleman lawyer," where I'd spout off schmaltzy colloquialisms. "Well, your honor, counsel has come to a gunfight with a knife." "Judge, he's not within spitting distance of the standard required for the relief he's seeking." In the summer, I'd even wear seersucker to court, like Matlock. Believe it or not, the bit gets results. A lot of judges seem bored—forced to listen to lines of fat little clods in ill-fitting suits and ketchup-stained ties stammering and fuming about low-rent slip-and-fall cases. If you entertain them and look like you've actually put some work and original thought into an interesting argument, they'll reward you, or at least hurt your client less than he deserves.

Unfortunately, I got to use the Southern-gentleman act a lot less than I'd like. Most commercial cases have clearly liable and clearly aggrieved parties. The lion's share of them are strategic business decisions, in which a company knowingly violates an agreement for economic reasons and anticipates responsive litigation or files an all-but-frivolous claim to gain some advantage over a competitor. In the context of business lawsuits, the enforceability of a contract isn't decided by the tightness of its language so much as by the pocketbook of the parties involved. Commercial litigation has a lot less to do with the substance of a claim or defense than it does with which side can more effectively manipulate the rules and outspend the other. Break the opponent's wallet and they have no choice but to settle on the terms you want.

The game plan in most of these cases is to be as difficult and confrontational as possible, while staying within the confines of the rules, raising dozens of procedural arguments laymen know as "technicalities." Object to everything, refuse to produce information, and file endless motions seeking all sorts of rulings and sanctions against the other side every chance you get. Sometimes, if you file enough, you can confuse the issues of a case and twist an utterly vacant claim or defense into something almost plausible. At a minimum, you'll bleed your adversary's bank account. I've been involved in cases where lawyers objected to the disclosure of records that would *help* their client just to force the opponent to incur the cost of filing a motion to force the disclosure. Huge firms routinely "wallpaper" opponents with hundreds of requests for material their clients don't need and they know the opponent can't possibly produce simply to run up the other side's fees. The only skill set you really need to be a crack commercial litigator is enough facility with the rules to ensure you use every bullet available and avoid missing any deadlines.

When I'd make those sorts of procedural arguments in motion hearings, I'd often knee-jerk into "Aristocrat" mode, snottily citing court rules and tut-tutting about my opponent's disgraceful disregard for them. "Well, perhaps Rule 16(c)(iii) means nothing to Mr. Featherstone, but it is a rule, and we are obligated to follow the rules."

I felt guilty putting on that act, since I was usually arguing for a hypertechnical application of some commonly ignored rule to excuse my client's atrocious behavior, a tactic that works a lot more than it ought to. I didn't like winning motions that way, because it made me feel like a sniveling playground monitor. But I have to admit, it was kind of fun playing a white-shoe buffoon against type, and when the only option was losing, jumping into any character wasn't a difficult leap.

So yes, I liked motions. And I'd argue anything. But $250,000? And *real money,* not some judgment my client would never pay anyway? That was heavy. I remembered the headhunter's warning before I took the job, "The associate training is trial by fire." Indeed it was.

With a motion of that gravity I needed to be absolutely lucid, clear, and concise in every argument and rebuttal. There was no room for error, no allowance for my chronic ADD moments. No daydreaming about a cute Latin clerk's tits or amusing myself with a short-reel fantasy about the courtroom erupting into a bar-room brawl from a spaghetti western, eyeing the people around me and handicapping who'd win in various head-to-head match-ups. I couldn't zone out and stare at the wall or hum "Hurdy Gurdy Man" in my head while opposing counsel called my client the business equivalent of a pederast, as he surely would. There was no allowance for even a momentary lapse; I had to be calm, collected, and razor-sharp in my reasoning.

The first step was the usual preparation, learning the argu-ment from all sides and compressing the points of law and fact that favored my client into a simple pitch a judge could easily swallow. But that was just shoring up on the substance. What about the delivery? How would I ensure that I came off as smooth as I needed to be? The solution there was obvious: Take one of those hangover pills before court.

"Fuck!" I woke up late on the morning of the argument, which wasn't unusual. "How do you lose a goddamned shoe?" I yelled over and over as I raced against the clock to get ready, rummaging through the pile of dirty socks and random foot-wear on the floor of my closet, as though the complaint would cause my missing black lace-up to materialize. By the time I found it under a garment bag it was after eight, barely time to run to the car and drive to court. I was halfway there before I realized I'd left without picking up a coffee and bagel sandwich from the corner deli. "Goddamnit!" It was another one of "those" mornings, by which I mean every morning. I turned on Howard Stern, flipped the pill in my mouth, and chased it with the last of a bottle of water lying in a pile of garbage on the floor of the pas-senger side of the truck.

Court opened at nine and I was second on the motion list.

Usually that meant an hour-long wait, but the motion before us settled, so we took the floor early.

My opponent was a well-known trial lawyer named Carl Mintz, an ex-prosecutor who'd put away high-level criminals before cashing in on the defense side. Carl was fifty-fiveish, thin, and balding, his last wisps of hair streaked back in the standard "shark" cut. He walked stiffly and rarely smiled, his mouth tightened in a permanent frown. Carl was fancy, but not in some cheap, exaggerated way. He spoke with a haughty lilt and wore simple but perfectly tailored suits, picked all but certainly for the snobbishness of the look. Where most of the lawyers around Philadelphia commanding Carl's $500-an-hour fee dressed like Guido pimps, Carl looked like Sean Connery in *Dr. No*. The man telecasted "Arrogant Dick," which seemed to be exactly the image he was cultivating.

You'd need an airplane hangar to house Carl's ego. Bloated self-perception and terminal narcissism are pandemics in the legal industry, but even in that deluded confederacy, he stood out. Every loose conversation I had with him turned into a story about some conquest, from being able to throw 85 miles per hour when he pitched in high school, to winning some case, to the classes on trial procedure he taught as a guest lecturer at several law schools. At one point he even offered to give me tips on how he would have handled our client's defense if he'd been on our side, effectively saying, "You're going to lose, and when you do, I'll tell you why." Carl probably thought that was polite, if not a downright generous offer.

On the morning of our argument, Carl strutted into court with his clients and pointed them to the first-row seats directly behind the plaintiff's table. "Where's Evan?" he deadpanned, all business.

"I'm handling this one."

"Oh, okay. Fine, then." From the response, I guessed he was insulted Evan would send an associate to battle him. That, or aggravated he wouldn't get to gloat in front of the managing partner after his impending victory.

Carl arranged his papers in neat piles across the table in front of him, pulled a pen from his jacket pocket and threw a quick half-smile at his client, certain he'd be celebrating with them after bludgeoning me. Shifting back to face the judge, he buttoned his jacket, righted its drape on his shoulders and thrust his chin in the air. The judge smiled, we exchanged the usual pleasantries, and then Carl took the floor.

"Your honor, my clients are moving to have two hundred and fifty thousand dollars currently frozen distributed to them because, in all likelihood, they will succeed at trial. The evidence of the defendant's breaches and fraud is simply astounding—overwhelming, and quite frankly staggering. I'm shocked, truly shocked, and I've been involved in many cases, your honor, and . . . Well, I'd like to recite some of it for the court . . . "

And on and on it went.

Carl's presentation was obnoxious, insulting to my client and patronizing to the judge. We all put on a song-and-dance for the court, but I never stoop to obsequious flattery. Carl all but offered the judge a hand release every time the old man interjected: "Excellent point, your honor," "Your honor anticipated where I was going next," "Very true, your honor. And you raise an interesting point." Every time the judge made a light comment, Carl laughed like it was the funniest joke he'd ever heard.

As I sat there listening to Carl argue, I realized I'd gotten very lucky. His argument was awful. He rattled off dozens of facts he claimed proved his clients' version of events and went off on one scathing diatribe after another. He probably figured he was on a roll, and I had to admit, his frothing rant did have an amusing flow to it. The problem was, every insult, over-the-top accusation, and slanderous description dug him deeper into a hole. If he'd presented a few of them in a measured fashion, he might have been able to convince the judge there was a reason to turn over some of that $250,000 in advance of trial. But Carl had offered so much overheated rhetoric that even if the judge had been inclined to grant the motion, now he had no choice but to deny it. No court can ever give off the appearance of being swayed by frenzied ad hominems.

I leaned back in my chair and watched Carl roll, seemingly oblivious to the fact that he was making an argument against his own motion. About two-thirds of the way through his presentation, he asked the court for a moment to review some notes before concluding. As he flipped through the papers on the table in front of him, he turned and shot me a grin. I guess he figured he'd won. I wanted to mouth "Thanks," in response, but I feared jinxing myself. Success is never "in the bag" in litigation.

And frankly, I wasn't sure my lips were even working. About that time I noticed the pill, which I'd all but forgotten, was beginning to really take effect. Watching Carl scan his notes, I realized I'd been leaning back in the defendant's chair at an angle almost parallel to the floor. My legs felt numb and the judge was blurring in and out of focus. Reaching for the water pitcher, I realized my arms were rubberized. They worked fine but felt heavy, as though I'd just done a hundred curls with forty-pound dumbbells. It was obvious the stuff had me by the balls, but I didn't panic. I couldn't. The higher-functioning portions of my brain were on overdrive, but the pill had switched off the adrenaline receptors.

How do I handle this? I'm going to fall down when it's my turn to argue. My head felt too heavy for my neck, and despite the fear gripping my brain, I felt myself sinking lower into the chair, the most comfortable piece of furniture I'd ever occupied. I wanted to go with the buzz, but I had no idea where that would lead. Was this the peak, or just the beginning? If half a pill brought me out of a staggering hangover, what did a whole one do sober? It seemed an awful lot stronger this time, immobilizing, and I didn't know how far that would go, how many of my systems it would compromise. Would I find myself a slurring, crippled fool, mumbling like some wino off the streets?

This was experimental territory for me. I wasn't a painkiller or muscle-relaxant person. Things like Percocet and Vicodin never interested me. The stuff always seemed a waste of time, a "medicated" high for the sort of parasites who feign back injuries to get themselves on government benefits. The way I saw things, if a drug didn't work on my brain, it wasn't worth taking. The only reason I'd eaten the pill that morning was to wipe the anxiety out of the moment, and now here I was, tattooed to the chair, feeling like I was suspended in some viscous gel and wondering if my knees would buckle when I stood to address the judge.

At least I was calm. If there was a fight-or-flight rush coursing through me, I certainly didn't feel it. During Carl's conclusion, as he machine-gunned my client with a litany of cheap, irrelevant criticisms, the judge glanced in my direction, inviting me to object. I smiled back, rolled my eyes and held my chin, running my tongue around the inside of my lips to make sure the muscles in my mouth were working.

When my rebuttal time finally came, I stood as quickly as possible, to gird against any appearance of sluggishness. Not a good idea. Everything in the room suddenly turned pink and fuzzy, as though I were viewing it through a thick red gauze, not unlike a sudden rush of blood to the head, only miles more intense and unabating. The initial sensation was similar to coming out of mild anesthesia, in that haze where every sense of time and its forward progression ceases, or a little like the tail end of a nitrous hit, only with a lot more lucidity.

"Nowww weee'll heecar frommm youuu," the judge said, turning toward me. The courtroom ran in slow motion, all sounds and movements drawn out as though it were a videotape playing a shade too slow. For a split second I grappled with the dueling concepts of the moment. On one hand, I was standing in a room full of my peers, arguing complex legal theories. On the other, I'd taken a very strange pill. *They must realize I'm tweaked here, those fuzzy pink bastards.*

When I started to speak I didn't know what to expect. The only thought in my head was, *Fuck it. You have to say something.*

There was no way to know if it would be gibberish or brilliance until I opened my mouth. I crossed my fingers and started talking, and the argument just flowed. From where, I had no idea.

"Your honor, I heard nothing but allegations from the movant, which, contrary to his argument, are not undisputed facts. He's asking the court to lower the blade without a trial. Everything he said supports the need for a trial, to determine what the real facts are. The court can't give him my client's money now, before those facts are decided . . . "

There were none of the usual synaptic misfires. No questioning every argument before I made it or deciding mid-sentence that I didn't like the sound of a phrase and restarting my point differently. No rambling asides or repetitive run-on points. All the usual demons running around in my head were gone. It felt like every one of the self-defeating tics that could have sunk me was turned off and I was fully in my element, in my world. The thing slid off my lips as though I were relating an anecdote at a bar with glass of scotch and a cigarette. So many times I'd thought, *If everything about this career weren't so formal and the people in it so uptight, if I could just feel at ease and talk the way I would with friends, this would probably be a really easy job.* Well, now I knew. It was a creepy realization, but if the ultimate question of the day was whether I was better stone sober or tweaked on that pill, the answer was obvious. The only problem was getting more. *I wonder if I know anyone who's terminally ill . . .*

Carl's clients didn't stick around to hear the ruling. By the time I was done, they were putting on their coats to leave. The judge wasted no time denying Carl's motion. I knew from the way he smiled and said my client would "be getting his day in court soon enough" that this was a successful battle in a war that might not go as well. But I paid that no mind. No use casting a pall over the moment. This was a win. My win.

"Good argument," Carl congratulated me, as tersely as he could, and stalked from the courtroom.

"Thank you." I sank back into the chair and reorganized my papers.

"Excuse me sir. Uh, sir." A clerk appeared at my shoulder.

"Yes?"

"The judge is hearing the next motion." I turned and saw a group of lawyers holding exhibit cases behind me. "You're in counsel's seat."

"Right. We're in court."

Definitely a half pill next time.

KEEP YOUR SHIT TO YOURSELF

Sometimes after you've been doing the same rotten, annoying work every day for long enough, the little things get to you.

"How are you, Maryann?"

"Good morning, Kathy."

"How you doing, Deana?"

I could hear Ernie twenty feet away. He was a partner during my first year at Miller Graham, and every morning, like clockwork, he'd walk down the hall, greeting the secretaries sitting in a row of cubicles outside my door. Ernie was always jovial, striding by with a broad, satisfied smile on his face, like he'd just settled some huge case. But as friendly as he appeared, Ernie never lingered or stopped to chat with any of the assistants. He was on a mission, heading to the men's room, with that newspaper tucked under his arm.

I couldn't miss Ernie's morning march. His office was just up from mine, and I was almost directly across the floor from the entrance to the men's restroom. He was older, old-fashioned, and probably figured it was just polite to say hello as he trotted past. Whenever I saw him coming I'd pick up the phone or turn my head. He probably thought me rude or snobbish, but I just couldn't look the guy in the eye, not under those circumstances. The morning was bad enough without having to talk to Ernie as he folded that newspaper in his hands and drove all those disgusting images into my head. Watching him pass, it was all I could do to not slap the pile of newsprint from his hand and shout, "Dammit, man. Have some fucking dignity."

Working in a law firm is having your mind assaulted in dozens of little ways every day. I'm not talking about the major annoyances like office politics, prima donna partners or the constant stroking of fragile male egos you have to engage in to get along in the field. These are smaller injuries, chronic little insults to the psyche, piling up day after day.

The list of ugly and disturbing images you run into regularly in a law office goes on forever. I could offer hundreds of examples from every firm in which I've worked, most of them fitting into archetypes we'd all recognize. There was the associate with pubescent acne who left at least one festering pea-sized white-head on his face at all times, the copy room guy with the serial-killer grin and teeth perpetually spackled with the remnants of Cheetos and Snickers bars, the mailroom assistant who'd never heard of deodorant, and, of course, the chain-smoking secretary who coughed, then swallowed, then recoughed back into her mouth the same slug of phlegm all day long.

And no one can forget the Dark Ages of corporate casual, that bleak period before firms developed guidelines for proper business attire. You had the grossly obese gave-up-on-life-at-nineteen assistants sporting the "office sweat suit look"—lumpy sweaters and stretch pants three sizes too small, displaying cavernous camel toes in their massive, udder-like genitals. There were the office "Chia Pets," those men who looked like chimpanzees in golf shirts, with layers of coarse, almost pubic hair sprouting from every exposed inch of flesh and pouring out of the tops of their collars. And who would forget the "Double Asses"—those androgynous middle-aged paralegals who wore snug-fitting, pleated Dockers highlighting "gunts" that protruded as much in front as their asses did in the back, making it difficult to tell from a distance whether the woman was coming toward you or walking away.* The list of aesthetic offenses in the average office would run on forever. It's not happenstance that *Vogue* and *GQ* have never done "Law Firm Style" issues.

Of all these sensory assaults, however, the worst is verbal, what I'd call "mental rape." Yes, the concept is just about as simple as it sounds, but giving you a dry definition does it an injustice. To truly understand the power of the thing, you have to experience it. Consider these statements, at least one of which could apply to your job circumstance:

- Your boss just walked into your office naked from the waist down, smiling, gripping a huge, throbbing purple erection.

- The creepy associate two offices down—the chinless guy who never talks to anyone and stares a lot—is surfing on-line swimsuit magazines and rubbing his nipples.

- You know that bald bookkeeper down the hall, the one with yellow teeth and sores on his scalp? He masturbated into his bathroom sink before leaving for work this morning.

You get the picture. You can't do anything to stop the mental rape. As soon as the words leave the speaker's mouth, your brain begins processing them and visualizing their substance. If the image upsets or disturbs you, you only think about it more. You may be stuck envisioning your boss's engorged member for several hours after you finish reading this piece. Hell, you might have already envisioned him firing off a money shot with it.

In the office setting, mental rapists are usually well-meaning people who don't realize they're battering your brain. Sometimes

---

*Basically, Homer Simpson's body with breasts and a Billie Jean King haircut.

it's a new mother talking to another woman with no idea of the volume of her voice. "It got so bad I was bleeding, so I just decided to use the breast pump." This woman has no idea she's just made it impossible for you to ever talk to her without picturing electric vacuums attached to her bleeding breasts, as though she were in some hard-core bondage video or snuff film.

Sometimes the offender will think his sharing of intimate details is hip or cool, "what the kids do." These people are often older men trapped in a midlife crisis, feeling their virility ebb and trying to reconnect with their inner stud—the sort of men who drive Jaguar convertibles, prop their sunglasses in their hair and wear dry-cleaned jeans on casual Fridays. "I miss anything at the meeting this morning? The kids are back at college and the wife held me up a little bit. A little morning surprise. Know what I mean?" *Oh yes. Tell me about your last colonoscopy as well. And your vasectomy.*

But of all these mental rapists, the very worst was Ernie's kind, the "Newspaper Guy." The Newspaper Guy is that chipper prick who marches down the hall to the men's room every morning, booming "Hello!" in a "Zip-a-Dee-Doo-Dah" tone to everyone he sees on the way with a newspaper folded prominently under his arm, telecasting to the whole fucking office:

"Hey! Guess what? Right now a huge fecal loaf is pushing against the sides of my bowels! I'm going to walk into the men's room, get in a stall, open the paper, fart a few times, read some articles, strain, moan, then squeeze a huge chocolate submarine into the water. When you see me on my way back, twenty minutes from now, I'll be sweating, and you'll know exactly why."

When I'd see Ernie walking by with the paper, all I could picture was his face turning purple as he arched forward on the bowl with his pants around his ankles. If I happened to be standing near my secretary's cubicle as he walked past, he'd say hello and I'd be forced to answer back in kind, biting my tongue to avoid loosing a sarcastic rant. *Best wishes on the shit, Ernie! Hope it's a smoothie, and remember, don't wipe too hard. That's how you get hemorrhoids!*

I've been videotaped having sex, been to nude beaches and

had physicals administered by female doctors. I wouldn't call myself "shy" or "reserved" in any regard. But I have never, will never, and could never even fathom allowing someone to see or hear me defecate. When I had to do that at the office, I'd search or wait for an empty men's room, even if it involved going to another floor. If people came in to use the urinal while I was in the stall, I'd become deadly quiet, not making a sound until they left. And if someone got in the stall next to me, to the extent I could, I'd pretend I was done, flush, and leave. Under no circumstances did I ever voluntarily listen to someone or allow someone to listen to me "dropping the kids off at the pool." Call me fancy. Call me a freak. That's just how I roll.

To me, the bathroom's a place to spend as little time as possible. I'm in, done, and gone. No tucking my shirt to get it just so and adjusting my pants thirty times in front of the mirror. That's all done before I leave the stall. And once I'm out of there, I head straight to the sink, wash my hands, then dart for the door. Why anyone would want to extend the time they had to spend in an underventilated room full of excrement receptacles baffles me. Aside from maybe a Counting Crows concert, I can't think of a single place on the planet I'd less want to be.

And the worst of the Newspaper Guys, a subset known as "Stall-Talkers," would actually engage or continue conversations with you after they'd entered the stall:

"Hey, did you hear about the Fletcher decision?"

"Uh . . . no. I, uh, hadn't."

"It's right here in the morning paper. Looks like the—[*heavy breathing*]—judge really, uh—[*agonizingly long pause*]—nailed them."

"Great. That's just great."

The dialogue is almost like a play-by-play. By timing the pauses and heavy breaths, you can pinpoint exactly when each part of the action's taking place, from the second his sphincter began loosening to that final release, all the way through to the wiping. Thankfully, blessedly, the sound of the toilet flushing usually covered that. Hearing even a hint of those surfaces rubbing against one another and imagining a guy like Ernie with his hand up his ass would have had me all but vomiting in the sink.

Still, as gross as all these images could be, I couldn't figure out why seeing Ernie carrying the paper made me so angry. It seemed such an irrational, disproportionate response. I was a live-and-let-live kind of guy. So he liked taking long shits. People have stranger hobbies. What was wrong with that?

Everything. Everything was wrong with that. When I really thought about it, I realized it wasn't Ernie's or any other Newspaper Guy's bathroom habits that annoyed me. It was the Celebration of the Shit. Defecating is a daily exercise, one of the few things Oprah Winfrey, the Dalai Lama and Chester the Building Super with the Hundred-Yard Stare all did this morning. It's an equalizer of sorts, more so than death or taxes or any of the other commonalities binding us on basal levels. At some point in the last day or so even the Queen of England had to wipe her ass, but it's no one's greatest moment. The fact is, if sitting in a hotbox of stale farts and acrid urine fumes provides an escape for you—enough to justify a ritual or reading materials—you need a fucking hobby, and probably a therapist.

And that's what drove me nuts about Ernie and all the other Newspaper Guys I'd known at various firms. Your morning shit should never be the best thing about your day. Every time I watched him pass I remembered a summer job I'd had between high school and college. For what I can only assume was the purpose of showing me just how bad life could be if I didn't study in school, my father got me a job working in his buddy's cold-storage warehouse, pushing around pallets of frozen chicken. My co-workers were drunks and burnouts who hated their jobs, and one of the chief hiding places where people would go to escape the maddeningly repetitive toil was the bathroom. They'd take magazines into it and hide, knowing they'd have at least fifteen minutes of peace before the foreman started banging on the door.

That's what I flashed back to whenever I saw a Newspaper Guy. Ernie and his kind were usually older, people who'd been practicing law for years, and watching them raised a question I didn't want to consider: *Would that be me someday?* I thought I'd learned the lesson that summer job was supposed to enforce. I'd gone to school, gotten good grades, gotten a professional degree. But now here I was, gone full circle, back in a gilded version of that warehouse, punching time cards in a field where pinching a loaf seemed to be the highlight of the day for a lot of people.

Getting Your Money's Worth

MAKE IT A DOUBLE, AND ANOTHER DOUBLE

T hey won't eat that." Lisa leaned across the table, trying to stop me, but she was too late. I hooked the foie gras on the end of my fork and catapulted it into the air. The sack of fat flipped end over end like a half-filled water balloon, then splashed into the koi pond below.

"You're right." The fish scattered from it like a tear gas bomb.

"And you're an asshole." She sat back in her chair and sipped a glass of champagne.

"What? I didn't want that on my steak. It's organ meat, like scrapple. People only eat that shit because it's French."

"Will you please act like an adult? People are looking at us."

"What? The fish are probably hungry. It's a win-win." I glanced right and caught a woman in a sequined American flag T-shirt at the table next to us peeking at me out of the corners of her eyes. The moment our glances met, she turned and pretended to be talking to her husband. "The steak isn't even good."

"Why did you order it? This is a seafood restaurant. We're on an island."

"The bastard tricked me. I should have known."

"Who tricked you?"

"Nobody. It's a long story." I reached over to grab a sip of Lisa's drink.

"Get your own." She slapped my hand.

"I would if the waiter would come back."

"Can I help you?" The Japanese man was suddenly hovering over the table.

"Jesus, you scared me. Triple Knob Creek please. And champagne, a white one."

"White champagne. I'll see what I can do. Oh, and sir . . . Please, we ask that you not throw food into the pond."

"They looked hungry."

"They're well fed, sir. Very well fed."

I wasn't really angry about food, though I do loathe foie gras. I was salty about a fax I'd received from the office informing me that when I got home I'd be facing a blinding shitrain of work on a massive, incredibly weak case.

Before Lisa and I left on our honeymoon, I'd used a hardball tactic on an opponent, unexpectedly pushing for a trial in a long-languishing case, hoping the sudden threat of going to court would shake his client into a settlement. The plan backfired. Instead of responding with an offer, while I sat on a beach ten thousand miles away, my opponent filed papers with the court demanding my client put his evidence on the table. If they won the motion, the case would likely go to trial, which would be a flat-out disaster. My client's case was technically valid. The claims were real and the other side had wronged him. The problem was, organizationally, due to the complex allegations and the history of convoluted business relations between the parties, the suit was a mess, the kind of action you'd need an army of lawyers to ready for trial. On top of that, my client was impossible to manage, the type I knew would wind up being the other side's best witness.

The path to this low point was simple, commonplace for an associate. From time to time we're all assigned a lead zeppelin of a case, some impossible patchwork of claims, old, byzantine and weak. The subject matter of the actions vary, but their posture is always the same. The evidence is spotty, the legal theories contradictory and the physical files a compost heap of torn papers, empty folders, busted binders, and boxes of sloppy documents covered in black-marker notations—"September 1995" or "March 1998 Doc Review: Tampa." The last letter from an opponent is dated ten months ago and a call to his firm elicits, "He doesn't work here anymore. Can I direct you to someone else?"

These "cold cases" always have a long, tortured history. Most have been passed around the firm, through half a dozen associates who've since left, finding a new home with each lawyer's departure. Every adoption's the same. "This would be a great claim if it were just on the right track." A partner hands the mess to its new babysitter with some tepid cheerleading. "You've done well in some other matters and we think you can get this one resolved." Translation: "Maybe you're the alchemist who'll turn this septic runoff to diamonds. See if you can raise Lazarus."

Lazarus in this case was "Office Data Systems, Inc.," a once-successful small corporation that leased electronic hardware to a number of Fortune 500 companies, including the defendant in our case, "Great Big Co." GBC had refused to honor a contract with ODS, severely damaging the company. ODS's owner was a wild Greek fireplug named George Bakalis. George was more salesman than manager, and he didn't keep the closest eye on his outfit, relying far too much on GBC's business. When GBC violated his contract, ODS's revenues tanked, and the company all but collapsed. George claimed all of his losses were GBC's fault, and that was largely true. The problem was organizing George's evidence, testimony and witnesses to support those claims. As tight and scary as his complaint might have been, George was loose and wild, with a reckless tongue and a minimal attention span—an exact opposite of the type of organized personality I needed to explain his nuanced allegations.

I smelled the stink of doom on George's case the moment I saw the massive size of the file, which filled an entire cabinet. There's no way to get your head around a bank of documents like that, particularly where half of them predated grunge music. It was immediately clear that the only way to win anything in the case was surprise. We had to get it set for trial in a posture where the other side had no idea how much of it was a bluff. But how? If I asked the court to set a trial date, GBC would demand time to subpoena witnesses, examine the proofs supporting our claims and take numerous depositions, including George's. I was tied in a Gordian knot. There was no rational solution, so I did the only thing any good lawyer could. Procrastinate.

You've probably heard someone complain about how slow the courts work. They blame the system, but that's just what their attorneys tell them. The real reasons for the delay are the lawyers. I've seen lawyers stall the signing of settlement agreements for weeks because they couldn't get to the painful task of analyzing, modifying and negotiating drafts of the thing. I've seen them reschedule depositions half a dozen times because they couldn't bring themselves to read a box of oppressively dull documents to prepare for it. I've personally asked for extensions of court deadlines simply because I couldn't force myself to respond to the other side's papers. Over and over, I'd start crafting some technical argument, and each time, inexplicably, as though I'd blacked out for a moment and come to, I'd find myself reading the newspaper under my desk.

Laziness becomes standard operating procedure after a while. Every day's a new mountain of gibberish on your desk, most of it angry, bloated missives from asshole opponents. And you're supposed to respond to all of it with letters aggressive enough to look like you care. After a while, the "ignore it" default switch in your head takes over. The daily letters keep coming but you don't reply, and before you know it, the backlog grows terminal. You stop pushing cases and start putting out fires, managing an inventory of actions just enough to avoid getting fired. A file of minor missed deadlines piles up in your head. You figure you'll get to them tomorrow. It's the 29th and you've got to fill out a pile of time sheets before the end of the month and your buddy just sent you a slide show of this impossible blonde with tits like cantaloupes and a coin-slot pussy. Who has the time for all that paperwork?

I worked enough on the ODS case to posture it for a settlement, but not force it into trial, since I was sure that would be doom. Then, out of nowhere, at an office meeting a month before my wedding, Evan boomed across the conference table, "What's the status on the ODS case? When's trial?"

Oh shit.

"Well, uh, there's lots of discovery to be done, and—"

"Get it listed for trial."

"I still need a lot of documents, and—"

"Get whatever you still need finished now and get it listed for trial."

"Understood." There was no debating, I could tell from his voice. This was a "do as you're told" situation. I walked back to my office after the meeting and looked at the piles of boxes of case files scattered about my floor, volumes of material I'd need to all but memorize for trial. So much goddamned work, such impossible claims, and all I could think the whole time was *Why?* The firm didn't need the business and the thing was clearly more trouble than it could ever be worth. *Why would someone take on a Titanic of an action like this?* I asked myself, as though I didn't know the answer.

Two of my close friends have taken acid on airplanes, one on a trip from Philadelphia to Paris, one on a flight from Los Angeles to D.C. On its face, the idea's so wrong and senseless that discussing it as anything but a wild hypothetical seems ridiculous. Trapped in a tube doing 400 miles per hour at 30,000 feet, there's no place to throw a Frisbee, stare at the trees, or run if things come unhinged. You're literally riding it out, among two hundred people in exactly the same physical circumstance as you, yet every bit as alone as you'd be in solitary confinement. You can't even dare eye contact with the person in the next seat. For all you know he's an evangelical pastor from Missouri. What would you say if he tried to engage you in small talk? What common ground would you have but your present location?

"So, uh, did you know the wings on this thing can bend so far that the tips can touch it without snapping?"

He'd slam the help button and claw over you into the aisle, screaming, "He's talking about the wings snapping! The wings!"

You'd hear an air marshal's pistol CLICK behind your right ear. They'd have you on the floor in zipper cuffs in seconds, drooling and begging for someone to shoot you with a tranquilizer gun.

Luckily, my friends didn't face those concerns. Each took the trip with a parent sitting next to him. The experiences were nearly identical.

Philadelphia to Paris: "I got bored and ate the thing about an hour or two into the flight. I ordered vodkas all the way across the water. My father kept giving me shit about drinking too much. When we landed I'd forgotten the time-difference thing. I was still tensed up from the strychnine and demanded we go to a bar. He freaked out. I didn't realize it was morning there."

L.A. to D.C.: "We got an upgrade to first class. I wound up going drink for drink with my old man until he passed out, somewhere around Kansas, so I started shooting the shit with the stewardesses. They were some real cool chicks. Fed me handfuls of those little plastic liquor bottles."

I had the same response to each story. "What the fuck were you thinking?"

International Flier: "That's a long flight, you know? It gives the mind something to do. But I don't think I'd do it again. Not being able to smoke in that condition is awful."

Domestic Flier: "You get free drinks in first class. I wanted to make sure I got my money's worth."

For most people, first class is reward enough. It's comfort, and for those who keep score, a perch from which to feel like you're ahead of a lot of Joneses. Then there are those who want to really get their money's worth. I'd like to say there's some complex explanation for what causes an otherwise sane person to eat a high-grade hallucinogen on an airplane, but the answer's pretty simple. Some folks just like to stand on the gas pedal. It's the only way they know to wring some emotional upheaval, a reminder they're alive, out of a terrible, dull routine.

Now, of course, Evan wouldn't eat acid on a cross-continental flight. But he was a tamer point on that broad continuum of thought. Being a respected litigator and having the money and the swanky offices wasn't enough for him. He wanted to gamble, street-fight, feel like he had something on the line. Where Evan really got his rocks off was trying extreme-underdog cases, tackling the steepest odds in the sort of brutal, vicious disputes where most people would say both sides deserved to lose. Evan made sure he *felt* his work, however nerve-racking or heart-attack-inducing it might be. He got his money's worth out of the job.

I used to whine when Evan assigned me to work on impossible cases, but that was just because they tended to be a lot of work. Substantively, even when we lost, they were as close to fun as civil litigation ever got. And ODS could have been one of them, except for one fact: We were the plaintiff. There's a whining element at the heart of plaintiff's law—running to the courthouse the way a child might cry to a parent to fight his battles. It seemed creepy, wrong, and underhanded, no matter how legitimate the case might be. Even in business litigation, being the "plaintiff" made me feel a little like a bitchy, greasy ambulance-chaser.

As Evan ordered, I promptly fired off a request to the court, asking it to set the case for trial. GBC responded by requesting additional time to prepare and take numerous depositions. I argued in reply that they'd had more than enough time already. The plan was to push for as close to a "Wild West" trial as we could get—one where GBC would have as little advance record of what we were going to say as possible—the sort of uncontrollable courtroom brawl big corporations fear most.

A week later I got hitched, and Lisa and I flew to Maui for our honeymoon. I figured when I got back we'd either be settling the case or I'd be preparing for a disastrous trial, after which I'd be looking for another job. Sitting in an airliner over the ocean on your third Dewar's, either is fine.

Sadly, gallons of liquor, champagne, and ten thousand miles of distance can't even cleave you from the job. After eleven drunken days on the beach and a Dylan Thomas bar tab, I had to call the office to find out where things stood in the ODS case. They faxed me a motion GBC had filed with the court. It was solid, reasonable, and right on every point of law. There was no way the judge wouldn't at least let them depose George and enough of his employees to find all the holes in our case. I threw the papers in the trash and headed for the pool bar.

"Triple Knob Creek, please, with a splash of ginger ale."

"We don't make triples, sir."

"Why?"

"It's a rule."

"That's the dumbest rule I've ever heard. I'm just going to get two doubles then, which will be even more."

"Two doubles then?"

"In one glass, please."

"Sorry. I can't do that."

"So you can't do quadruples either?"

"No. I don't think the glass will hold that much."

"So you'd give me a quadruple, but not a triple?"

"Why not just get it on the rocks?"

"Maybe I will. Is that as big as a triple?"

"Maybe. Depends on who's pouring. It could be more than a triple."

"You're pouring."

"In that case it would be bigger than a triple."

"So then why not a triple?"

"I don't know. It's not my rule."

"Fine. Can I have it in a to-go cup?"

"Two doubles or on the rocks?"

"Just fill the glass as much as you can. I'm late for dinner."

"Where are you eating?"

"Place up the street."

"You don't know the name?"

"The seafood joint, the first one up the beach."

"Oh yes. I eat there often. Order the steak. It's wonderful."

"Thanks. Sorry about the confusion. I really need a drink."

"Have a nice dinner."

Two days later I was on a plane home. Three days later I was in the office, jet-lagged, rummaging through documents, trying to figure out a way to submit a court-ordered report to the other side explaining how ODS had suffered $3 million in damages as a result of GBC's conduct. It was coherent on its face, but the numbers in the thing were crazy, footnoted with assumptions and meandering formulas all culminating in the only clear line item on the page: "Total—$3,000,000." I prayed the other side wouldn't request the accounting documents supporting it, and amazingly, they didn't. But they did request to depose George.

The junior partner who'd previously been handling GBC's defense had just been replaced by a senior partner named Randall Raleigh. Raleigh was learning the facts on the fly, and during a phone call he casually admitted that he hadn't litigated or tried a case in a few years. I immediately assumed Raleigh was a rusty paper-pusher. He'd ask George a few hours' worth of general questions and we'd be done.

George's deposition was on a Monday morning. The view from the conference room in GBC's lawyers' office where it was being held was a panorama of Philadelphia's dank west side. Not the prettiest sight, but good enough to stare at and daydream. I sank low in a leather chair next to George, one hand on my coffee, the other propping up my jaw, readying myself for one of those "eyes-open" naps I'd learned to take during long meetings.

That was my last pleasant moment of the day.

I was dead wrong about Raleigh being a lightweight. He tore into George like a quarry drill, and the guy knew his shit. He didn't ask a pile of disconnected shotgun questions, start arguments or run down the hopeless red herrings George hung in front of him as so many lawyers would have. After a few background questions he just ran the ball straight up the middle, relentlessly grilling George on every basis for every one of his claims. George stammered, deflected, changed the subject and poured on jokes and asides. Raleigh just smiled. "Thank you, George. Now please answer my question."

By lunch, George had pissed away $1.5 million of his claim running his mouth off. By my calculations, if he kept going at that rate, we'd owe GBC a couple million by the end of his deposition. By noon I was sweating. I'd expected to "zone out" through the morning, but instead had been forced to throw one objection after another at Raleigh's questions to protect George.

During the lunch break, I ran a few blocks to a nearby hotel to have lunch with my mother, who was in town on business.

"You look stressed."

"My client is getting killed and all I can do is sit and watch the case go down the tubes. It's maddening."

"I never hear you say 'everything's great.' Is that ever going to happen?"

"You know any lawyer who says that?"

"If you're not happy you need to quit. I've told you that a thousand times."

"And pay the bills how exactly?"

"You're always finding excuses not to do something. If you don't have the guts, just admit it."

"I've put eight years into this career, and—" I choked on a mouthful of poached salmon, forcing it down with an Amstel.

"Slow down, will you? Finish your food, then talk."

"I was saying I've invested a decade in this career. What would you have me do, just walk away?"

"It's always easy to come up with reasons to stay put."

"The issue is cash flow. How do I pay the bills if I quit?"

"If you really want something better, you'll find a way."

I downed the end of my beer and stared into the traffic on the boulevard outside, going over my finances in my head. She was right. The primary problem was lack of guts. I could have quit and lasted a few months, even with Lisa in grad school, but I'd gotten used to blowing money, addicted to the six-figure income. You could live nicely in Philadelphia on that kind of float, and Lisa and I spent every dime of it. Could I really give that up? Live like a schnook while I ramped up a new career? And a new career doing what? I was thirty and still didn't know what I wanted to be when I grew up.

"I'll think about what you said." I shoveled the last of the lunch in my face, stuck my mother with the tab and ran back to the deposition.

When I got back from the break, George was waiting for me in the lobby with his usual hundred questions about nonissues. "Can I correct something I said about my education?" "My damages aren't just three million. They're much higher than that." "Why did the lawyer ask me about what medication I'm on?" "Why can't I ask him questions?"

Damages . . . Damages . . . Damages. The rest of George's commentary was white noise, but that word struck me, popping out of the stream of non sequiturs and hanging in the air. George had been demanding that I amend his damages claim, from $3 million to $8 million. For weeks I'd blown off his directive, thinking it was reckless and would poison any hope of settlement. George couldn't explain the numbers we were asking for already. I figured I'd look like a pig or a clown or both nearly tripling them.

But now, after the morning's disastrous testimony, facing ruin, why not? Maybe an obscene damages claim was what we needed—a napalm bombing to burn off all the ancillary arguments over whether we could actually prove GBC's wrongdoing and startle everyone into focusing sheerly on the numbers. Sure, it seemed lunacy, but so was the rest of the case, and the decision to suddenly turn on a dime and throw the damn thing into trial. We were running a two-minute offense and the only chance we had was momentum, to keep the defense moving even if it meant throwing bombs into triple coverage. This was gambler's territory, a tightrope walk only a hopeless adrenaline junkie could enjoy. At a normal rate of speed, a case can turn from gold to shit or ruin to pay dirt in a heartbeat based on any of a million unpredictable events that can come out of nowhere without the slightest bit of warning. Driving one at this frantic pace was blazing through an asteroid field. No time to turn. One bad move and you're dust. This was where we'd get our money's worth out of the case. Or go down in flames. But really, there was no other way. Where a rational, conservative approach would guarantee failure, prudence is malpractice.

As soon as I could, I prepared a new damages claim listing George's losses at $6 million and faxed it to Raleigh's firm. A message hit my answering machine a short time later. "We're going to ask the court to let us take another deposition of your client regarding these new damages," they replied when they saw it. I didn't respond. If they wanted another crack at my client, they'd have to get an order from the judge. I liked George and I always will, but if I had to sit through another deposition with him, he wouldn't leave the room alive.

A couple of weeks later, we had a settlement conference before a retired judge. He was employed as a mediator, to settle claims by telling both parties how bad they'd do if they went to trial and then finding a number they could agree on to make the case go away. The process couldn't hurt us, but I didn't expect much to come out of it. There was no undoing George's testimony, which was an all but terminal cancer on our claims.

The mediator took us into a back room one party at a time. We pled our cases to him in private, first us, then our opponents. He nodded, made some notes, and grinned at our papers and damages estimates. The process repeated a few times, with no promising developments. Then, suddenly, on our third or fourth turn with the mediator, he stared at George, then Evan, then me.

"They'll put one million dollars on the case. That's as good as it gets. You know you need to take that."

I could barely keep my jaw from falling onto my chest. Half of me waited for the mediator to break his straight face, crack up and tell us he was kidding—"Just screwing with you. This thing's going to trial. You're fucked." Try as I might, I couldn't understand the result. It felt like the semester of college where I missed half my classes, ate mushrooms every other day, and wound up on the dean's list.

It was maddening to wonder why they settled and realize I'd never know the answer. Never know if it was the hardball play of pushing them into a quick trial, fear of Evan or maybe, just maybe, George's crazy damages claim. But ultimately, the answer to that question was secondary. The bigger realization was that George got a million dollars—after saying anything and everything to hurt his case.

I'd won with lousy cases and lost with great ones before, but not like this. If this kind of payday was possible in a dry business dispute, I could only imagine what was possible in a catastrophic injury case in front of a jury. Perhaps I'd judged tort lawyers too harshly. Maybe personal injury law was the answer to the cash-flow problem with quitting. All I really needed was that one home-run case. Luck into that $5 million bombshell settlement and I'd be out. Done. Retired. Gone.

There was a good bit of celebration back at Miller Graham that day. After I'd told the story of the amazing result half a dozen times I settled back in my office and called a friend who was doing personal injury work.

"How hard is it for a commercial litigator to switch over to your field?"

My Fifteen Minutes of Fame

(Well, More Like Ten)

CHEVY CHASE, ANAL RAPE

AND THE BIG COMEUPPANCE

Make a fucking point already. I mean, for God's sake man, show you can finish a thought, that you can cough up some hint of a clear opinion. Try as I might, nothing coherent followed. I just kept flailing, spitting syllables—a city's worth of people watching, figuring me a fool, wondering how a mongoloid who couldn't form a basic response to an idiot simple question got himself a law degree, a job, and a commentator gig on national television.

I've had a lot of low points in my life, but this one took the cake. It was a public vetting, for friends, family, and everybody I'd bragged to about doing television appearances that yes, I was an idiot.

Well, I guess it's due. How's the rule go? The more you get away with, the bigger the one that bites you in the end?

The worst part of being two people isn't the splintering. It's not the tearing yourself down the middle or jumping in and out of character between your life and the office. That's actually kind of amusing, a feeling you're getting away with something, even if you're really just another paycheck slave who thinks he's beating the system. No, the bitter pill of it is having the two sides of your reality collide at the worst possible time, when it really matters.

My first real attempt to escape from the legal business started somewhere in the middle of a vodka marathon in the Mayflower bar in Washington. It was the summer of 2003, when the bastards still let you smoke in the place.

"Why are you still fucking around with law?" Paul, my sister's boyfriend, had been badgering me on that topic every time we met.

"What else am I going to do?"

"So you're afraid of losing the money."

"I've invested a lot of time into the career." I tapped my glass at the waitress.

"You'll run out of that soon enough."

"I hear you." I shrugged as I always did in this conversation.

"No you don't." Paul spit a cloud of cigar smoke in my face. "If you did, you'd understand the urgency."

"Well, I'm trying to get out. I'm thinking of switching into personal injury or class-action work. Hit one big case and quit."

As I'd gotten better at the job, I started thinking I might actually be able to land that mythical "home run" case, a settlement that would give me enough money to get out of the field for good. Sure, it wouldn't be tomorrow or next week, but if I kept rolling the dice I figured it was bound to happen. The ODS case had ruined my view of the career. No matter how well the billable hours paid, I always felt like I was selling out cheap, taking the easy guaranteed money when I should have been gambling in contingency cases with the personal injury sharks who were cranking out seven-figure settlements every couple of weeks. The dream was something out of a bad heist movie—that final huge score before I'd go straight and walk away from the racket for good. And just like a heist flick, it was pure fantasy.

"You don't really think that plan will work, do you?" Paul laughed.

"I know it won't happen billing my hours like a factory worker."

"The lawyers who hit those jackpot cases live for the work. It's like everything else: the people who least enjoy the money get the most of it. If you just want the cash, you never get it."

"There are exceptions to that."

"Yeah. They're called investment bankers."

"I've met a few lawyers who've lucked out."

"Sure, anything can happen. And if you want to wear fancy suits and run around playing 'lawyer' in a place like Philadelphia, fine. But from talking to you, and reading the emails you send, you see things as a writer. That's what you should be doing."

"I'm already working around the clock."

"What about television? You could make a name for yourself as a commentator, then write a few opinion articles for a local paper. They'll take freelance stuff if you have a byline saying you do television spots. Can you do commentary on criminal law?"

"I'm a little rusty, but I still do some of that work."

"You'll get over that. Just be yourself." I figured Paul knew what he was talking about; he was a correspondent for a news network.

Three weeks later I was in a studio in Philadelphia's China-town, appearing live on national television, on one of the network's hour-long news programs. I didn't know exactly what I'd be discussing or what would be expected of me. The only directions I received were to wear a dark suit and be ready to talk about police brutality. I got there around seven. They painted my face with blush, led me down a hallway and put me in a small, dark room lined with monitors on one side and a faux skyline of Philadelphia on the other.

"Please put your earphone in your left ear and clip the microphone on your jacket." The cameraman left the room. In the earpiece I could hear the sound of the television show playing in front of me, the one I'd be appearing on in minutes.

"Can your hear me?" the cameraman's voice boomed into my ear. "What I need you to do is stare at the red light above the camera lens. Don't look around. Oh, and you might want to fix your tie." In the background I could hear the show's host questioning a guest, her raspy baritone folding behind Paul's last advice replaying in my head: *Don't shift your eyes. It looks dim and sleazy. Stare straight into the camera.* I sat with my neck rigid, training myself to stare at the little red dot.

"Do you know what I'll be talking about?" I asked the cameraman.

"We're just the studio. You look good."

A voice came over the earpiece. "Ready?" The cameraman picked up his headset.

"Ready."

They didn't say "You're on!" or do any grand countdown. Somebody said "We're going live in one . . . two . . . three . . ." The cameraman dropped his arm on four.

Then there's nothing. You're live in front of half a million people, yet a tumbleweed floating through the studio wouldn't seem out of place in the least. Everywhere and nowhere at once. You see a blurry image of what you know is you on the monitor, but you can't focus on it. No deviation from the red dot. It's like you're talking to HAL 9000, from *2001: A Space Odyssey.*

The host immediately introduced the panel, a cute fortyish ex-prosecutor turned pundit, and a media magnet defense lawyer famous for defending notorious wealthy clients in sensational criminal cases. And then I heard my name.

Nod. Smile. Good.

The host set the tone early. "We're going to show you some shocking images of police abusing a man they were apprehending on suspicion of drug possession." I watched the officers dragging a man on the ground, punching and kicking and screaming at him. When the tape was done, the host and the victim's lawyer appeared on a split screen. They did a little back-and-forth about the "horrifying" images, and then the discussion passed to us. "Let's ask the panel. Do you think this was a case of police brutality?"

The ex-prosecutor cautioned us to reserve judgment on the police, as her part dictated. The other defense lawyer on the panel dove in headfirst, assailing the treatment as clear-cut brutality. For a second I was confused. These people weren't hedging their words or trying to come up with some dazzling, complex analysis to look smart. Then I remembered my circumstances. This wasn't a law firm. I was wearing makeup. My hair was lacquered to a Gordon Gekko helmet and the mood lighting tanned me like George Hamilton. Analysis? Fuck analysis. This was entertainment. I was introduced as a defense lawyer, so I said what defense lawyers are supposed to say.

"It's clear brutality. You don't do that to any suspect. The police were acting far outside their bounds." Pure knee-jerk opinion. No thinking or worrying about what some opponent would say. I just ran my mouth off—everything I'd wanted to do as a lawyer but couldn't because of all the silly rules and procedure in the system. The freedom didn't feel good, it felt like a calling, like I'd finally discovered what I wanted to be. *God, if I could only find a way to get paid to do this.*

When they cut to a commercial, a producer came over the headset. "Can you stick around and do another case for us? It's an invasion of privacy thing."

"Sure."

The cameraman put his clipboard down. "That was really good for a first-timer."

"I didn't say anything."

"The delivery was great."

"What's the next piece on?"

"Hidden video recorders in locker rooms," somebody on the headset feed answered. "A school superintendent put cameras in a high school girls' changing area. People were able to get access to them over the Internet."

"Are you serious?" *Do you have a link?*

"And we're on in one . . . two . . . three . . ." BOOM. The sound effect signalling we were back on the air shook my head and the video began to roll, showing pictures of a locker room, followed by a lawyer complaining about how his clients had been damaged.

"We don't know how many people have had access to the video. How many people had the password, how far it's circulated. We have no idea who was looking at these pictures. These were teenage girls. Teenage girls filmed in all levels of undress. It was a terrible invasion."

The host threw me a softball. "What do you think about this videotaping?"

Legally or as a masturbatory aid? I volleyed back a pile of words I'd heard over the past several minutes, arranging them in a coherent string as I went. "It's clearly a violation of these girls' privacy, and the fact that it appears on the Internet is outrageous. It probably opens the school to damages." No pauses or asides. No deep insight. Sound bites, always sound bites, and I spit the pap fast, clipping off the urge to say anything profound.

The host finished the piece, thanked the commentators and closed the show. The lights came on in the room and HAL went black. The cameraman laughed as he fiddled with the videotape machine. "You're good. They're going to call you back."

Three weeks later I was asked to go to a studio on a Sunday afternoon to discuss the Kobe Bryant rape investigation with the same panel of lawyers. This was big, a real story. Unfortunately, on Saturday of that same weekend I found myself forced to attend a dinner at the Union League in Philadelphia.

"Come on, you have to go." Harris had been insistent. He'd been talked into the dinner by a business acquaintance, but his girlfriend canceled at the last second. He needed a "date," and that turned out to be me.

"It's a couples' dinner. Are we gay?"

"They're trying to recruit people to join the place. A white-bread fucker like you should already be a member."

"To wash the dishes? I'm Irish."

"You look Aryan enough."

"Will I have to wear a jacket?"

"Otherwise you can't get into the bukkake room."

"Real Asians?"

"Only for members. Guests get crackheads. But it's comped."

"Lemme think about it. I have to do that TV thing early to-morrow. I can't get crushed." I had a bad feeling about the whole concept, like it was going to erupt into a bender. There was no proof of that, but I had a sense for these things, and I had an aw-ful feeling about the words "Union League." It sounded too stodgy and uptight, a playground for the stifled set—the kind of surface hiding a filthy, sordid underbelly. I pictured *Town & Country* types watching cockfights in a secret basement, with white slaves in pasties handing out cigars and juleps. It was a scene that would surprise me, I was certain—turn into a night of bathroom drug orgies, soft-swinging and "Liquor Olympics." I couldn't be around that. I had to stay healthy, clear-eyed and sane. I'd be on television the next day.

"All right, I'll go. But I'm getting out of there early. I'm not going nuts tonight."

"Don't worry. We're not talking about a bachelor party here."

The League's a huge old mansion on Broad Street, the sort of place you need to go to with a member, and there are no prices on the menu. The food's Episcopalian Thanksgiving/Golf Course Wedding Fusion, the decor from WWII and all the dust deliber-ate—real geriatric chic. I didn't feel the slightest bit self-conscious wandering the place sockless in a stained seersucker suit.

As in any WASP-themed restaurant, the food at the League's irrelevant. They pour the whiskey heavy and the only object seems to be numbness, surgical grade. It's near impossible not to get flattened in the place. There are three attractions to any res-taurant: People-Watching, Eating Something You've Never Tried Before and Being Served. As People-Watching, there aren't any women or freaks to survey in the League. You get a generic pa-rade of potbellied men in blazers and blue-haired wives with em-broidered muumuu dresses hanging like curtains over what appear to be randomly assorted layers of breasts, interrupted by the occasional younger family outing—a thirty-sevenish bond lawyer with an SS haircut and Stepford wife. As to Eating Some-thing You've Never Tried Before, if you haven't had minestrone, you're in for something special. But on the Being Served end, I have to admit the place is Michelin four-star. Shoeshines are on the appetizer menu. Having him call you "Colonel" during the process is an extra five dollars.

Dinner passed in a flurry of liquid orders. "Another? Yes." "Sure, one more." "Yes, a double." I checked my watch every half hour or so, making a note of the time, aiming to leave by ten. That came and went, then eleven, then twelve. By one I was back in my neighborhood ordering Basil Hayden and Red Bulls with Harris at a restaurant up the street. By two I was in my living room loaded out of my mind, arguing about music.

"I don't like the Flaming Lips." Harris turned down the stereo. "They're Hollywood garbage."

" 'Do You Realize' is like a modern version of 'The Sound of Silence.' " I turned it back up. "You have to listen to it."

"I hate Simon and Garfunkel."

"They're not my favorite either, but they did write some classics."

"Hugely overrated. Simon couldn't sing. He talked, like Lou Reed does, but not as good, and Garfunkel whispered really close to the microphone. One guy whispering, one guy talking, and people call them geniuses? Bullshit."

"I didn't mean the Lips sounded like them."

"They also can't play live. I can't respect any band that can't play live."

"What are you taking about? The Lips play live all the time."

"No, Simon and Garfunkel. You're never going to hear Simon and Garfunkel tear into a jam in the middle of 'Scarborough Fair' or 'Teach Your Children.' "

"I should hope not. 'Teach Your Children' is a fucking Eagles song."

"Jesus, what are you doing?"

"My hands aren't working." Actually, I could never roll a joint.

"Give me that." Harris pushed me away from the stash. "You're an embarrassment."

"I need a cigarette."

"I only have five left."

"That hollandaise sauce from dinner is churning in my stomach. I need to kill the taste."

"It was béarnaise sauce."

"What's the fucking difference?"

"Béarnaise is French. Hollandaise is Dutch."

When I finally remembered I had something to do the next day, I was alone, watching the beginning of *Apocalypse Now*. *Shit, I have to be on television tomorrow.* As I listened to Martin Sheen's opening narrative—"Saigon . . . Shit, I'm still only in Saigon"— the first gray glimpses of the dawn started sneaking through the edges of the blackout curtains in the living room. *Correction: I have to be on television today.*

I woke up somewhere in the afternoon, with that miserable booze migraine, the shooting pain behind the left eye that digs in and doesn't leave for twenty-four hours. I tried reading a few articles in Sunday's *Times*, but I was totally unable to concentrate. The words flowed as prose, but nothing else, like those times you're reading a book and start drifting, thinking about another subject, then realize you've somehow processed two pages of text and don't have a clue what any of it said. I was jelly-headed, temporarily retarded—still pickled from the night before. I couldn't go on television in this condition but I didn't have time to sweat out the poisons at the gym and I was too jittery from the hangover to fight it with coffee. The only way out was visiting the little tan "Pillbox" in my underwear drawer.

You collect a lot of drugs in the law business. I've been offered acid as a Christmas present by an IT worker, dope from a secretary for my birthday and seen mushrooms delivered to people in firm envelopes. Ecstasy was all over the place, a weekend ritual for a lot of the summer beach rental crowd. One paralegal I knew used to run out and buy coke at lunch before she melted down and was fired, and a summer clerk I knew kept film cannisters of "kief," hyperconcentrated pure THC crystals created in a centrifuge. Law's the perfect hiding place for closet drug monkeys. If firms ever started testing employees the way corporations do a quarter of the industry would be forced into rehab.

And that's just the illegal stuff, for the getting-high set. The bigger dope sector in law is the coping crowd, the lawyers taking prescription meds to get through the day. These people split into two camps. There are the hard-core depression cases who take Prozac and Zoloft. And then there are the people who are just fried—burned out by the constant stress and impossible deadlines. These people just need an occasional mickey to check their anxiety, make the job tolerable. They take Ativan, or if they have a really kind psychiatrist, Xanax.

Xanax is the Rolls-Royce of functioning-but-don't-care-about-anything pills, what a fellow associate at one firm who used to keep the drug in a locket around her neck called the "kill switch." Those times where a ten-minute flurry of phone calls, faxes, and emails turns a perfectly calm week into a shitrain of idiot paperwork? Those moments where you can actually feel your face turning purple as some Napoleon threatens you over the phone? Flip the "kill switch," and they're drowned in fathoms of apathy you didn't know existed.

People gave me Xanax from time to time, often at the end of a brutal weekend in New York, the sort where I'd find myself getting on a train in Penn Station on a Sunday afternoon, exhausted and nauseous after being up for thirty-six hours. "Here, take a couple of these," a friend would say. "Otherwise you're going to lose your mind on the train." I didn't waste those little gems. I'd take one for the ride and put the others in the Pillbox. They were worth saving—a get-out-of-jail card for those horrible Monday mornings where you think you're going to have a nervous breakdown.

Maybe I'll take just one. I opened the Pillbox and pulled out a folded business card holding Xanax tablets. *Calm the mind, kill the hangover.* I shoved the card in my pocket and called for a cab to the television studio where I was doing a live feed for the show.

"How you doing today?" The driver was a fiftyish black man

with a strong voice, the kind that filled a car—the friendly, talk-ative kind I didn't need at that moment.

"Why are you all dressed up?"

"I'm doing a thing on television."

"Really? What?"

"Talking about the Kobe Bryant case."

"You know what happened there, right?"

"She's a gold digger, a groupie. He didn't rape anyone. He's not the type."

"Ha ha. You're close. I know a bodyguard for Patti LaBelle who works with a guy who does guard work for Kobe. Guards are freelancers, you know. Anyway, this guy heard from one of Kobe's guards that the girl went crazy after Kobe did her in the back door. He didn't want any paternity suits, you know? That's why there was all the blood on the sheets."

"The guy never heard of condoms?"

"I don't know. Maybe that's how he likes it. All I heard was he tore her up."

A disgusting story all around. Horrible racial overtones, rape, and the unspoken image of an NBA forward's member tearing open a hopeless teenage starfucker. The images alone were agi-tating, without the creepy backstory and all the strange ques-tions it raised. How was I going to discuss something like this? This wasn't a matter of legal issues. This was an episode of *CSI* mixed up with something out of *Hustler*. I pulled out the busi-ness card and unfolded it. The pills were mashed to dust and jagged nuggets from being in my pocket for too long at some point. Did I have one, two, three in there? *Fuck it.* I licked the card. You can always self-animate on a sedative. You just have to know how to tap the adrenaline spigot.

"Thanks." I tipped the driver and walked into the studio. A skinny tech walked me through a dingy room with a remote-controlled camera. "You'll have to wait a few minutes. They're running late with your segment."

I called Harris from the greenroom. "Hey, give me something on the Kobe Bryant case."

"Like what?"

"Anything. Are there any developments in the story? I heard he fucked her in the ass. Is that on the news?"

"CNN's reporting he gave her a Hot Plate. Say that."

"I'm serious."

"Actually, it was a Little Jack Horner."

"What the hell is that?"

"You've never stuck your thumb in a girl's ass?"

"Excellent. That's what I'll say."

"If you want my opinion, Shaq's behind the whole thing. It's a frame-up."

"You asshole, this your fault." As I clicked off my phone, the cameraman came into the room.

"You know how to set up your mic, right? Just look at the red light. Holler if you need anything." The lights went down. Just HAL 9000 and me, alone, eye-to-eye.

The cameraman suddenly came over the headset. "We're going on in about thirty seconds." *All right. Get organized. Smile for the camera and collect your thoughts.* I tried to block it from my mind, but I couldn't shake the image of Bryant sodomizing this hopeless oakie waitress, wearing his Lakers jersey the whole time. And every time I thought about a Lakers jersey I immediately pictured Chevy Chase in *Fletch*.

Yes, that was the short film playing in my head as I waited to go live on camera—Kobe Bryant sodomizing a drunk girl bent over the side of a bed, with Chevy Chase appearing in the scene every now and again, randomly, as though he were a spectator or part of some hideous gang bang. And in the background, repeating over and over, was the cabdriver's commentary: "He did her in the back door . . ." "Blood on the sheets . . ." "Tore her up . . ."

Okay. I took a breath. *Stop trying to think and just listen. You'll know what to say when the time's right. It'll just flow, like it always does.*

Suddenly we were on. The host introduced us and then started asking the ex-prosecutor on the panel questions about two acquaintances of the accuser who had just emerged, supporting the accuser's version of events, and verifying that she looked terrible after the alleged assault.

"What could Bryant's people say about these two potential witnesses?" The host then turned to me.

"Well, these witnesses are both friends of the accuser—"

"Not necessarily." The host cut me off. "One is an 'okay' friend and the other just works with her."

Thanks. Thanks for taking that point and shoving it up my ass.

Silence. I pursed my lips for a moment and tried to figure out a response. The only problem was, I'd already forgotten the question. My short-term memory was gone. The minute the host took me off script I was cooked. It was barely a moment on tape, but television's measured in nanoseconds. The slightest delay is an agonizing intermission—the sign of an amateur, a person who hasn't learned to think in "TV time." And when you're sitting there, praying for something to say, the thinnest sliver of a moment feels like a day.

All the imaginable responses I could offer seemed to smash together on my tongue. Or there might have been none at all. I can't recall anything from the exact moment but dead clear space, beyond a blank canvas—the picture you get attempting to imagine total nothingness. For the first time in my life, I was speechless. I mean, I started talking, forming words, but none of it made any sense. More an automatic survival instinct—making sounds, tethering fragments of thoughts together and hoping they'd go somewhere as I kept rambling.

"Well, uh, you could also take the position that, uh, what the witnesses saw under the circumstances was somebody upset that she had, uh, a consensual relation with someone that upset her—" I remember stopping midphrase and shifting in my seat, nervously searching for something to say—any relevant point. *You're flailing. Use the anal story. It's the only way to salvage this—obliterate all memories of the rest of your gibberish.* "It's, uh, hard to make a judgment based on appearance that someone was the victim of assault versus something that they, um . . ." At this point my mouth was full of marbles. I was blinking a lot, smiling and trying to look collected, hoping someone would interject, because I hadn't a clue how to finish my comment. *Do not use the anal thing. You'll never be asked back if you drop that here.* The argument in my head was relentless. *Bullshit! Using the anal rumor is the only prayer you have of being asked back.* " . . . [T]hat, uh, she did not enjoy the sex that took place, but it might not have been a full-blown sexual assault. I guess that's a very fine line there."

You can say anything on television as long as you sound like an expert. Substance has its place, but cadence, certainty and speed are paramount. Looking like someone who knows what he's talking about is five times the value of actually knowing. Babbling and stuttering, running off course on a litany of clipped asides—these are mortal sins. Lose the seamless flow of syllables and a tube junkie suddenly remembers he's supposed to be cleaning the birdbath or waxing the El Camino. Fumbling also cracks the medium's illusion of omnipotence—the notion that the people inside the box are smarter or a thousand times more knowledgeable than the people watching it.

I'd sounded like John Kerry after a bowl of hash. There's no dancing around anal sex. Talking about it's the same as doing it—you're either in or out. Teasing around the precipice only brings shame and second thoughts. All those half-assed attempts to find a polite segue into the topic painted me an idiot, and rightly so. There aren't many feelings worse than looking into the camera and knowing hundreds of thousands of people were reaching the conclusion you've got shit for brains.

The host must have either sensed me a moron or saw where I was going and had the good sense to jump to another commentator. The other defense lawyer on the panel quickly responded, offering a coherent explanation of the point he assumed I was trying to make.

After the segment ended I sat in the room for a moment, wondering what had just happened. *Christ, how did I collapse like that?* This was a hell of a comeuppance. For the first time, my synapses had let me down. I had nothing, and the normal adrenaline rush

I relied on was stunted by the pills. At least I looked calm making an ass of myself.

On the walk home, I ran a postmortem in my head, constructing explanations. I blamed the pills, the hangover and bad luck, but those were just deflections, diversions—parts of a broader, obvious answer. I'd been living in two worlds and getting away with it for years, and this sort of royal fuckup was inevitable. It was a simple matter of statistics. The only anomaly in the thing was that I'd blown up on television.

And the really rotten part of the mess was that I'd actually wanted to be good at this. It was a possible way out, a chance to be something more than just another fucking lawyer. This was all grandstanding and arguing—the fun part of being an attorney I'd wanted—with none of the tedium, wretched personalities, and niggling procedural horseshit. As far as escape plans go, it was far from airtight. But it was a start, and doing something, anything, on television seemed a hell of a lot more plausible an exit than sticking it out in law, waiting for that monster case to walk through the door and drop a mother lode of money in my lap. This was a chance to work at something people actually want to do, and don't spend half of their working hours dreaming of fleeing.

But now what? There was no second chance on television, I knew that. There was always a way to spin or bullshit my way out of fuckups in the legal world. Law's just paper, and even the worst mistake is always curable with a motion, pleading, or letter, or in the worst case, an appeal. Not here, though. Not in television. At long last the wheels had come off, and the proof was broadcast to everyone I knew. I'd bombed. I needed a Plan B exit strategy now, and I didn't have one.

Paul called my home phone an hour later. "Well, you fucked that up nicely. What were you thinking?"

"I wouldn't use the word 'thinking' to describe today."

"Nobody wants to hear you analyze what witness's appearances *might* indicate. You're a defense lawyer. You say the girl could have looked upset for a million reasons and it doesn't prove anything. Done."

"I don't imagine I'll be getting asked back."

"Well . . ." Paul hesitated. I knew what he was going to say next. "It's a good idea to start writing those newspaper articles we discussed, while you can still say you recently did commentary for a national news network."

Last Roulette Wheel on
the Way Out of the Casino

OUT OF THE BILLING MACHINE,

INTO THE LAWSUIT MACHINE

I knew I wasn't going to like Bill Janus the minute I saw him. Sitting in the waiting room, I watched the guy walk to and from the receptionist's desk—robotic, always staring forward, deadly serious and never deviating from the task at hand, stomping through the motions of his day. I was the only foreigner in the waiting area, a space as big as a large walk-in closet, and the guy didn't look at me once, not even to nod hello.

Fuck. Another "Machine." You see a lot of lawyers like that, processing one task after another and just rolling forward, never stopping to consider anything but the next reminder in their calendar. It's a coping mechanism—constant rote motion taking the mind out of the moment.

Generally I didn't mind Machines. They're easy to read and you always know what you're dealing with. The only problem is, there's nothing but the work—their endless, grinding execution, attacking everything in the same deliberate fashion. For a person like me, they raise a litany of horrible questions? *Isn't there more than just performing, efficiency and production? Isn't there a hope that on some simple level, a job might be creative? Maybe even enjoyable?*

"Hello," he finally addressed me when it was time to start the interview. "Bill Janus." The minute I looked him in the eye and shook his hand, every survival mechanism in my body immediately screamed, *Run, now.*

Bill's firm, Janus, Carson & Malloy, did personal injury work, the last practice area I hadn't tried, and the last chance I had at cashing out in law, or so I thought. Whatever my instincts said, if he offered me the job, I was taking it.

Most of 2004 had been low point. I didn't write newspaper articles after my failed television appearance in 2003, and, as Paul had guessed, he couldn't get me any more airtime. In January of 2004, Martin had moved away from Philadelphia, and three months after that, Harris was transferred out west by his company. Just like that, in a period of seven months, my hope of an escape from law and the safety net of friends that had kept me in suspended adolescence both evaporated.

That spring, Lisa and I moved out of the city, to a home in the western suburbs, to the world of mortgages, property taxes and lawn care. Every morning I drove to the train station, jumped on the seven forty-five express and did the half-hour commute into Philadelphia. When the train stopped, I'd march with a herd of bodies through a filthy underground tunnel to my office tower—another anonymous blue suit, aging into everything I'd feared.

It went on like that for half a year until one day, in October of 2004, something snapped. I was just sitting upstairs in my house, drafting a pointless brief for some client, when I decided I'd had enough—that I couldn't hold all of the rancid anecdotes and images piling in my head a moment longer. I set up a website under the name "Philadelphia Lawyer" and started writing what I was thinking, three hundred pages of text before I was done.

The site grew a cult following, enough that one night my sister and Paul called from a bar in Washington and put me on the phone with a couple of Air Force officers they'd overheard talking about the website.

"Dude, I love the site," the voice screamed over the crowd in the background.

"You have a following at the Pentagon. The stuff is great. I laughed my ass off."

"I'm just writing what everyone's thinking."

"That's why it works. It speaks to people."

You could take every legal victory I'd been involved in and every dollar I'd made as a lawyer and they weren't worth a tenth of that comment.

But then, just as the site was peaking, reality dragged me back to the ground. In early 2005, a lawyer friend called me with a tip about Janus, Carson & Malloy seeking an associate. The position had just opened, and if I sent in a résumé immediately, I had a decent shot at the job. This was a chance to learn how to find and prosecute those huge personal injury claims that garnered seven- and eight-figure settlements they wrote about in the newspapers. The issue now was, did I stay in place, in a job I knew well enough that I could keep writing on the side, see if I could get noticed and find a way to make a buck as an author? Or did I give up the writing and take on the learning curve of a new legal job, for what I thought could be a boatload of cash down the road?

I did the lawyerly thing and took the path most chosen.

A week later I found myself sitting across from Bill Janus, trying to find something to talk about. The burden was all on me because Bill didn't say much of anything. He was one of those deliberately quiet sorts, the kind where you could see the gears rolling in his head, and the only question was whether he kept his mouth shut because he was really smart or just didn't have anything to say.

Either way, Bill's lack of a tongue made my job impossible. For an applicant, the trick to any interview is saying as little as he has to. Of the three categories of responses to interview questions—Nothing, Something, or Anything—Nothing's always optimal. Something shows a level of knowledge, but that inevitably begs some follow-up questioning, which eventually shows that you don't *really* know what you're talking about. Anything's death, the nervous gibberish a fool spouts in a pregnant pause, fragments of phrases he thinks better of speaking a couple of words in or canned replies from career guides. Anything sits in the air like a fresh wet fart, and nobody can even look its speaker in the eye. Nothing's the only sure bet. It offends nobody and there's no follow-up. Once you've given up trying to say Something and learned to avoid the impulse to say Anything, you can get through any interview.

Unless you're interviewing with a guy like Bill, where you have to fill a lot of dead air. "So why are you looking to leave your firm and your practice area?"

"Because yours is the last industry left that makes economic sense. What's my option? Be one of these suckers billing 2,400 hours a year for two hundred grand when he's fifty?" It was a slightly aggressive way to start things off, but after taking quick measure of Bill, I figured I could use the "money" angle. He was dressed right out of one those Neiman Marcus catalogs Lisa got in the mail, with a coaster-sized diving watch hanging from his wrist, just north of his manicure.

"You're pretty sure of yourself," he responded. "Not that that's necessarily a bad thing . . ."

Confident's an easy act when you've got nothing to lose. I'd given up on law, but after sucking down nine years of aggravation in the job, I wasn't going down on a called strike. Janus, his firm and what he did was the last roulette table on my way out of the casino, and I intended to bet every chip in my pocket on one last spin of the wheel.

Daniel Malloy, one of Janus's partners, came in about half-way through the interview. Malloy was the opposite of Janus, instantly taking over the room the minute he opened his month. In every way Janus was methodical, Malloy was loose, unpredictable, and arrogant—but in a charming, smartass way, disarming enough that he took me off my game. When he asked me if I had any questions about the firm, my mind went blank, so I stupidly made up a nonsense question on the spot. "Are you approachable if I have questions? You know, is there an open-door policy in that regard?"

"No." He laughed at me. "We expect you to figure out every-thing on your own. Is that a serious fucking question? Are you really asking that?"

Malloy didn't give a damn what you thought of him and he seemed pretty sure he knew more than everybody else in the room. The guy was smart, you could tell that immediately, and he might have been quicker than everybody else. Whether he was sharper in his rapid assessments is another matter. I've no doubt he summed me up in an instant and was half right in every conclusion. Still, I liked him. But I'd have liked anybody. Pulling conversation out of Janus had been like mugging the homeless.

"What we're looking for is passion." Malloy got right in my face. "We do what we do for money, but we need someone who really, really wants to do this job—someone who truly feels passion for being a plaintiff's attorney."

I waited for a hint of sarcasm. *He's fucking with me.* I didn't know all the nuts and bolts of bringing plaintiff's cases, but I had friends who did it and I knew the economics of the thing. JCM was a top-notch outfit and handled difficult cases, but on a macro level, for the less successful firms that make up the majority of the business, the model is filing all sorts of claims and seeing what sticks. "Specious" is an exotic concept in the field. There are a fair number of real personal injury claims out there, but they're not the majority. In Philadelphia, we're talking about an industry where a lot of firms' bread-and-butter revenue comes from lawsuits for strains and sprains suffered when 300-pound terminally unemployed daytime television addicts get into 10-mile-per-hour fender benders or twist their ankles on loose gravel in liquor store parking lots—hardly the sort of work aligned with notions of "passion."

Everything in law is soft lying, but could Malloy really be serious? Had he cribbed that pap from *Profiles in Courage*? *Jonathan Livingston Seagull*? Was it sarcasm? A trick question? You get so cynical and used to constant bullshit in the legal business anything that sounds like true sentiment overwhelms the brain. If he were being intentionally sappy and I didn't spot it, I'd look dim. If he were serious and I gave a smartass response, the interview was over. I did the only thing I could, volley back in kind:

"I really want to make a difference. I feel like I need to make some sort of constructive change through what I'm doing, and I think plaintiff's work would allow me to actually make a change in someone's life, to feel like I made that difference."

Making a difference as a Philadelphia PI lawyer? Did I actually say that? How many times have you said "I love you" just to get in her pants? When you're done there, you can run to another room, get a beer, fix a sandwich, or just leave, usually with the benefit of a good buzz. I had to sit stone sober and ponder that thunderhead of schmaltz, hanging over me like an essence of festering rot. *Fuck it.* What else was I going to do? Tell the truth?

"'Passion'? Are you fucking serious, Dan? What I'm looking for here is that one monster claim. A chemical company dumping dioxin next to a kindergarten . . . A drunken hedge fund manager pitching his cigarette boat through a sloop full of nuns on a church retreat . . . A tanker company allowing ergot fungus to seep into industrial sugar shipments, causing thousands of people to hallucinate after eating Twinkies . . . I want a claim I can pimp to twelve Jerry Springer fans for a barrel of dollar bills big enough to buy myself a compound near a beach and never have to walk into an office or sit through one of these things again for as long as I live."

That's what we all want. We just can't say it.

"Let me ask you another question." Malloy ran his fingers over his chin. "Who do you think has more at risk here, you or us?"

I did, as far as he knew. Personal injury law is all about the end-of-year bonus, and JC&M paid $30,000 less in base pay than I was getting at Miller Graham. But beyond that, if I didn't succeed here, the business litigation bar would never have me back. I'd be a pariah, a victim of the "Once you leave, you're out for good" childishness that permeates that practice area. Seven out of ten lawyers in billable-hour firms would quit if they could find the same money doing anything else, and nothing reminds them just how tight their "golden handcuffs" are like an escape artist, even a failed one. The other issue was the Scarlet Letter personal injury law would put on my résumé. Fair or not, it's seen as a bottom feeders' market. Once I'd shifted to that side of the world, it would brand me, and not in a good way.

Malloy had raised a valid question. But at this point, at this late inning, risk wasn't even part of the equation anymore. I wasn't going back to a business litigation job if this one tanked. "There are a million ways to make money with a law degree," people told me when I was heading to law school. I'd go looking for the other 999,999.

"Who has more to lose?" I stared back at Malloy. "I do."

Everybody loves a gambler. And how else would he expect me to answer that question? Who hires a chickenshit?

They asked me to come back a week later, and I knew it was to offer me a job. Suddenly I had to ask myself, Could I really be a personal injury lawyer? Selling out was easy in theory. I'd paid a lot of lip service to the idea of being a PI lawyer, but having the offer staring me in the face made the whole thing concrete, dredging up the old second guesses I thought I'd dismissed. *Am I jumping too hastily? Giving up a well-paying gig to chase a perfect career that doesn't exist? What are the chances I'm really going to hit that magical seven-figure case? Is this just another pipe dream?*

I had to step back from the decision, get some outside advice. First I called Harris:

"It's about time. Aren't you supposed to change jobs annually?"

Then I called Bennett:

"You have to take a thirty-thousand-dollar base cut? Sounds like *they're* good lawyers."

The last person I called was Alex, the only one who gave me any real constructive response:

"I say do it. It's a perfect fit for you."

"I wonder if I'm buying a pig in a poke. What if I hate it? What are the real chances I'm going to strike it rich?"

"What are the chances you're going to strike it rich sitting where you are?"

"I'm going to take it, I just don't know if I can really hack it in that world."

"Look, I bust your balls a lot, dude, but honestly, seriously, you have to stop underestimating yourself."

"Thanks."

"You're a lot sleazier than you think."

"Justice" Junkies

TRAPPED ON KOOL-AID ISLAND

It only took one testimonial dinner for me to realize I'd never survive as a plaintiff's lawyer. As I stood in line at the hotel bar, the words kept repeating in my head. *I'm fucked. I'll never make it in this job.*

I'd gone into personal injury law knowing it was a long shot, a terrible fit in every regard. Still, I thought I could make it work, at least for a few years—long enough to build a reservoir of cash to allow me to pay bills while I took time off to find another career. The concept seemed simple. The execution was another matter. It hadn't been as easy as I expected. The first six months had been grueling. Janus got under my skin in a way no lawyer had before, to the point where merely seeing his face irritated me, grating on my every nerve. And what really drove me nuts was that I couldn't figure out why. I could only hope it was a temporary personality clash, something I'd adjust to, get over in time.

Standing in that hotel, however, in a collection of all the biggest personal injury lawyers in the city, I began to see the problems were a lot bigger than my relationship with Bill. I'd woefully overestimated my acting chops. This wasn't just playing a part like I had at the other firms. There was no shared background, no common thread I could build on to craft myself into an acceptable office caricature. I didn't have the slightest hint of a connection with these people. I was further from them than any other lawyers I'd worked with before, on many levels their polar opposite.

Normally this wouldn't be a huge deal. Except for one small problem: Lisa was pregnant. We'd been planning to have a kid since the summer, but for one reason or another, mostly a lack of schooling in simple biology, I figured it would take a few months, maybe even a year. I was wrong. She went off the pill in July and was knocked up by September. Quitting wasn't an option now, and a mercenary like me, with four firms on his résumé in less than a decade, couldn't just jump back into the job market in short order. I had to make this gig work, one way or another. That meant doing everything the firm requested, including "chair-filler" duty at industry testimonials.

Once a year all the plaintiffs' lawyers in town got together at a local hotel for a rubber-chicken dinner to honor some politician or crusader. It's a standard honorific with hours of speeches and awards and presentations, the sort that only become tolerable after a handful of drinks. The minute I got to the hotel I sprinted to the bar to lay down a primer. Predictably, the line was deep, and I wound up waiting in it for what felt like an hour, taking in the scenery, surveying my new peers.

Half the place was filled with generic lawyer types in drab gray-and-blue uniforms. Nothing interesting or unusual—a typical pack of paunchy, middle-aged men. As to the other half, well, plaintiffs' attorneys are the self-proclaimed "lawyers of the people." And they looked it. Milling around the bar area felt like the scene in *GoodFellas* where Henry Hill describes each of the members of Paulie's crew, the camera rolling past every toupee, pompadour, pinkie ring, sharkskin suit and all the cake-faced goomads in press-on nails and fire-engine red lipstick. The room was chock-full of "bling," but it was stale, confused and slapped together—the "Jersey" kind.

The hotel was a Super Bowl of people-watching. Just waiting in line I saw Johnnie Cochran's doppelgänger in gold-plated Puff

Daddy glasses and a vertical-striped tie, an old man in a baby-shit brown version of Tom Wolfe's three-piece suit and a woman who was a dead ringer for Milton Berle, dressed in what looked like a geisha-themed ball gown. A couple of cigarette girls in pasties and dwarves on miniature ponies would have rounded out the atmosphere perfectly.

When I finally reached the bartender, I had to yell to him over the sound of a lumpy man with a recessed chin barking into a cell phone to my left, gesturing with his free hand to impress the people around him. "No, the settlement is never going to work with thirty thousand dollars! I need thirty-six!" It was hard not to lean over and squeeze his cheeks. *Hey Spanky, I know you're a big-time wheeler and dealer, but how about taking it outside?* To the right a couple of "playas" in brand-new suits, deep October tans and Andrew Dice Clay haircuts were angling into my space at the bar, laughing loudly and posturing for phantom paparazzi. It was all I could do not to tap one on the shoulder and ask for a favor. *Hey Fonzie, how about elbowing the jukebox? It's stuck on "Piano Man" again.*

I'd say the scene was Gatsbyesque, but that seems cruel to Fitzgerald. A better analogy would be Rodney Dangerfield's "Regular Guy" fashion show from *Easy Money*. There's no way to be kind about it—this was a crowd for radio. If I hadn't been dragged to the damn dinner, I'd have had that queer guilt you feel rubbernecking past a car accident or watching some horrible show on celebrity plastic surgery gone wrong. And the only thing more comical than the scene was the conversation, the sort of political sermonizing you'd expect from a freshman at Sarah Lawrence.

"These companies don't care about the workers. They just move everything overseas. Everything's about profit!"

"It's criminal that an oil executive gets paid $30 million and forty million people have no health insurance."

"The least Bush could have done was meet with Cindy Sheehan. Her only son died so Bush could avenge Saddam's attempt to kill his father."

You get used to hearing that sort of stuff quickly in the personal injury world. The industry's filled with left-wing "movement minds." Some are true believers. Others are cynical opportunists who realize liberal politicians are a contingency lawyer's best friends. A few of them are both at once, or one or the other depending on the moment or issue at hand. I never told anyone in the firm I was a registered Libertarian. "Political agnostic" doesn't play well in a crowd like that, and you never win an argument with anyone who fucks you or signs your paychecks.

I fired back one last drink and settled into my seat as the dinner was about to begin. A bigwig from a national plaintiffs' lawyers association started the evening off, peppering the floor with opening remarks in a folksy Southern drawl.

"Ahh really love coming up here to Philadelphia. You are the heart and soul of the Personal Injury Bar." He was smooth, and his presentation was well polished, spraying all the proper buzzwords and slogans. "We will keep fighting to ensure that access to justice remains a hallmark of this nation. They can't close the courthouse doors on us when people who are willing to stand up for the voiceless fight back." I tilted my wine back and forth as he rambled along, watching its silky residue slide down the sides of the glass.

After two or three more attorneys spoke, the honoree finally took the stage. A pudgy intellectual with an *Eraserhead* haircut, he prattled on in an NPR broadcaster's affectation about the David-and-Goliath conflict trial lawyers faced in 2005. "The corporations are being heard above us. They have the strongest PR campaign in history demonizing trial lawyers right now. This is the moment when we need our strongest voices!"

It was funny to sit there as a third-party skeptic, listening to the religious revival tone of the speech. I'd never seen people so high on victims' complexes. And as I sat there, absorbing the sermons, I finally understood why I loathed working for Bill so much.

Bill rarely came into my office, but every now and again he'd stop in to talk, usually about some heated case where the other side had refused to settle and wasn't intimidated by our claims.

Generally the guy was pragmatic, even keel—icy and detached in many regards. But when we discussed those difficult cases he'd often shift, dropping his cool and getting angry about how some defendant was playing hardball. It was as though he was offended the other side would raise a defense where he was clearly on the side of "justice."

I remember him once telling me how appalled he was that a landlord we were suing had watched tenants go back into a building in which carbon monoxide fumes might have been present. "Can you believe the audacity? To just stand there and watch them?" I sat there thinking, *Get off the soapbox, will you? The guy probably didn't know what else to do. And how was he going to stop them? Tackle them in the street?* I handled one deposition where opposing counsel and Bill couldn't be in the same room because of the bad blood between them. When I went to the lawyer's office I expected to run into some horrible, fire-breathing lunatic. He turned out to be polite, businesslike. We fought and he was difficult, an asshole at times, but nothing personal or ugly erupted. He was doing his job and I did mine. It was just business.

I'd listen to Bill take umbrage and wonder how he expected me to respond. Was I supposed to clap? Shake my head and tell him how appalled I was, too? The whole spectacle scared me. I saw both sides of every case, which seemed to me the only honest position. Yes, sometimes defendants are liable, but in my experience, having worked on both sides of the aisle, most of them aren't. The plaintiff's been damaged as a result of some freak set of circumstances, and there's a good argument to be made that the defendant's only sin is being in the wrong place at the wrong time and having money or an insurance policy a personal injury lawyer can tap into for a settlement. That anyone could turn those kinds of claims and that business model into a battle between right and wrong and claim to be wearing the white hat in the disputes all but tripped my gag reflex.

And that's what irritated me about the whole legal industry and everything I was sitting in that room listening to. On one level I was galled anyone would think me dumb enough to buy into such cheap sloganeering. On another, it was a perfect crystallization of everything that had driven me nuts about law in general. There's a tragedy in virulent advocacy, in all of the pretexts and self-deceptions that go along with it. I'd gone into law thinking that would be amusing, but now, staring at its wages—a roomful of industry hacks loaded on the proverbial Kool-Aid—I wanted to jump out of my skin. What kind of rational, reasonable people bullshit themselves with myths? It's embarrassing, painful to watch. I felt dirty and shameful just being part of that carnival, like I'd never be able to shower enough to clean off the stench of the thing.

As I listened to the honoree prattle on, I knew the question had shifted. It wasn't *if* I'd be leaving the career, just a matter of when, of how long I could stick it out. The industry had turned me into a "Reverse Zelig," a photographic negative of the famous Woody Allen character who took on the physical characteristics of whatever groups of people he was around. The closer I'd gotten to all these advocates, the more skeptical I became, the more holes I saw in their arguments and justifications, and the further I moved away from them. Law's no place for a person refusing to suspend disbelief, at least on the surface. Particularly personal injury law. I had to get out, and not just to another practice area. But to what? To where? I didn't have any other skills, and I had a kid on the way.

Eraserhead's speech finally wound down to its closing sound bites: "corporations hurting people . . ." "protecting rights . . ." "workers being trampled in the new economy!" Shades of Che Guevara, with a twist of Abbie Hoffman. When he finally bowed out, the place erupted in applause. I stood with everybody in the crowd, clapping, toasting the speech and nodding along with all the other lawyers around me, wondering to myself, *How the fuck are you going to get out of this mess?*

Plan B

t was the last week of April of 2006, maybe Monday, maybe
Thursday. I was just sitting at my desk staring out the window
when the email prompt came onto my computer. A lawyer friend
in New York who knew about my old website emailed me a link
to a story about a lawsuit in federal court in Philadelphia involving a notorious writer and Internet personality, Tucker Max. A
local guido with a public relations company was suing Max for
allowing people to post insulting comments about him and his
company on a heavily trafficked Internet chat board Max maintained. In response, Max had decided to throw a fund-raising
party for his defense at a bar in Philadelphia, right in the plaintiff's backyard.

I knew Max's board well. A year and a half before, it had published a link to my since-defunct website, driving tens of thousands of readers to it overnight. I read a few stories about the
lawsuit and shot Max a message offering free legal advice. He
turned that down and instead proposed I sign a contract with him
and launch a new website. I didn't know what to think at first.
The idea took me by surprise, but after considering his work, I
could see there was a synergy of sorts. Max initially gained fame

for being fired from a summer associate position at one of the top law firms in the country for persistent drunk and belligerent behavior. After shifting to writing, among stories about sex with amputees, tackling the team mascot at a professional hockey game and filming anal sex, Max gave speeches about how working in a law firm had been an utterly soulless job he'd never recommend to anyone. After a few emails and five minutes on the phone with the guy I confirmed, yes, he was a lunatic, but a shrewd fucker. If I was going to get the attention of a publisher to get a book deal, this guy could do it. Hell, his book was on the *Times* bestseller list.

We struck a deal, and Max set me up with a literary agent to see if there was a book in my stuff. The agent signed me up, and a week later I started putting together a proposal to submit to publishers. Between relaunching my website, working on the book pitch and managing my caseload at the office, I slept maybe four hours a night through April and May of 2006. At the time, Janus's practice had become all but unbearable, an avalanche of paper burying me deeper every day. Every time I turned around, an opponent was filing something against one of my clients in a case, or Janus was asking me to prepare some monstrous trial submission in his cases on short notice. The work was brutal, twice as hard as anything I'd done before.

That wouldn't have bothered me under normal circumstances. Janus was a capitalist and it was his right to bleed as much labor as he could from his workers. The problem was, he still hadn't paid me half of my bonus for the previous year, and I was beginning to feel like I had the word "sucker" tattooed on my forehead.

When I'd walked into my annual review the previous December, Janus told me he was very pleased with my work. In fact, when I asked him what I could improve upon, he said, "Nothing." Then he gave me less than half of what I deserved, along with a story about how he'd give me more cash in March. As I listened to him without saying a word, he probably figured I was mad about the money. Actually, the biggest annoyance was the lack of respect. That wasn't the sort of thing you just sprang on an employee. Hitting me with that surprise a week after the holidays made me feel like Chevy Chase in *Christmas Vacation*. Sure, it wasn't a membership to the Jelly-of-the-Month Club in lieu of a bonus, but it sure felt like it. And Janus was so smug about it. No "I'm really sorry about this" in his explanation, just a "Here's what you're getting. Deal with it."

I smiled and said, "Thank you," but that's not what I was thinking. *I'm not forgetting this, Bill*

March came and went, then April. The work kept coming, piling on top of me, but that second slug of money still hadn't materialized. Every day that passed, that "sucker" tattoo I'd imagined on my forehead got bigger and bigger, morphing into what felt like a billboard over my eyes, broadcasting the word in blinking neon lights, reminding me the whole wretched mess was my own damn fault. *Never trust a lawyer.* I'd told myself that a thousand times. *You thought you were going to make out on this deal, and here you are, working twice as hard and getting paid less. You got taken, dumbass.*

I don't believe in fate or destiny, but there was a strange timing in my connecting with Max at that time. Where I could have snapped and been jailed for throwing Janus through his office window, instead I channeled all my energy and every spare moment into the new website and getting a book deal. I'd work at the office until seven or eight, stay up until two or three in the morning doing my "second job," then wake up at six forty-five and do it all over again. Lisa was seven months pregnant at the time, and I knew this was a last-chance opportunity. If I didn't get a book deal now, I probably never would.

Where I'd been two people before, the work me and the real me, now I had a third self—the prospective author, learning a business he doesn't know shit about on the fly. I'd be at a deposition questioning a witness on some detail of a case and excuse myself to take a cell phone call from my agent. I'd be writing a brief in one window on my computer screen while trading corrections for stories and essays with my website editor. On the train to and from work I'd slave away at a legal pad. People probably figured I was another young go-getter trying to squeeze an extra half hour of billable time from my day to make partner. Most of the text was actually about anal sex, misadventures on nude beaches or nitrous oxide.

On the last day of May, Janus finally gave me the second half of my bonus. Coincidentally, that was the same week my agent and I finalized the book proposal and sent it to publishers. I opened the envelope Janus handed me and looked at the bonus check. It was sizable, enough to buy a decent used car, but at that moment it was just a piece of paper with some numbers and a signature scribbled across the front. I was a million miles away, half of me with Lisa at home, wondering when she'd be going into labor, half at my agent's office in New York, wondering whether the book proposal would sell.

In mid-June I made up an excuse for not being at work and hopped on a Metroliner to New York to meet with potential publishers. Two months earlier I'd been just another suit on the morning train to an office tower in Philadelphia. And now here I was, a suit on the train to Manhattan to pitch a book about the last ten years of his life. The whole day was surreal, like I'd stepped through a wormhole into a different world. But the odd thing was, it seemed more real than anything I'd done in the office in the last decade, as though all the years in law had just been a long coma, a hibernation I'd fallen into after college.

At one point in the morning we met with a publisher who said she had a friend practicing at a law firm in Philadelphia. "So a lot of lawyers would like to know who you are." She grinned.

"Really? What do they think of my stuff?" I half expected her to laugh and admit something like, "Well, they don't really like it," assuming it asked the sorts of questions people coping with the career would rather keep buried. That, or most didn't read it at all, Philadelphia being pretty much resigned to its situation, and most locals not too interested in being reminded about it.

"From what I know, I think most of them would like to buy you a drink."

If I had any doubts left about what I was doing, that was the end of them.

After finishing the meetings I grabbed dinner with friends, then caught a late train home. Alone, somewhere between Newark and Philadelphia, rolling through the desolate Pine Barrens and dingy strip malls of central New Jersey, the adrenaline rush of the day finally faded, replaced by the realization I'd now done all I could. If I got an offer, I was one step closer to a jailbreak, using all the rotten and silly shit I'd seen in the job to buy a ticket out of it.

"How'd it go?" Lisa called me.

"I think it went well. How are you doing?"

"He's kicking a lot, but nothing's happening yet. Did any publishers buy the book?"

"I don't know. We won't know until next week or so."

"How did it feel?"

"It felt good . . . Liberating."

"That's positive then, isn't it?"

"That's the therapeutic side of it. Whether I made a sale is a different issue. I don't know how to read these people. They're totally different from lawyers."

"Someone will buy it. It'll work out."

"It better." I didn't know what I'd do if I didn't get a book deal. There was no way I could pimp legal paper in Philadelphia for the rest of my life. Writing about the scene had destroyed me for the career, at least in a place like Philadelphia. But all I could do now was wait. Go back into the office and act like everything was normal. Sit across from Janus and take his directives, listen to him talk about his cases and pretend to give a shit. It's a strange thing to work at a job as demanding as law, acting like you're a lifer, totally invested in the career, all the time knowing at any moment the phone might ring and someone would offer you a pile of money to write a book savaging exactly what you were doing.

Everything Went Wrong

ESCAPE'S REAL EASY, ON PAPER

The plan was idiot simple. Get the book advance, plunk down a resignation letter, tell Janus to kiss my ass and run off into the sunset. On paper it seemed foolproof. What could go wrong?

Everything.

In a life littered with one awful decision and mistake after another, and all the nervous, sweating last-minute saves in their wake, the last six months of my legal career were the worst of my life.

The odyssey started in June, the 28th to be exact, in a hospital outside Philadelphia.

"Can you please come over here, sir?" An assistant appeared behind the screen of my laptop. I was just sitting there, punching search terms into Google: *"Angus Young Guitar"* . . . *"Model guitar played Angus Young"* . . . *"Guitar Angus AC/DC."* I'd been working on a piece for my new website, an essay about American class anxiety, arguing that you could measure the level of a person's social insecurity by his like or dislike of AC/DC. I'd been researching the band's history for two weeks. I knew *Back in Black* had sold 40 million copies worldwide, that only one member of the band, Cliff Williams, had actually been born in Australia, and that original singer Bon Scott died of alcohol poisoning on February 19, 1980, sleeping off a drunk in a Porsche. All this minutiae and I couldn't remember the model of Angus Young's fucking guitar.

I was probably preoccupied.

"Yes, of course." I folded the computer and jumped up. She turned and guided me to the side of the bed, near a video screen of a heart beating fast, then slow, then fast again. I stood there mute, shocked, unable to form a word. I couldn't even watch the film. Everything was surreal. *How did this happen?*

Well, I knew how it happened. But still, I was young, in the prime of my life. I didn't belong in this freak-show scenario. It was too early, too much, too real.

The sort of people who bring burlap grocery bags to Whole Foods and the Prozaced soccer-mom set will tell you it's "wonderful" or a "miracle," something that "defines" a life or their "greatest moment." Crazy revisionist gibberish. The only accurate description of seeing your child being born belongs to a salty friend of mine from South America—"a horror movie . . . where your wife's the star."

"Are you done writing?"

"What?" I pretended not to hear Lisa.

"You looked busy, asshole. I didn't want to—Ohhhhh God, this hurts!" She sneered. She'd been in labor for the previous twenty hours, the last twelve of them excruciating. "I didn't want to disturb your writing. I was waiting until—Oh God, this hurts!—Until you were finished."

"Nice to see you haven't lost your humor."

"No. Just—" She growled and leaned forward. "Just my dignity."

"Push! Come on! Push! Breathe! Push!" A nurse handed me one of Lisa's legs and told me to pull it back, then yelled the sort of slogans you might have heard in a high school football weight room. After ten or so minutes of that, the doctor dragged over a huge vacuum, shoved it between Lisa's legs and pulled out a bloody, raisin-like alien with a yarmulke ringed into the top of its head from the suction.

"Congratulations! You're a father!"

Holy fucking shit. Now I've really done it.

This is where everything's supposed to change—your life suddenly affirmed, all the holes and gaps filled, everything rounded out in a way you could never have imagined a moment before. Bullshit. There's no grand epiphany or realization that this was the most important thing you'd ever witnessed, at least not in that exact moment. You're shocked, scared, struck with a numbing fear you've just done something a dozen times more irrational than the most reckless thing you'd done before. Yes, it's moving, and yes, you fall in love with your wife on a whole different level. But that's only half the story, the half struggling to punch through a deafening alarm ringing over and over in your head. *What the fuck do I do now?*

Indeed. What would I do? It was easy to say I'd grab the book advance and trash the legal career when it was just a plan. But now, on top of all the other bills and obligations, I had a kid. I'd spent ten years slugging it out in the trenches of a wretched industry in a desperate city, clawing to a point where I didn't have to worry about money, and now I was just going to throw it all away? How would I pay for the kid's tuition? How would I ever practice law again if I needed to after writing a book pissing on the field?

It's second nature to see all the downsides when you're a lawyer. I'd been taught to see danger and loss around every corner, the glass eternally half empty. That was what had me second-guessing the plan as I drove home from the hospital to pick up a bag of clothes for Lisa. But on the drive I passed four different train stations, including the one just below my house—the one I trudged to on so many mornings. As I drove by them, I thought about what the easy path would be, what it would look like. I saw myself in my fifties and sixties, an absentee lawyer-dad paying tuitions with bonus checks. Gray and paunchy, fiddling with a BlackBerry and filling out time sheets on the train. An aging partner with high blood pressure, a corner-office physique, and bottles of pills—some to numb me, some to get me hard. Then what? Seventy on a deck in Florida, fumbling through a medicated haze to remember some book I had the chance to write? Fuck that. Better to go down swinging than live in the slow suicide of *What if?*

In a period of three weeks Lisa and I had a kid, put our home up for sale, and I started writing a book that would probably kill the only career I'd known. I accepted an offer from a publisher quickly, but the contract was immediately hung up on language regarding television and film rights. On top of starting the book and buying and selling homes on the sly, now I had to learn entertainment law.

While that was going on, the real estate market took a nosedive, shaving $60,000 in value off my home, part of which I'd planned to live off while I wrote the book. At the same time, I had contractors and inspectors coming through the place every other day, doing repairs and touch-ups we needed to sell the property. Between that and the prospective buyers coming through, Lisa and I were barely able to spend any time in our own house. I'd sit in the backyard writing on a laptop while she took care of the baby.

For reasons I could only attribute to a cruel and petty God, in August an overheated electric switch started a fire in the attic. I woke up one morning—a Saturday, of course, so I couldn't even use the incident as an excuse to take a day off—to smoke all over the second floor. Two fire departments came to our home, parking huge hose trucks in the street and running inside with the usual axes and oxygen tanks. I remember standing in the backyard talking to a fireman as Lisa held the screaming baby in her arms, on the verge of tears from lack of sleep. "Once the smoke clears out, your house is going to smell pretty bad for a while." The fireman smiled grimly. "Do you folks have anywhere else you can stay?"

"No."

September was a little easier. We only had a tree fall on the house. I was sitting in a bedroom, writing, when I heard a tremendous crash and felt the home shake. When I ran outside, forty feet of oak branches and leaves were hanging over the side of the house and blocking my driveway. "Hey baby," I remember calling Lisa, who was visiting with her parents. "Do your folks have a chainsaw?" Potential buyers would be parked in front of the property with their real estate agents and see me driving across my lawn to reach the street, which was the only way I could get in and out while the tree blocked the way. I'd smile and wave out the window. "Go inside! Have a look!"

While all this was going on, I was still battling through the staggering workload Janus was laying on me. I'd argue motions on Monday, handle an arbitration in a personal injury case in Atlantic City on Wednesday, and take depositions of defendants in a complex business tort case on Friday. On the days in between I'd try to keep up with endless threat letters, motions, and thirty-page document requests fired at me by one of the most ruthless business litigators in the city in a horrible contract claim involving an ex-affiliate of the firm. I wasn't just the firm's associate. I was also its defense counsel.

The easy course would have been half-assing everything, but I didn't know how to do that. In September, with the help of a great local lawyer, I managed to turn around a multimillion-dollar products liability case by getting a federal judge in New Orleans to transfer it back to Philadelphia over the objections of one of the biggest law firms in the country, one of only a handful of plaintiffs in the country to succeed in doing so. On the plane ride down I remembered reading over the legal papers and thinking, *Why am I putting in this effort? What do I care?* It was the kind of motion I could afford to lose, where the cards were stacked against us and failure wouldn't impact my bonus. But at this point the career was a game, and going out on a high note was the only proper kiss-off. Leave the bastards baffled when I split—a parting mind-fuck in exchange for all the annoyance of the previous year and a half.

Finally, in late October, the book deal was signed and my house put under contract for sale. I came home one afternoon and found a copy of the book contract in a FedEx box on the steps, along with a check for the first installment of my advance. Sitting in my car holding the check from the publisher, my first urge was to run. Pick up the BlackBerry, fire off an email to Janus and take the rest of the year off:

Re: FYI

Bill:
Figured I'd let you know I won't be in tomorrow. Or the next day. Or any after that. Send whatever's in my office to the Salvation Army.
Best,
P.J.
P.S.: Go rub your knuckles in shit.

It was damn hard not to send that message, but I knew no matter how annoying the next sixty days might be, I couldn't go just yet. If I did that, I'd forfeit my end-of-the-year bonus, and there was no way in hell I was walking away from something I'd bled for so close to the end of the year. I'd served just shy of a decade in the field at that point. I could do a couple of months more.

Gone

If I had to pick the beginning of the end, those last few yards to the finish line, I'd start with the office Christmas party. It was the usual setup, the one everybody knows. The firm rented out a room in a swanky downtown steak joint and everybody got loaded and discussed what they'd be doing over the holidays. Most of the night was standard red-wine talk, how many presents people still had to buy, how many crazy relatives were coming to visit. Every now and again, though, someone would talk business—where the firm was headed, how much we had to look forward to. That was a little awkward for me. It was odd drinking to future success, knowing I'd be gone in two weeks. I listened to Malloy repeat several times how great the new year was going to be, which I knew was a soft setup for bad news on the current bonus. "To the new year!" I held up my glass and toasted back.

Two weeks earlier Lisa and I had made a down payment on a new house closer to a job she'd taken after graduate school. I knew JC&M gave out bonuses on the last workday of the year, so my plan now was to get the bonus check on the last day of December, confirm it cleared, resign immediately, move everything out of the house we were selling over the next week, close on the sale of our old house and the purchase of the new one a few days after that, then move everything into the new home the next day. A week before the Christmas party, my mortgage broker had asked me how much cash I'd have at closing for a down payment on the new property. I gave her some savings, what we'd make on the sale of our old home, plus exactly half of what I reasonably thought I was entitled to as a bonus. Sitting at the Christmas party listening to Malloy talk about how great the upcoming year would be, I knew my conservative estimate was the right course.

Janus and I exchanged some small talk at the dinner, which inevitably turned to shop, as it always did. He told me a story about how a trial judge wronged him with an unfair ruling and he'd shown that judge who was boss by filing and winning an appeal. I was loaded, and I'd heard the story three or four times before. Hell, I had parts of the narrative memorized. I sidestepped pretending it was new to me by commiserating, throwing out a story about how some judge had treated me unfairly in a case involving a company's loss of a shipment of $10,000 watches made by some Swiss company called Vacheron Constantin.

"I wonder what they put in a watch that makes it that expensive."

Janus pulled back his cuff and smiled. "This is one."

"Nice watch." Looking at the thing, I couldn't help wondering why a guy with that kind of scratch was repeating stories about a run-in with some local judge. If I had that float, I'd be in a resort town somewhere, stumbling around ripped, talking to trees and hanging out with shoestring Kennedys. I certainly wouldn't be in Philadelphia, grinding my days out suing people.

A week after the Christmas party, Janus brought me into a conference room and told me the size of the bonus I'd be receiving. "We've had a year I'd say was on the high end of 'decent,' and we're going to do something we did last year that I think worked well. We're going to give you a portion of the bonus now and distribute the rest to you at some point in the future."

"Okay. I understand."

"And there's no set date. I can't tell you when." Janus quickly spit out the caveat, probably expecting me to ask when I'd be getting that second distribution.

"Okay." It took everything in my power to stop myself from grinning. For a second I felt bad for Janus. Here he was, figuring he had the leverage to dictate when I'd get that second slug of money and I'd just accept it. I was just an associate. How could I complain? My only option was to say, "Thank you."

You're in for a surprise next week, Bill.

On New Year's Day I called my bank, confirmed the bonus check had cleared, and drove to a Kinko's down the street, just off Villanova University's campus.

"City and state please." The information prompt came over the cell phone as I wheeled the car into the parking lot.

"Four Seasons Hotels. Can I have the number for the Great Exuma location, please."

"Thank you, sir. We're connecting your call to area code 242-XXX-XXXX."

"Good evening. Four Seasons Great Exuma," the staticky voice came over my cell phone.

"Yes. Hello. Can I please have your fax number?"

As I fed my resignation letter through the fax machine, fighting the last vapors of a horrible New Year's hangover, I expected some emotion, a bit of remorse that things hadn't worked out differently, or at least some last-minute second thoughts. Nothing came. Pulling that trigger was the easiest thing I've ever done. Ten years litigating in Philadelphia is thirty doing anything else. There was no looking back, no worries or nostalgia, none of the regret you'd feel over a failed relationship or shattered business venture. No lamenting what might have been or thinking I was pissing anything worthwhile away. Until they find a way to pay you in time and satisfaction, law will be a fool's bargain, at least for people like me. And once you're past upper-middle-class fears like golden handcuffs and the delusion that you can't switch careers after thirty, the notion of sticking it out as a hired bullshitter in a place like Philadelphia is so wrong and senseless the only question left in your head is why you stayed as long as you did.

Beep. The fax machine spit out a confirmation page marked "OK" along with the letter.

> Dear Bill:
> I am resigning from Janus, Carson & Malloy and leaving
> the practice of law.
> I wish the firm luck in future endeavors.

Less words, more weight, and there really wasn't anything else to say. I folded the fax into my pocket and walked out the door.

"It's done." I called Lisa and relayed the message.

"Fantastic! So what now? Do you still have to go in tomorrow?"

"I think I'm just going to shut off the cell phone for a few days."

I didn't go to work the next day, or the day after that. The staff from the office emailed me a couple times, mostly concerned about my health. Everyone thought I'd gone crazy. Lawyers don't just walk away from bonus money and leave all their cases in the air. They love money, and they live for the job. It's their *life*.

Eventually Malloy had an associate ask me to call him, which I did. "So you're done? You're serious?"

"Yep."

"You're a lawyer." He sounded baffled. "What are you going to do with yourself?"

"The question is: What *won't* I do?"

"Well, as somebody who considers the bigger picture, I understand that. What I don't understand is—"

"The issue's simple." I cut him off. He was going to try to get me to reconsider, to assure me he'd fix whatever had caused me to resign. But there was nothing for Malloy to cure. My gripe wasn't limited to the firm. In fact, though he was a prime reason I was leaving, at that point my gripe wasn't even with Janus, at least not personally. He was more a symbol—an example of everything that made me want to run from the industry—than any sort of congenital irritant. "It's just irrational to work so hard at something you loathe."

"I hear you there. I can't argue with that."

I knew he couldn't. Standing in the front yard of my house listening to Malloy talk as I pored over revisions of the first chapters of this book, I finally understood his comment at my interview about needing to have "passion" for what you do. He was right, and that truth explains the desperate lives of so many bodies packed away in cubicles and offices all around the country. A friend of mine once explained the average life of toil by quoting his father, a psychiatrist. "People hate their jobs. We call it depression and give them drugs." "Do anything solely for money and you'll never be rich," my father used to tell me when I was young. I'd nod and laugh to myself. *Whatever. You're a fucking banker.* Now the lesson was finally sticking. A little late, a little costly, but I was still lucky. For a lot of people, it never registers at all. They piss away the only irreplaceable resource they'll ever have.

For a second I thought about asking Malloy how anyone could have a passion for something as annoying and corrosive as law. *Isn't there a good case to be made that loving this shit is proof of mental illness? What kind of person wants to spend his life arguing and tearing things down?* But I held my tongue. The guy was being open with me, and there was no point in starting that debate. A thin minority actually like the practice. A thin minority also like to get whipped, vote for Lyndon LaRouche, think evolution's fiction and shoot up high schools with automatic rifles.

I finally met with Janus a week later, when he got back from his vacation. "Why like that? I got a message in the middle of the night and the concierge brought your letter to me. I figured, *I must have done something to really piss this guy off.*"

When you're leaving, the power dynamic is totally inside out. Without a paycheck to dangle over your head, a partner doesn't have a shot glass worth of leverage. There's no deference granted out of politeness or some notion of respect for an elder. On its best day, law's a tenuous dance of mercenary greedheads, the older milking the younger for labor and the younger plotting how to take what the older's got. Janus wasn't the man who'd told me how things were going to be just a week before. The playing field was reversed. I could have said anything I liked, and he'd have no choice but to sit there and take it.

But in that moment, when you have that power—what all the Napoleons of the industry crave and get off on throwing around—the only thing worth saying is goodbye. Realizing the difference between Janus and me, the strongest urge was just to run. Being a "Philadelphia Lawyer" was his world. His kind lived, ate, and died as part of a thing the average decent person avoids like a necrotizing flesh virus. What purpose would clawing into him serve? It'd be cheap and incomplete, and he'd never understand a stitch of it anyway.

"Why did I resign as I did? Because I'm done. I'm sick of the field, and all the senseless arguments and annoyances, and the people in it more than anything. It's a shitty life and I'm not doing it anymore."

"Well, when that happens, I agree, you have to go. What I get out of it is seeing a change. When I sue a business and they make a change as a result of what I did, that's fulfilling."

I just smiled. What did I care why he did anything anymore?

"Well, that's fine, but let me tell you this: That splitting-the-bonus thing without notice, that isn't making friends."

"Well, you have to understand that—"

"Actually, I don't. You don't owe me an explanation. It's your business and I was an employee. You make your choices and I make mine."

"Every year isn't a great year. It's an up and down business."

"I understand. But there are two schools of thought on that. One says the partners pay in good times and bad because they get the biggest chunk of the spoils when things are up." I knew Janus would never give me another penny, but I figured raising the bonus issue might get him to throw some additional cash to the other associates. The way I figured it, he'd run the numbers and probably assumed he was making out well on my departure. Finding and training my replacement would be a nightmare, but he'd saved himself the second half of my bonus payment.

A different auditor might have concluded I was up, having used my time in the firm to round out the last bit of industry experience I needed to snag an advance for a book deal. There are a million ways to make money with a law degree. I doubt Janus imagined this one.

I left town a few days later, for good. And driving around City Hall taking in the scenery, all the buildings I'd trudged past every day for a decade, a fleeting pang of regret did slide past me. On balance, Philadelphia's not a good city, but it's not a bad city either, and law, if you could kill 70 percent of the people in the business and start over, well, it might not be a terrible career. But that wasn't my experience. I'd seen both from their lowest angles, in a rotten, desperate culture, and I wouldn't miss either. My last memory of the city was gunning the truck down the Schuylkill Expressway, humming along with "Statesboro Blues" and watching the skyline disappear in the rearview mirror. Gone . . . Another busted shyster . . . one more casualty of the circus, with barely the sense left to run.

Acknowledgments

Most of the people who inspired or made this book possible are described in it. I can't name them here, but the guilty bastards know who they are.

In addition to them, these people deserve a hand (I know I'll miss a bunch of you here, but it's late, I'm burned and the deadline's tomorrow).

My folks (Sorry, Mom)

My sister

"Paul"

"Alex"

Matt

Donika

Byrd

Tucker

Alicia

Russ